The Lying Pen
of the Scribe

by Rav Sha'ul

To my family and all Nazarenes, nothing will ever come between us no matter what anybody says or does, you will always be in my heart forever, and your spot will never be replaced!

Special thanks to my family for all your love and support. I dedicate this book to my King who makes all thing possible. And to the Nazarenes who make this ministry possible. Special thanks to Bruce Piatt for dedicating his time to teaching this book series to hundreds of Nazarenes daily. I dedicate this book to my wife Stephanie Fox Sides and children Stephanie Yates, Ashley Black, and Dayne Sides, and all those who have contributed to this cause below; may you all walk the path of Righteousness and be granted a place in the Kingdom.

Sherry Shaw	Andrew Genova	Lelia Dela Cruz	Bruce Piatt Sr.
Christinah Curtis	Deborah Bat Yah	Robin Beard-Fogg	Marie-Louise Muehlemann
Patrick & Gerdien Mosch	Lorry Stepp	Beth Batista	Ed Hall
Palmira Casanova	Ron Parker	Malakyah Malachi Malcolm	Gold Mountain Shepherds
Wang JANE	Joseph Franson	Joshua & Marvah Pilkerton	Alona Pakome
Andrew King	In Him Ministries	Ernestine James	Laura Ausmus
Robert Braun	Frances Frankie Oja	Scott Thompson	Roland Atencio
René and Carmen Spatz	Imad Laham	Ernest Hasler	Patrick Squire
Grace Whittaker	Sandra McGruder	Gareld McNeil	Matt Vader
Willie Koh	Nadybah Bat Yahuah	Nicholas Maalouf	Natzaryahu Ban Yahuah
Max Ard	Craig Mikic	Ariel Devar	Diversified Hawaii Consulting
Julie Ann Fureigh	Joseph Putol	Pato Zazzini	Jennifer Stewart
Raquel Bermyol	Judy Gaudet	Neville & June Shaw	Robin Beard-Fogg
Robert Arney	Frankellys Pena	KellyRae Breining	Jared London
Greg Bates	Tiffani Austin	William Netherly	Maria Acres Holst
Ma Durnford	Debra Docis	Gregrey Mitchell	Peggy Berger
Jerri Talbot	Judy Williams	Stacy Leazer Ray	John Fausett

Table of Contents

Chapter 5

About this Book

About this Book: Purpose

Rabbi Joel C. Dobin

"<u>Astrology was so much part of Jewish life and experience and so well respected in our tradition and law that the abandonment of Astrology to follow the chimera of scientific linearality was one of the greatest religious tragedies that ever befell our people.</u> For in so doing, we abandoned as well the mystical realities of our faith, our abilities to balance our lives and attain Unity, and <u>we have created of our synagogues and temples arenas of contention for power and concern for financial sufficiency</u>.... I write as an astrologer, seeking to turn all those whose various faiths have seemed to abandon them back to their own faith."

The purpose of this book is to expose the Lying Pen of the Scribe and then re-establish the written texts in light of their source... The Heavenly Scroll. My intention is not to diminish the confidence we all have in the Tanakh and New Testament writings of the Nazarenes. Rather, I intend to defend the Messiah against Rabbinical Judaism's assault on the New Testament and Yahusha as their Messiah.

We are going to examine the historical record to see if there is evidence the Scriptures were "made into a lie" at the hands of scribes and translators.

I am going to compare the standard of judgment that is used to declare the New Testament is a work of fiction with the Tanakh. I will show that the Tanakh fails every test used to disqualify the New Testament (only in a greater fashion)! If we are discrediting the NT then based on those same standards the Tanakh must be rejected as well. We are dealing with the transliteration of dead languages and ancient traditions mingled with pagan worship and oral traditions into our modern texts of Scripture. All are

15

transliterated by scribes with competing interests as Rabbi Joel C. Dobin pointed out. Interesting to note the definition of "confusion":

Confusion

Confusion | www.dictionary.com/browse/confusion
from Latin confusionem (nominative confusio) "a mingling, mixing, blending; confusion, disorder," noun of action from confundere "to pour together," also "to confuse" (see confound). Sense of "a putting to shame" (a sort of mental "overthrow") is late 14c. in English,

"Confusion" is the exact definition of transliteration... "a mingling, mixing, blending" together of a myriad of dead languages and oral traditions into some modern form from unreliable texts passed down from error-prone Hellenized Jewish scribes. <u>Most of what we base our current traslations on are notes discarded by scribes for reasons unkown!</u> Who is the "author of confusion"? Exactly my point. These modern translations were penned by men filled with The Spirit of the Dragon and they were designed to be confusing!

We are now coming face-to-face with what the Bible calls "***the Lying Pen of the Scribes***". Both on purpose and inadvertently by Hellenized scribes and committees of intellectual "experts" through transliteration trying to create a "word-for-word" rendition from an ancient dead language to modern languages when that is quite simply... IMPOSSIBLE. The inevitable result is "syncretism" which mirrors the definition of confusion.

Syncretism

Political ideology
Description: *Syncretism is the practice of combining different beliefs and various schools of thought. Syncretism involves the merging or assimilation of several originally discrete traditions...* Wikipedia

16

When attempting to overcome the Lying Pen of the Scribe the written texts must be re-established in light The Heavenly Scroll. It is the Testimony of Yahuah written in the stars/constellations that will ultimately declare who the Messiah is. We must revearse engineer the Scriptures past down to us to discover the Truth held by the first century Nazarenes called *The Way*.

Mislead by Written Texts

Most of us have been raised to believe the Bible is without error. "God-breathed", it is said, and in no need of untwisting or any further translation. It is complete and everything we need to know to be confident we have the truth. Unfortunately, this is not only a fallacy, but it contradicts the clear declarations in Scripture!

ISAIAH 9:16
FOR THOSE WHO GUIDE THIS PEOPLE MISLEAD THEM, AND THOSE THEY MISLEAD ARE SWALLOWED UP

MATTHEW 23:24
YOU BLIND GUIDES! YOU STRAIN OUT A GNAT BUT SWALLOW A CAMEL.

LUKE 6:39
YAHUSHA ALSO TOLD THEM A PARABLE: "CAN A BLIND MAN LEAD A BLIND MAN? WILL THEY NOT BOTH FALL INTO A PIT?

JOHN 9:39
THEN YAHUSHA DECLARED, "FOR JUDGMENT I HAVE COME INTO THIS WORLD, SO THAT THE BLIND MAY SEE AND THOSE WHO SEE MAY BECOME BLIND."

We read on the pages of the Bible that we would only "think" we have His Word (Jeremiah 8:7-9). However, the written word would be twisted into a Babylonian lie through translation and syncretism. This would be done at the hands of pagan astrologers (wise men) who twist The Word of His Testimony written into the stars into what we today think of as The Zodiac over time! Then abolish that "Word" altogether because it is the basis of all pagan religions. We are not taught the reality which is all religions including the faith of Abraham are based on The Heavenly Scroll.

Why twist the Zodiac into a pagan lie? Because the written scriptures are based on the Plan of Salvation written in the stars!

Water down the meaning of the stars/constellations, associate it with pagan worship. Then abolish The Heavenly Scroll alltogether, deny its message, and make the texts confusing; without a foundation the Scriptures can be mistranslated and handled falsely by scribes:

JEREMIAH 8

7 BUT MY PEOPLE DO NOT KNOW THE WORD OF YAHUAH (*eternally preserved in the stars - Psalm 119:89*). 8 "HOW CAN YOU SAY, 'WE ARE WISE MEN (*h2450 chakam - astrologers*), AND THE WORD OF YAHUAH'S TESTIMONY IS WITH US'? BUT BEHOLD, THE LYING PEN OF THE SCRIBES HAS MADE MY WORD (*Logos/Dabar - 'spoken promise in the beginning'*) INTO A LIE. 9 "THE WISE MEN (*astrologers*) ARE PUT TO SHAME, THEY ARE DISMAYED (*by the constellations/stars/Sun to worship them - Jeremiah 10:2*) AND CAUGHT (*in idolatry - Deuteronomy 4:19*); **BEHOLD, THEY HAVE REJECTED THE WORD OF MY TESTIMONY** (*The Heavenly Scroll the ancient path - Jeremiah 6:16*), **AND WHAT KIND OF WISDOM DO THEY HAVE?**...

Above we see the "wise men" who made His Word, preserved in The Heavenly Scroll, into a lie and are put to shame by their efforts to preserve His Word and "*dismayed and caught up*" in idolatry. They began worshipping the constellations. We see this later in Jeremiah:

JEREMIAH 10:2

THUS SAITH YAHUAH, LEARN NOT THE WAY OF THE HEATHEN, AND BE NOT DISMAYED AT THE SIGNS OF HEAVEN (CONSTELLATIONS); FOR THE HEATHEN ARE DISMAYED AT THEM.

In Deuteronomy, we see that while we are to look up and read The Heavenly Scroll, we must be careful not to be caught up in idolatry by worshiping the constellations.

DEUTERONOMY 4:19
AND WHEN YOU LOOK UP TO THE HEAVENS AND SEE THE
SUN, THE MOON, AND THE STARS—ALL THE HEAVENLY
SCROLL—DO NOT BE ENTICED INTO BOWING DOWN TO
WORSHIP THE CONSTELLATIONS (they are pictographs not
gods) FOR YAHUAH YOUR GOD HAS APPORTIONED SUN,
MOON, CONSTELLATION, AND STARS AS SIGNS TO ALL THE
NATIONS UNDER THE HEAVENLY SCROLL.

Nothing but Lies

In Jeremiah, we read that our faith today is based on "Nothing but lies". That there would be no truth in the twisted Scriptures we have had handed down to us as we come out of the nations.

JEREMIAH 16:19

18 "I WILL FIRST DOUBLY REPAY THEIR INIQUITY AND THEIR SIN, BECAUSE THEY HAVE POLLUTED MY LAND; THEY HAVE FILLED MY INHERITANCE WITH THE CARCASSES OF THEIR DETESTABLE IDOLS AND WITH THEIR ABOMINATIONS." 19 O YAHUAH, MY STRENGTH AND MY STRONGHOLD, AND MY REFUGE IN THE DAY OF DISTRESS, TO YOU THE (*lost sheep scattered among the*) NATIONS WILL COME FROM THE ENDS OF THE EARTH AND SAY, "*OUR FATHERS HAVE INHERITED NOTHING BUT LIES, IDOLS AND WORTHLESS THINGS OF NO PROFIT.*" 20 CAN MAN MAKE GODS FOR HIMSELF? YET THEY (*make for themselves based on the constellations as gods - Deuteronomy 3:19 - and Babylonian incarnation of the Sun "in the flesh"*) ARE NOT GODS!

We read from the Nazarenes in the N.T. that as the Greeks conquered the faith and gained possession of the original Hebrew texts, they twisted those originals into a pagan lie to conform to their existing pagan beliefs. In this way, a false religion could be created incorporating all other religions into a "Universal Religion":

---

2 PETER 3:16

SHA'UL WRITES THE SAME WAY IN THE MYSTERY LANGUAGE IN ALL HIS LETTERS, SPEAKING IN LETTERS OF THESE MATTERS. HIS LETTERS CONTAIN SOME THINGS THAT ARE HARD TO UNDERSTAND, WHICH IGNORANT AND UNSTABLE PEOPLE (*Greeks*) TWIST, AS THEY DO THE OTHER SCRIPTURES, TO THEIR OWN DESTRUCTION.

This is exactly what happened at the Council of Nicaea. A false religion was born, a false messiah was created, and all the pre-existing pagan rituals and holy days were kept. Everything Holy to the Creator was turned into an abomination based on these twisted Scriptures and lies were then passed down to us today.

Where did we get our English Bibles? Pagan Greeks and hellenized Jewish scribes are to blame! This led to scribes and translators over the past 3000 years passing down these abominations! This is also brought out in the historical context and openly admitted by the ones who did the translating! The Catholic Church took the Hebrew texts and twisted them into Greek/Latin to assimilate all pagan religions into one Universal Church.

> **The Catholic Encyclopedia, Volume 6,** page 136 ----
> *"Substitution of false documents and tampering with genuine ones was quite a trade in the Middle Ages. Innocent III (1198) points out nine species of forgery [of ecclesiastical records] which had come under his notice. But such frauds of the Church were not confined to the Middle Ages; they begin even with the beginning of the Church and infest every period of its history for fifteen hundred years and defile nearly every document, both of "Scriptures" and of Church aggrandizement. As truly said by Collins, in his celebrated Discourse of Free Thinking: "In Short, these frauds are very common in all books which are published by priests or priestly men... For it is certain they may plead the authority of the Fathers for Forgery, Corruption and mangling of Authors, with more reason than for any of their Articles of Faith..."(p.96.)"*

It is, for this reason, we have gone astray from the true Faith of Abraham found in the stars, abolished The Law, violated The Sabbath, and kept pagan holidays instead of Yahuah's Holy Days. For more on that topic, read my book *Christianity and the Great Deception*.

The Word of Yahuah's Testimony

Is the written Scriptures, let's call them the Bible, literally God-breathed by the Holy Spirit? Is the Bible infallible? Inerrant? Or is it the product of human endeavor and therefore prone to error and interpretation?

The Word of Yahuah's Testimony concerning His coming King who would rule creation is found in The Heavenly Scroll and the foundation the Earthly written scrolls. We see in Isaiah 48 below that The Heavenly Scroll is Yahuah's "Divine Counsel" that ministers the Good News when summoned together by the Sun as it moves across the sky.

ISAIAH 48

11 FOR MY OWN SAKE, FOR MY OWN SAKE I WILL DO IT; FOR HOW COULD DISHONOR COME TO MY NAME (*Yahuah*)? I WILL NOT GIVE MY GLORY (*as Creator*) TO ANOTHER! 12 LISTEN TO ME, O YAAQOB AND YISRAYL, MY CALLED; I AM HE; I AM THE ALEPH, I ALSO AM THE TAV. 13 MY HAND HAS LAID THE FOUNDATION OF THE EARTH (*all by Himself - Isaiah 44:24*), AND MY RIGHT HAND HAS SPANNED (*spread out like a tent*) THE HEAVEN(*ly Scroll - Psalm 19*); WHEN I SUMMON THEM (*stars/constellations*) TOGETHER, THEY WILL MINISTER TOGETHER (*to proclaim the Messiah/Plan of Salvation - Psalm 19*). 14 ALL OF YOU, GATHER YOURSELVES TOGETHER AND HEAR (*what the stars proclaim day after day, night after night - Psalm 19*)! WHO AMONG THEM HAS FORETOLD THESE THINGS (*written in the stars*)?

ISAIAH 40:25-26

"TO WHOM WILL YOU COMPARE ME? OR WHO IS MY EQUAL?" SAYS THE HOLY ONE. LIFT YOUR EYES AND LOOK TO THE HEAVENS (*H 8064 - shamayim*) WHO CREATED ALL THESE (*stars/constellations*)? HE WHO BRINGS OUT THE STARRY HOSTS (*constellations host stars*) ONE BY ONE (*as the*

Sun moves along the Ecliptic) AND CALLS THEM EACH *(constellation)* BY NAME. BECAUSE OF HIS GREAT POWER AND MIGHTY STRENGTH, NOT ONE OF THEM IS MISSING *(there are 12 major constellations along the ecliptic).*

JOB 38:32
YAHUAH SAID TO HIS UPRIGHT SERVANT "CAN YOU BRING FORTH MAZZAROTH *(The Heavenly Scroll)* IN THEIR SEASON *(to minister the Gospel - Isaiah 48:11-14).*

DEUTERONOMY 3:19
WHEN YOU LOOK UP TO THE SKY *(sky is Hebrew shamayim/Zodiac)* AND SEE THE SUN, MOON, AND STARS — THE WHOLE HEAVENLY CREATION *(The Heavenly Scroll)* — YOU MUST NOT BE SEDUCED TO WORSHIP AND SERVE THEM *(constellations)*, FOR YAHUAH YOUR ELOHIM HAS ASSIGNED THEM TO ALL THE PEOPLE OF THE WORLD *(they were created by Yahuah to proclaim the coming Messiah Yahusha - Psalm 19 - they are not gods).*

ENOCH 35:3
I BLESSED YAHUAH OF GLORY, WHO HAD MADE THOSE GREAT AND SPLENDID SIGNS *(of the Zodiac)*, THAT THEY MIGHT DISPLAY THE MAGNIFICENCE OF HIS WORKS *(The Plan of Salvation Psalms 19)* TO ANGELS AND TO THE SOULS OF MEN; AND THAT THESE *(splendid signs in The Heavenly Scroll)* MIGHT GLORIFY ALL HIS WORKS AND OPERATIONS; MIGHT SEE THE EFFECT OF HIS POWER; MIGHT GLORIFY THE GREAT LABOR OF HIS HANDS; AND BLESS HIM FOREVER.

This is "the Word" Yahusha came to fulfill!

DANIEL 4:35
"ALL THE INHABITANTS OF THE EARTH ARE ACCOUNTED AS NOTHING, BUT HE DOES ACCORDING TO HIS WILL WRITTEN IN THE HOST OF HEAVEN *(The Heavenly Scroll which hosts constellations. Constellations "host stars")*

HEBREWS 10:7
THEN I SAID, 'HERE I AM–IT IS WRITTEN ABOUT ME IN THE HEAVENLY SCROLL– I HAVE COME TO DO YOUR WILL, MY GOD! (*Matthew 6:10*)

MATTHEW 6:10
YOUR KINGDOM COME, YOUR WILL BE DONE, ON EARTH AS IT IS (*written*) IN (*the*) HEAVEN(*ly scroll*).

Hebrew people over time rejected The Heavenly Scroll (the ancient path) and the message in the stars was carried forward in secret by the Zadok Priesthood:

JEREMIAH 6:16
THIS IS WHAT YAHUAH SAYS: "STAND AT THE CROSSROADS AND LOOK; ASK FOR THE ANCIENT (Enochian) PATHS, ASK WHERE "THE GOOD WAY" IS, AND WALK IN THE WAY (*of Enoch*), AND YOU WILL FIND REST FOR YOUR SOULS. BUT YOU SAID, 'WE WILL NOT WALK IN IT.'"

ISAIAH 48:3-6
3 I FORETOLD THE FORMER THINGS LONG AGO (written in the stars on Day 4 of Creation), MY MOUTH ANNOUNCED THEM (*to My Prophets via The Heavenly Scroll*) AND I MADE THEM KNOWN (*to all mankind written in the stars - Psalm 19, Enoch 35:3 - given to all mankind - Deuteronomy - 3:19*); THEN SUDDENLY I ACTED, AND THE MESSAGE PROCLAIMED BY THE STARS/CONSTELLATIONS CAME TO PASS (*at the end of the Age of Aries*). 4 FOR I KNEW HOW STUBBORN YOU WERE; YOUR NECK MUSCLES WERE IRON; YOUR FOREHEAD WAS BRONZE. 5 THEREFORE I TOLD YOU THESE THINGS (*in The Heavenly Scroll*) LONG AGO (*at Creation*); BEFORE THEY WERE FULFILLED I ANNOUNCED THE PLAN OF SALVATION TO YOU (*in The Heavenly Scroll*) SO THAT YOU COULD NOT SAY, 'MY IMAGES BROUGHT THEM ABOUT; MY WOODEN IMAGE AND METAL GOD ORDAINED THEM.' 6 YOU HAVE HEARD THESE THINGS (*that the stars proclaim day after day, night after night to all mankind as a witness - Psalm 19, Isaiah 48:111-15,*

26

Isaiah 40:26); LOOK AT ALL THE STARS AND CONSTELLATION. WILL YOU NOT ADMIT THEM (*the Sun/stars/constellations are The Word of His Testimony called The Way*)?

Zodiac means "the way or path of the sun" as it travels through the 12 major constellations. The question is "what did the Nazarenes believe in regard to The Heavenly Scroll?" Sha'ul was a leader of the "sect of the Nazarenes" who followed *The Way* or "Ancient Path" of Enoch:

ACTS 24:14
HOWEVER, I ADMIT THAT I WORSHIP THE GOD OF OUR ANCESTORS AS A FOLLOWER OF THE WAY (*foretold in The Heavenly Scroll, the ancient Enochian Path*), WHICH THEY CALL A SECT.

Beliefs of the Nazarenes

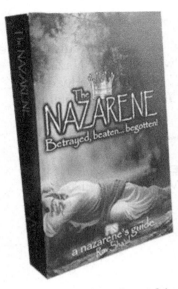

For more on this topic, read my book **The Nazarene**. Concerning the Nazarenes in the first century, the Christian Church father Epiphanius tells us:

Epiphanius; Panarion 29:9:4, A.D. 374.

"But these sectarians... did not call themselves Christians – but "Nazarenes" [Natsarim] . . . However, they are simply complete Jews. They use not only the New Testament but the Old Testament as well, as the Jews do... They have no different ideas but confess everything exactly as The Law proclaims it and in the Jewish fashion – except for their belief in Messiah, if you please! For they acknowledge both the Resurrection of the dead and the Divine Creation of all things, and declare that God is One, and that His son is Yahusha The Messiah. They are trained to a nicety in Hebrew. For among them the entire Law (Torah), the Prophets, and the... Writings ... are read in Hebrew, as they surely are by the Jews. They are different from the Jews, and different from Christians, only in the following. They disagree with Jews because they have come to Faith in Messiah; but since they are still fettered by The Law – Circumcision, the Sabbath, and the rest – they are not in accord with Christians . . . they are nothing but Jews... They have the Gospel according to Matthew in its entirety in Hebrew. For it is clear that they still preserve this, in the Hebrew alphabet, as it was originally written."

28

Based on the above historical account, a Nazarene was what Epiphanius called "a complete Jew". But what else did they believe?

John the Baptist rose to the position of Zadok High Priest with the Spirit of Elijah, the "Great Nazarene Teacher of Righteousness". Those who followed John were originally of the sect of the Essenes. This new sect that followed John the Baptist became known as **Nazarenes**. John taught them The Heavenly Scroll where the Messiah is called The Branch:

ALMAH (VIRGO) — MAIDEN, VIRTUOUS BRIDE
A YOUNG MAIDEN (*Hebrew 'almah'*) WILL GIVE A VIRGIN BIRTH (*he will be her firstborn son to open up her virgin womb*) TO A BEAUTIFUL GLORIOUS AND RIGHTEOUS *BRANCH*. THE SEED (*star Spica*) OF THE WOMAN WILL BE A MAN OF HUMILIATION (*Suffering Servant/Spring Feasts*) TO RISE TO BE THE DESIRE OF NATIONS (*King of Kings*) AND WILL BECOME EXALTED FIRST AS SHEPHERD (*High Priest*) THEN AS HARVESTER (*Conquering King/Fall Feasts*).

John was a prophet and High Priest, the son of the Priest Zechariah. We see that John taught The Way as "the rising sun (zodiac) will come to us from Shamayim/stars" called The Heavenly Scroll.

LUKE 1:76-79
[76] AND YOU, MY CHILD, WILL BE CALLED A PROPHET OF THE MOST HIGH (*for proclaiming The Heavenly Scroll/Plan of Salvation*); FOR YOU WILL GO ON BEFORE THE MESSIAH TO PREPARE THE WAY FOR HIM, [77] TO GIVE HIS PEOPLE THE KNOWLEDGE OF SALVATION THROUGH THE FORGIVENESS OF THEIR SINS (*through MIKVEH called The Way*), [78] BECAUSE OF THE TENDER MERCY OF OUR ELOHIM, *BY WHICH THE RISING SUN WILL COME TO US FROM THE*

HEAVENLY SCROLL (*Psalm 19, Enoch 35:3, Isaiah 48:3-6, Isaiah 40:26*)!

We know more about the Nazarenes by examining their origin as Essenes and Ebionites:

> **From "Ebionites & Nazarenes: Tracking the Original Followers of Jesus" by James Tabor:**
> *This Ebionite/Nazarene movement was made up of mostly Jewish followers of John the Baptizer and later Jesus, who were concentrated in Palestine and surrounding regions and led by "James the Just" (the brother of Jesus), and flourished between the years 30-80 C.E. Non-Jews were certainly part of the mix but the dominant ethos of the group was an adherence to live according to Jewish law (Galatians 2:14). They were zealous for the Torah and continued to observe the mitzvot (Commandments) as enlightened by their Rabbi and Teacher...*
>
> *- Nazarene comes from the Hebrew word Netzer (drawn from Isaiah 11:1 and the Constellation VIRGO) and means "a Branch"—so the Nazarenes were the "Branchites" or followers of the one they believed to be the Branch—that is the Davidic Messiah...*
>
> *- Referred to themselves as The Way, Perhaps their most common designation was the Yachad–the brotherhood*
>
> *- They were bitterly opposed to the corrupt Priests in Jerusalem, to the Herods, and even to the Pharisees whom they saw as compromising with that establishment to get power and influence from the Hellenistic/Roman powers.*
>
> *- They had their own developed Halacha (interpretation of Torah)*

30

- They accept Paul (with caution) and believe in some aspect of the divinity of Jesus (after his resurrection), even possibly the virgin birth (as simply a sign) but viewed him as "adopted" as Son of God at his baptism.

- <u>Belief that Jesus as a human being with a father and a mother</u>

- Sought out the "Path" reflected in the pre-Sinai revelation, especially the time from Enoch to Noah.

- Dedication to following the whole Torah, as applicable to Israel and to Gentiles, but through the "easy yoke" or the "Torah of liberty" of their Teacher Jesus, which emphasized the Spirit of the Biblical Prophets in a restoration of the "True Faith," the Ancient Paths (Jeremiah 6:16; Matthew 11:28-30; James 2:8-13; Matthew 5:17-18; 9:13; 12:7), from which, by and large, they believed the establishment Jewish groups of 2nd Temple times had departed.

- Rejection of the "doctrines and traditions" of men, which they believed had been added to the pure Torah of Moses, including scribal alterations of the texts of Scripture (Jeremiah 8:8).

From these historical records combined with the proper interpretation of the Scriptures, we can confidently say Sha'ul:

- Put his faith in The Heavenly Scroll called the ancient path where the Plan of Salvation is laid out and Yahuah bears witness of Yahusha.
- Believed in the intent of the written Torah and rejected the human traditions of Rabbinical Judaism known today as The Talmud.

31

- Believed that Yahusha the Nazarene was the Messiah.
- Rejected the labels "Jew and Christian".
- Rejected the worship of the Messiah and later the name "Jesus".
- Believed the Messiah was born to two human parents.
- Rejected the efforts of the Christopagans to drag believers into Lawlessness and pagan rituals.
- Called upon and spoke the full Name of the Creator Yahuah.
- Kept and taught his assemblies to keep the Sabbath and Holy Days.
- Observed the sacred Enochian calendar not the solar calendar.
- Rejected Incarnation.
- Taught the 'intent' of The Law over the letter.
- Believed that Yahusha is Yahuah's Firstborn AGAIN Son, adopted upon his Mikveh!
- Rejected the Greek Hellenistic Mindset.
- Kept Circumcision, the Sabbath, and Holy Days.

Scholars Admit Sha'ul's Writings Were Twisted

What we find today is a "movement" among almost all Scholars who have come to recognize that Sha'ul's writings were twisted, mistranslated, and intentionally altered by Christianity to "do away with The Law"! Textual Critics found many instances in the modern English translations as well as with the Greek copies of the original Hebrew scripts, where the translators subtracted words and then added words and phrases to twist Sha'ul's writings to create **The Pauline Doctrine**.

It is admitted among scholars that Sha'ul <u>did not intend to teach against 'The' Law, Feasts, and Sabbaths of the Most High</u>. Let me quote from The Jerusalem Perspective which is a Christian site of true scholars and textual critics:

> <u>Source: 'The Western Captivity of the Apostle Sha'ul' by Jack Poirier columnist for The Jerusalem Perspective.</u>
> *"No area of modern textual criticism is more prominent, and theologically momentous, than the developments that have taken place in the past forty years concerning our understanding of what the books of Romans and Galatians are all about.*
>
> *"It is now a commonplace observation among scholars that Sha'ul's most basic convictions were misrepresented by the most dominant streams of Western theology. Although a more detailed discussion would include a number of lesser figures as well, it is significant that the principal culprits in the Westernization of Sha'ul (e.g., Augustine, Luther, Calvin, Karl Barth, et al.) are all deserving of chapter (on how Sha'ul's was misrepresented in their teachings) in a general history of the Church. This shows how central the*

33

> *interpretation of Sha'ul is to the Christian history of ideas.*
> *As it goes with Sha'ul, so with the Church."*

And there you have it... Sha'ul's writings were twisted by the Greeks as Jeremiah, Isaiah, Yahusha, Peter, and Sha'ul warned us they would be.

---

1 *CORINTHIANS* 1:23
BUT WE PREACH THE MESSIAH CRUCIFIED: A STUMBLING BLOCK TO JEWS AND FOOLISHNESS TO GREEKS--

2 *PETER* 3:16-17
SHA'UL WRITES THE SAME WAY IN ALL HIS LETTERS, SPEAKING IN THEM OF THESE MATTERS. HIS LETTERS CONTAIN SOME THINGS THAT ARE HARD TO UNDERSTAND, WHICH IGNORANT AND UNSTABLE (*Greek*) PEOPLE DISTORT, AS THEY DO THE OTHER SCRIPTURES, TO THEIR OWN DESTRUCTION. -- THEREFORE, DEAR FRIENDS, SINCE YOU HAVE BEEN FOREWARNED, BE ON YOUR GUARD SO THAT YOU MAY NOT BE CARRIED AWAY BY THE ERROR OF THE 'LAWLESS' AND FALL FROM YOUR SECURE POSITION.

We must keep the warnings in Jeremiah in mind.

JEREMIAH 8:7-9
[7] BUT MY PEOPLE DO NOT KNOW THE ORDINANCE OF YAHUAH (*Eternally preserved in the stars - Psalm 119:89, Psalm 89:2*). [8] HOW CAN YOU SAY, WE ARE WISE MEN (*h2450 chakam - 'astrologers'*), AND THE WORD OF YAHUAH'S TESTIMONY (*that Yahusha is The Branch foretold in The Heavenly Scroll*) IS WITH US? BUT BEHOLD, THE 'LYING PEN OF THE SCRIBES' HAS MADE MY WORD (*LOGOS/DABAR - 'Spoken Promise in the beginning' Eternally preserved in The Heavenly Scroll - Psalm 119:89*) INTO A LIE (*by removing The Word of His Testimony*). [9] THE WISE MEN (*h2450 chakam – 'astrologers'*) ARE PUT TO SHAME THEY ARE DISMAYED (*Jeremiah 10:2*) AND CAUGHT (*in idolatry - Deuteronomy 4:19*); BEHOLD, THEY HAVE REJECTED

34

THE WORD OF MY TESTIMONY (*The Heavenly Scroll - Isaiah 48:3-6, Jeremiah 6:16*), AND WHAT KIND OF WISDOM DO THEY HAVE?

Sha'ul was a Nazarene and as such followed the Ancient Enochian Path called "The Way" and proclaimed The Heavenly Scroll the foundation of our faith. That is the Gospel message that Sha'ul based his faith and teachings on. Faith in The Heavenly Scroll is 'the faith of Abraham" as well as "The Great Commission".

Sha'ul the Leader of the Nazarenes

Rav Sha'ul was a Nazarene or Notsri not what we would consider a Christian. The fact that Sha'ul was not only a Nazarene, but the "Leader of the Sect of Nazarenes" indicates what Sha'ul believed and taught in the letters that survive today. We must go back to the first century to identify what the Nazarenes believed and put Sha'ul's writings in that context. This is called the "language and cultural matrix".

Each letter we have written by Sha'ul to the Nazarene assemblies was written to a unique audience with unique challenges he addressed. When attempting to understand any one letter, we must put them into the context of all his writings and teachings. What Sha'ul mentions in passing in one letter is explained in more detail in another. What the assembly in Rome faced, believed, and required was different than what the assembly in Galatia faced, believed, and required.

We must assume there are many letters written to these assemblies we do not have. What he taught each assembly was most probably taught to all, we just no longer have those letters. For this reason, a solid understanding of all his surviving letters must be brought to bear on each individual letter.

Sha'ul was a leading Pharisee of his day meaning he was an expert in the Torah and Prophets. Being a high-ranking Pharisee, he was also intimately familiar with the oral traditions and human commands keeping the Jews (the House of Judah) in bondage to the establishment. This "establishment" of Pharisees, Sadducees, and Levites who controlled the synagogues and Temple had lost their way by denying The Heavenly Scroll coming out of Babylonian captivity.

As we come out of our paganism (Christianity) and realize that we are to keep The Holy Days of Yahuah, we naturally look to

Judaism for the answers. What we do not realize is, Judaism is a Hellenized pagan religion as much as Christianity!

Hellenization - Wikipedia

"The twentieth century witnessed a lively debate over the extent of Hellenization in the Levant and particularly among the ancient Palestinian Jews that has continued until today. The Judaism of the diaspora was thought to have succumbed thoroughly to its influences. Bultmann thus argued that Christianity arose almost completely within those Hellenistic confines and should be read against that background as opposed to a more traditional (Palestinian) Jewish background"

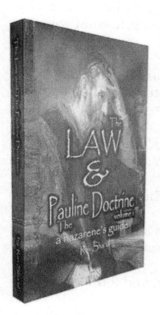

Being mentored by Gamaliel who was the most famous Rabbi in Jewish history; there was no one more qualified to break these bonds and confront the establishment than Sha'ul the Apostle. All accusations that Sha'ul was a "false teacher" are based on mistranslated texts by the pagan Roman Christian Church.

Please see my book **The Law and The Pauline Doctrine** for the truth of what Sha'ul taught and to overcome the twisted Greek appropriate lie that is ... *The Pauline Doctrine.*

Sha'ul was not a Roman Hellenized Christian but a Hebrew Nazarene. This is stated clearly in the Book of Acts:

ACTS 24:5-6
"FOR WE HAVE FOUND THIS MAN TO BE A PEST AND A MOVER OF SEDITION AMONG ALL THE JEWS THROUGHOUT

THE WORLD, AND <u>A RINGLEADER OF THE SECT OF THE
NAZARENES</u>: WHO ALSO HATH GONE ABOUT TO PROFANE
THE TEMPLE: WHOM WE TOOK, AND WOULD HAVE JUDGED
ACCORDING TO OUR LAW"

Sha'ul, like John the Baptist and Yahusha the Messiah, was the leading figure in defense of the Ancient Enochian Path (The Heavenly Scroll), the written Torah, Prophets, and Messiah. That is what being a Nazarene was all about 2000 years ago and remains true today.

All Nazarenes kept the hidden mysteries of Yahuah dating back to Enoch. They were to guard these mysteries, watch over and protect them! They were fierce opponents of all forms of paganism including the Babylonian Talmud and Hellenism (the worship of Greek gods and twisting of The Heavenly Scroll into what we know as the Zodiac today).

As I demonstrated a few pages back, the Nazarenes rejected Incarnation outright and any concept associated with Babylonian demi-gods:

- They rejected the Virgin Birth and the Trinity
- Proclaimed the Name of The Creator Yahuah and that He is the only God
- followed the ancient Enochian Path (Enoch Calendar and Enoch Zodiac)
- rejected the worship of the Messiah as a demi-god believing him to have been to two human parents a mother and a father
- refused the label "Christians" outright and felt it slanderous

The word Nazarenes means "followers of the Branch" which was foretold in what the Bible calls The Heavenly Scroll given to Enoch. They "admit" the stars and constellations proclaim a message to all mankind and followed The Ancient Way of Enoch they called *The Way*. This ancient path was rejected by the people of Israel.

The Ancient Path of Enoch

When Sha'ul refers to having faith and calls it the Faith of Abraham or just **The Faith**; what exactly was he referring to? He is referring to the original Gospel written in The Heavenly Scroll he calls "The Faith of Abraham".

PSALM 89:2
I WILL DECLARE THAT YOUR LOVE STANDS FIRM FOREVER, THAT YOU HAVE ESTABLISHED YOUR FAITHFUL PROMISE (*LOGOS / DEBAR*) OF SALVATION IN THE HEAVENLY SCROLL ITSELF.

PSALM 119:89
YOUR SPOKEN PROMISE (*LOGOS / DEBAR*), YAHUAH, IS ETERNAL; IT STANDS FIRM WRITTEN IN THE HEAVENLY SCROLL.

DANIEL 4:35
"ALL THE INHABITANTS OF THE EARTH ARE ACCOUNTED AS NOTHING, BUT HE DOES ACCORDING TO HIS WILL WRITTEN IN THE HOST OF HEAVEN (*The Heavenly Scroll which hosts constellations. Constellations "host stars"*)

This ancient path of Adam-Enoch is called "The Way" that we are to seek, Yahuah spoke to Jeremiah calling it "The Good Way":

JEREMIAH 6:16
THIS IS WHAT YAHUAH SAYS: "STAND AT THE CROSSROADS AND LOOK; ASK FOR THE ANCIENT (*Enochian*) PATHS, ASK WHERE "THE GOOD WAY" IS, AND WALK IN THE WAY (*of Enoch*), AND YOU WILL FIND REST FOR YOUR SOULS. BUT YOU SAID, 'WE WILL NOT WALK IN IT.'"

The Nazarenes understood that Yahuah's Will and Plan of Salvation was written in The Heavenly Scroll and purposed to be fulfilled in covenant with the Messiah.

EPHESIANS 1:9-10
9 HE MADE KNOWN TO US THE MYSTERY OF HIS WILL ACCORDING TO HIS GOOD PLEASURE, WRITTEN IN THE HEAVENLY SCROLL WHICH HE PURPOSED TO FULFILL IN THE YAHUSHAIC COVENANT, 10 TO BE PUT INTO EFFECT WHEN THE AGES REACH THEIR FULFILLMENT (*Age of Aquarius*)
—

The Hebrews as a whole and even more so later the Hellenized Jews rejected that ancient path and refused to walk in it. Judaism "thoroughly succumbed" to the influence of the religion of the Greeks, called Hellenism. The oral Torah with no foundation in written texts is used to justify these pagan doctrines and beliefs.

Hellenization – Wikipedia

> *"The twentieth century witnessed a lively debate over the extent of Hellenization in the Levant and particularly among the ancient Palestinian Jews that has continued until today. The Judaism of the diaspora was thought to have succumbed thoroughly to its influences. Bultmann thus argued that Christianity arose almost completely within those Hellenistic confines and should be read against that background as opposed to a more traditional (Palestinian) Jewish background"*

Abraham and all the prophets, then through the Zadok Priesthood later John the Baptist, Yahusha and his disciples, then under Sha'ul; all the Nazarenes accepted the ancient path called **The Way**.

ACTS 24:14

HOWEVER, I ADMIT THAT I WORSHIP THE GOD OF OUR ANCESTORS AS A FOLLOWER OF THE WAY (*foretold in The Heavenly Scroll, the ancient Enochian Path - Jeremiah 6:16*), WHICH THEY CALL A SECT.

This "ancient path" passed down through Enoch is that Yahuah laid out in the stars/constellations the Plan of Salvation.

ENOCH 35:3

I BLESSED YAHUAH AUTHOR OF GLORY (*The Heavenly Scroll - Psalm 19:1*), WHO HAD MADE THOSE GREAT AND SPLENDID SIGNS (*of the Zodiac – Genesis 1:14*), THAT THEY MIGHT DISPLAY (*to all mankind - Deut. 4:19*) THE MAGNIFICENCE OF THE WORKS OF HIS HANDS TO ANGELS AND TO THE SOULS OF MEN; AND THAT THESE (*splendid signs in The Heavenly Scroll*) MIGHT GLORIFY ALL HIS WORKS AND OPERATIONS; THAT WE MIGHT SEE THE EFFECT OF HIS POWER (*as Creator to Write His Plan into the fabric of Creation on Day 4 and control the flow of history and fulfill His Promises*); AND THE HEAVENLY SCROLL MIGHT GLORIFY THE GREAT LABOR OF HIS HANDS; AND BLESS HIM FOREVER.

In Romans, Sha'ul confirms Isaiah 48 by quoting King David in Psalms 19:4 where David describes the Zodiac and declares the heavens/Zodiac are pouring forth speech day after day to all mankind as the Sun passes across the sky.

ROMANS 10

17 CONSEQUENTLY, FAITH COMES FROM HEARING THE MESSAGE OF THE GOSPEL (*proclaimed in the heavens*), AND THE MESSAGE IS HEARD THROUGH THE ABOUT THE MESSIAH WORD (*HEAVENLY SCROLL*). 18 BUT I ASK: DID THEY NOT HEAR? OF COURSE THEY DID: "THEIR (*stars and constellations of The Heavenly Scroll*) VOICE HAS GONE OUT INTO ALL THE

EARTH, THEIR WORDS (*concerning Yahusha*) TO THE ENDS OF THE WORLD." (*Sha'ul quotes Psalms 19:4*)

Sha'ul says the message is heard through the word about Yahusha. What "word about Yahusha"? Maybe Sha'ul is referring to the prophecies in The Torah and Writings? No. The "message that is heard through the word about the Messiah" Sha'ul says is... **the Zodiac**, The Heavenly Scroll; the Original Revelation to all mankind, the first and most complete Gospel of Yahusha the Messiah! After asking the question "did they not hear" the message of the Gospel above in Romans 10:18, Sha'ul quotes Psalm 19 where David declares the stars/constellations proclaim the life of the Messiah to all mankind.

PSALM 19:2-6

2 THE SHAMAYIM/HEAVENS (*the place in the sky where the stars are located i.e. Zodiac*) ARE TELLING OF THE GLORY OF YAHUAH (*the Glory of Yahuah is Yahusha! - Hebrews 1:3*); AND THEIR EXPANSE IS DECLARING THE WORK OF HIS HANDS (*Enoch 35:3*). 2 DAY TO DAY POURS FORTH SPEECH, AND NIGHT TO NIGHT REVEALS KNOWLEDGE. 3 THERE IS NO SPEECH, NOR ARE THERE WORDS; THEIR (*signs of the Zodiac/Constellations*) VOICE IS NOT HEARD. 4 THEIR LINE (*ecliptic*) HAS GONE OUT THROUGH (*and seen through*) ALL THE EARTH, AND THEIR (*constellations*) UTTERANCES TO THE END OF THE WORLD. IN THEM (the constellations) HE HAS PLACED A TENT FOR THE SUN (*the Zodiac*), 5 WHICH (*as it travels through the constellations or 'signs'*) IS AS A BRIDEGROOM (*Yahusha*) COMING OUT OF HIS CHAMBER; IT REJOICES AS A STRONG MAN TO RUN HIS COURSE (*through the ecliptic*). 6 ITS RISING IS FROM ONE END OF THE HEAVENS (*stars*), AND ITS CIRCUIT (Zodiac means circuit or path) TO THE OTHER END OF STARS IN HEAVEN; AND THERE IS NOTHING HIDDEN FROM ITS HEAT.

We were told the Zodiac is Yahuah's gift to all mankind, and we were not supposed to worship it. We abandoned the message told

43

by the meaning of the constellations and made gods out of them to worship:

> ### DEUTERONOMY 4:19
> WHEN YOU LOOK UP TO THE SKY (*sky is Hebrew shamayim/Zodiac*) AND SEE THE SUN, MOON, AND STARS (*speaking of the Zodiac*) – THE WHOLE HEAVENLY (*Hebrew shamayim*) CREATION – YOU MUST NOT BE SEDUCED TO WORSHIP AND SERVE THEM (*constellations*), <u>FOR YAHUAH YOUR ELOHIM HAS ASSIGNED THEM</u> (*the constellations*) <u>TO ALL THE PEOPLE OF THE WORLD</u> (*they were created by Yahuah to proclaim the coming Messiah Yahusha, see Psalm 19, they are pictographs they are not gods*).

Then, because we chose to idolize the constellations, we reversed course and declared The Heavenly Scroll itself pagan. This was a major mistake!

Rabbi Joel C. Dobin
> "*<u>Astrology was so much part of Jewish life and experience and so well respected in our tradition and law that the abandonment of Astrology to follow the chimera of scientific linearality was one of the greatest religious tragedies that ever befell our people.</u> For in so doing, we abandoned as well the mystical realities of our faith, our abilities to balance our lives and attain Unity...*"

The Heavenly Scroll or Zodiac was revealed to Enoch and later to Abraham and was the "source of their faith":

> ### GENESIS 15:5
> AND YAHUAH BROUGHT ABRAM FORTH ABROAD (*out under the stars*), AND SAID, LOOK NOW TOWARD HEAVEN (*shamayim/Zodiac*), AND (*see if you can*) TELL (*what*) THE STARS (*proclaim*), IF THOU BE ABLE TO NUMBER THEM (*read them in order, there are 12*): AND HE SAID UNTO HIM, SO (*what they*

44

proclaim) SHALL THY SEED (*Yahusha*) BE (*they tell the story of his life*).

Everything that was done in creation was done according to a predestined plan written into the fabric of Creation "in the beginning":

JOHN 1
1 IN THE BEGINNING WAS THE PLAN OF YAHUAH, AND THE PLAN WAS WITH YAHUAH (*and defined His purpose in creation*), AND THE PLAN WAS YAHUAH'S. 2 THE SAME PLAN WAS IN THE BEGINNING WITH YAHUAH. 3 ALL THINGS WERE DONE ACCORDING TO THE PLAN OF YAHUAH, AND WITHOUT THE PLAN OF YAHUAH NOTHING WAS DONE, THAT WAS DONE. 4 IN THIS PLAN WAS (*predestined*) LIFE (*through a human Messiah's sacrifice*), AND THAT LIFE WAS THE LIGHT (*revelation*) TO MANKIND.

That "plan" or "spoken promise/LOGOS/DABAR" is called The Heavenly Scroll and there is nothing done by Yahuah that is not written in the stars at creation.

DANIEL 4:35
"ALL THE INHABITANTS OF THE EARTH ARE ACCOUNTED AS NOTHING, BUT HE DOES ACCORDING TO HIS WILL WRITTEN IN THE HOST OF HEAVEN (*The Heavenly Scroll which hosts constellations. Constellations "host stars"*)

Yahuah didn't just name these stars and constellations for identification purposes; but for signs to be used as prophetic markers for coming days, seasons, and years ... but also as signs with meaning called **pictographs** that tell the story of Yahusha the Messiah as the Sun passes through them each year!

GENESIS 1:14
AND YAHUAH SAID, "LET THERE BE LIGHTS IN THE EXPANSE

OF THE SKY TO SEPARATE THE DAY FROM THE NIGHT, AND
LET THEM SERVE AS SIGNS, AND TO MARK SEASONS AND
DAYS AND YEARS."

Sha'ul taught the Nazarene assembly in Galatia it was Abraham's
faith in The Heavenly Scroll that was credited to him as
Righteousness!

GALATIANS 3

5 SO AGAIN I ASK, DOES YAHUAH GIVE YOU HIS SPIRIT AND
WORK MIRACLES AMONG YOU BY THE WORKS OF THE LAW,
OR BY YOUR BELIEVING WHAT YOU HEARD (*proclaimed by the
stars - Psalms 19*)? 6 SO ALSO ABRAHAM "BELIEVED YAHUAH
(*when Yahuah told him to read The Heavenly Scroll - Genesis 15:5*),
AND IT (*his belief in The Heavenly Scroll's Gospel message*) WAS
CREDITED TO HIM AS RIGHTEOUSNESS." 7 UNDERSTAND,
THEN, THAT THOSE WHO HAVE FAITH (*in The Heavenly Scroll*)
ARE CHILDREN OF ABRAHAM. 8 SCRIPTURE (*the word
contained eternally in The Heavenly Scroll - Psalms 119:89*)
FORESAW (*from the foundation of the world - 1 Peter 1:20*) THAT
YAHUAH WOULD JUSTIFY THE GENTILES BY FAITH AND
ANNOUNCED THE GOSPEL IN ADVANCE TO ABRAHAM (*telling
him to read the stars - Genesis 15:5 - which minister the Gospel to all
mankind - Isaiah 48:11-15*): "ALL NATIONS WILL BE BLESSED
THROUGH YOU." 9 SO THOSE WHO RELY ON FAITH (*in the
Plan of Salvation written in The Heavenly Scroll*) ARE BLESSED
ALONG WITH ABRAHAM, THE MAN OF FAITH (*in what he read in
the stars - Genesis 15:5*) ...16 THE PROMISES (*Logos/Dabar
means "spoken promises"*) WERE SPOKEN TO ABRAHAM (*via The
Heavenly Scroll - Genesis 1:15*) AND TO HIS SEED. SCRIPTURE
DOES NOT SAY "AND TO SEEDS," MEANING MANY PEOPLE,
BUT "AND TO YOUR SEED," MEANING ONE PERSON, WHO IS
THE MESSIAH (*is what the Stars told Abraham, Isaiah, the
Galatians, and you and I today!*).

Only once The Ancient Path of Enoch (The Heavenly Scroll) is restored to Sha'ul the Nazarene can his writing be properly understood.

In Chapter 1 we will examine the translation issues that have given us written Scriptures that have been altered through syncretism to lead us all astray.

Chapter 1
Transliteration

Chapter 1: Transliteration

Biblical Hebrew has been a dead language now for 2,000 years. All we can do is reconstruct the best we can with what few incomplete discarded scripal notes, scrolls, inscriptions, etc. have survived passed down from error-prone scribal zealots. All with competing interests, beliefs, and oral traditions!

Worse yet, our efforts to achieve an English version have come at the hands of transliteration over time from what fragments we have in ancient Hebrew into Greek and from there into Latin, and from there into English then modern Hebrew. With each iteration of transliteration, we lose the authenticity, flavor, intent, and context that was The Hebrew Language and Cultural Matrix of the ancient Hebrews.

Source: https://en.wikipedia.org/wiki/Romanization_of_Hebrew
> *"In the cases of Hebrew transliteration into English, many Hebrew words have a long history of transliteration and were in many cases first transliterated into Greek and Latin before English."*

At issue is the concept of transliteration as the Scriptures are not "translated" they are "transliterated". There seems to be little standardization in the community of translation experts.

Biblical Hebrew is a Dead Language

Biblical Hebrew is a dead language! The language ceased to exist and was no longer spoken for more than 1,000 years.

HTTPS://WWW.BIBLICALARCHAEOLOGY.ORG/DAILY/BIBLI CAL-TOPICS/HEBREW-BIBLE/WHAT-IS-THE-OLDEST-HEBREW-BIBLE/

THE EARLIEST VERSION OF THE COMPLETE "OLD TESTAMENT" SCRIPTURE DATES BACK TO THE 10TH CENTURY AD WRITTEN BY THE MAORETES (NOT NAZARENES) AND WAS TRANSLITERATED FROM GREEK, NOT ANCIENT HEBREW. THE OLDEST COMPLETE OT IS THE CODEX LENINGRADENSIS DATING TO THE 13TH CENTURY AD....

While the Dead Sea Scrolls date back before the first century, they are far from complete. They are small fragments (a few complete books) and have to be reconstructed through "educated guesses" as to the massive missing parts to try and piece them back together.

We are constantly lied to about how the Hebrew OT was passed down to us today. Judaism became the standard Jewish religion but was their "Torah" the Torah used by Yahusha the Nazarene? Where and how did we achieve the Jewish Torah? Have the scribes meticulously maintained the Scriptures as we have been told by Judaism?

We will answer those questions in this book as well.

The Hebrew Scriptures Were NOT Meticulously Maintained by the Scribes

We are led to believe the Jewish Torah was meticulously transcribed down through history by dedicated scribes under the threat of death for the most minute mistep.

That could not be further from the truth!

Worse yet, far from being meticulously and in a consistent way passed down by Jewish scribes, they were mangled by those very scribes the same way the Catholic Church mangled the New Testament scripts. The result... a transliterated mixture of omissions, additions, twisting, and mangling to ensure the beliefs of the scribes were written into the text. Causing 2000 years of "interpretation" leading to a splintering of those with a desire to know the Truth. We now have many various sects within Judaism and hundreds of Christian denominations. This is because the "transition of the texts from one scribe to the next was fluid".

source:https://www.baslibrary.org/biblical-archaeology-review/41/6/4

"The earliest texts of the Hebrew Bible—or the Old Testament, as Christians call it—are found among the Dead Sea Scrolls, which include more than 200 Biblical texts ranging from a few words to almost complete books, such as a nearly undamaged copy of the Book of Isaiah (1QIsaa).a The dates of these ancient Bible manuscripts range from c. 250 B.C.E. to 115 C.E., so they are much older than the Ashkar-Gilson Manuscript. **In this early period, the texts were not yet completely fixed; their transmission was still fluid. Copyists made mistakes, wanted to improve or expand a**

text, or adapted the spelling of certain words. Sometimes the copies could be quite different versions of the same text—for example, the Book of Jeremiah"...

Not only are the Hebrew scriptures we read in our Bibles today only a few hundred years old and written by scribal error and manipulation of fragments passed down... No one speaks Biblical Hebrew/Aramaic today. Don't fall for all those "Hebrew experts" who claim they know better than everyone else and simply because they speak Modern Hebrew. They are as in the dark as someone who has nothing more than a good interlinear at their fingertips.

Source: https://www.ancient-hebrew.org/language/is-ancient-hebrew-a-dead-language.htm

> "*Strictly speaking, classical biblical Hebrew is a dead language. It is as dead as Akkadian, Ugaritic, Sumerian, or koiné Greek. We are dealing with a fixed set of texts, not the Hebrew spoken in the nation of Israel today. Israeli Hebrew has significant differences from biblical Hebrew. While the verb forms are by and large biblical, "not only were all the archaic forms of BH rejected . . . but also the consecutive tenses, the cohortative, the infinitive absolute more or less, and the infinitive construct (except for the plus [lamedh] and plus [bet] infinitive forms." The syntax is heavily influenced by a combination of Mishnaic Hebrew and European languages;[14] some biblical vocabulary is either rejected or substantially modified as to its usage; and "it has been calculated that some ten percent of the words in Hebrew dictionaries might be of foreign, usually Western, origin." Further, the pronunciation system is basically Sephardic, not Ashkenazic or Yemenite.*"

Different Publishers have Different Transliteration Rules

While our modern-day "Hebrew experts" in Judaism try and convince us we have The Word of Yahuah all we need to do is speak modern Hebrew, this is far from the truth. In fact, transliteration from Hebrew (which itself was reconstructed from transliterations into Greek/Latin i.e. the *Septuagint*) is far from a science. It is not even an art form. It is more of a "guess" and depends on who is doing the "guessing" from error-ridden sources and there is no standards or systems or rules by which various "experts" transliterate from one language to another.

Source: https://en.wikipedia.org/wiki/Romanization_of_Hebrew
> *"There are various transliteration standards or systems for Hebrew-to-English; no one system has significant common usage across all fields. Consequently, in general usage there are often no hard and fast rules in Hebrew-to-English transliteration, and many transliterations are an approximation due to a lack of equivalence between the English and Hebrew alphabets...*
> *Conflicting systems of transliteration often appear in the same text, as certain Hebrew words tend to associate with certain traditions of transliteration.*
> *These discrepancies in transliterations of the same word can be traced to discrepancies in the transliterations of individual Hebrew letters, reflecting not only different traditions of transliteration into different languages that use Latin alphabets."*

53

Example #1: A Rightful King by My Decree

Psalm 110:4 is used to link the King of Salem to Yahusha through some form of Divine re-incarnation carrying forward some type of "eternal priesthood", outside of that defined by Yahuah in Scripture (the bloodline of Aaron through Zadok).

However, what we do not realize is the Hebrew text of that Psalm is not so crystal clear! There are several ways of transliterating that Psalm.

Most translations that follow the Greek Old Testament (Septuagint) read "THOU ARE A PRIEST FOREVER AFTER THE 'ORDER' OF MELCHIZEDEK". However, the 1917 translation by JPS (the most trusted source at that time) recognized the word "order" was not what the Hebrew text implied at all. The "experts" got it wrong across the board for over a thousand years!

The meaning was more along the lines of a priest in the "manner" of a Melchi (righteous) Tzedek (King). It is not referring to King David (and by extension Yahusha) being a Priest in some other priestly order passed down from a dead pagan King of Salem! Below is how it is translated in the JPS 1917 Bible:

> **_Psalm_ 110:4** (JPS 1917 TRANSLATION OF TANAKH)
> THE LORD HATH SWORN, AND WILL NOT REPENT: 'THOU ART A PRIEST FOR EVER AFTER THE MANNER OF MELCHI TZEDEK.'

So what David was expressing is that Yahusha would be an Eternal Priest in like 'manner' (or like unto) a Righteous King. Psalm 110:4 has no significance to the King of Salem at all other than like Sha'ul explained, there is a comparison to be drawn, but nothing more. The new translation by JPS is far more accurate to The Plan of Salvation or Scarlet Thread of Redemption as Yahuah made the Promise of an Eternal Throne to David, and Eternal Priesthood to Zadok (David's close friend and High Priest). So Yahusha would Fulfill that Promise to the House of Zadok and be the Eternal High Priest but in the 'manner' of a Righteous King fulfilling the Promise to David. Yahusha would be BOTH.

Recently, the JPS (Jewish Publication Society) has gone back and completely re-translated the Tanakh.
The 1917 translation was based on The American Standard translation; they did not go back to the original text themselves in that 1917 version. We see from their website, that their NEW Translation is totally new and completely unrelated to the 1917 version as they did not follow The American Standard (derived from the Greek OT) but went back to the original Hebrew text themselves.

> *"The New Jewish Publication Society of America Tanakh, first published in complete form in 1985, is a modern Jewish translation of the Masoretic Text of the Hebrew Bible into English. It is based on revised editions of earlier publications of subdivisions of the Tanakh such as, the Torah and Five Megillot, which were originally published from 1969–1982. It is unrelated to the original JPS Tanakh translation, which was based on the Revised Version and American Standard Version but emended to more strictly follow the Masoretic text, beyond both translations being published by the Jewish Publication Society of America."*

How once going back to the original language and Masoretic text, they transliterated that Pslam below:

Psalm 110:4 (JPS 1985)
YOU ARE A PRIEST FOREVER, A RIGHTFUL KING BY MY DECREE.

This one example (of many) should cause us all to hit the pause button on the idea that "we have the Word of God IF you speak modern Hebrew"!

This sheds some serious "New Light" on this teaching of an external "Melchizedek Priesthood"! Because what David said has nothing to do with the King of Salem or some external pagan priesthood outside of Aaron called "The Melchizedek Priesthood" which relies 100% on a MISTRANSATION of Psalm 110:4. Yahuah was simply telling Yahusha that he was the Fulfillment of the Promise to the House of Zadok line of Aaronic High Priest, NOT some mythical extra-Biblical priesthood based on re-incarnation of an Ancient King!

The word translated "priest" in that verse is Hebrew 'kohen' ("כֹהֵן"). The term 'kohen' bears the connotation of priesthood, also servitude to the deity, and, less frequently, RULERSHIP! We see this in (II Sam. 8:18): "and David's sons were kohanim (chief officers not priests)". Below are a few examples of this interesting variation in transliteration:

2 *Samuel* 8:18 (KJV)
AND BENAIAH THE SON OF JEHOIADA WAS OVER BOTH THE CHERETHITES AND THE PELETHITES; AND DAVID'S SONS WERE CHIEF RULERS (KOHENIM).

2 *Samuel* 20:26 (KJV)
AND IRA, ALSO THE JAIRITE, WAS A CHIEF RULER (KOHEN) ABOUT DAVID.

1 *Kings* 4:5 (KJV)
AND AZARIAH THE SON OF NATHAN WAS OVER THE OFFICERS: AND ZABUD THE SON OF NATHAN WAS PRINCIPAL OFFICER (KOHEN) AND THE KING'S FRIEND.

The FIRST definition of Kohen is not 'priest' but "Chief Ruler" i.e. KING! Also note, that Kohen can also be a Priest of OTHER RELIGIONS (such as Salem):

H3548 '*Kohen*' - *Strong's Exhaustive Concordance*
chief ruler, own, priest, prince, principal officer. 2) priests of other religions

When speaking of the Hebrew word "kohen", Christian translators translated as "priest" in Psalm 110:4, it is often translated as "ruler" in many places in Christian translations. The Hebrew word is kohen and while commonly translated as "priest" it may have other meanings. The word appears 750 times in the Masoretic Text. In 5 cases the KJV translates it as "officers". Therefore, Psalm 110:4 could read:

Psalm 110:4
YOU ARE A RULER FOREVER, A RIGHTFUL KING BY MY DECREE.

This is the intent as it was spoken about King David (and by extension the Messiah), not the dead Priest/King of Salem.

Example #2: Let Us Make Man in Our Image

Getting back to my recent post on "us" and "our" in Genesis 1:26. A brother made the comment:

> *"You are missing the plural form of the verb after elohim in verse 26, as well as the plural possessive of the image and likeness. This is why the US and OUR must exist. Hebrew grammar demands this."*

"Hebrew grammar demands this" not sure I agree. Sounds more like a "guess" to me... see the attached image where the "experts" say "most likely derived" ... in other words "we really aren't sure."

The prefix נ (Nun) means 'we'.

This prefix was most likely derived from the Hebrew word meaning 'we' because sometimes the first letter א is dropped and it is simply spelled נחנו .

אנחנו   ANChNW   we

אני = I + ה = separate + נ = ahead + ו = add to

– meaning: 'I with others separate of me'.

The prefix שׁ (Shin) means 'who'.

The letter shin is attached to a verb to turn it into who (or what) does the action. For example, in English we would say that someone was a 'maker' of something, however, in Hebrew the phrase literally says 'who makes'. The reason the letter Shin is used for this purpose is unclear. It is most commonly found in the scriptures that the method of inserting a Yod or Waw as the second letter of the verb is used to turn the word into a person.

We cannot make a statement like "Biblical Hebrew demands it" because that language has been dead for 2000 years and then transliterated through 4 dead languages based on error-ridden fragments by opportunist Hellenized Jewish Scribes no earlier than the 10th Century.

Per the image above, the best we can say is "most likely"... I don't know about you, but "most likely" is far from "Hebrew demands it" and FAR from good enough for me in my search for understanding.

As I showed in example 1 Psalm 110:4 our so-called Hebrew experts never went back to Hebrew at all and used the Greek OT to arrive at a completely bogus translation for over over 1,000 years before JPS finally decided to get it right.

In our English Bibles, Genesis 1:26-27 reads:

Genesis 1:26-27

26 THEN GOD SAID, "LET US MAKE MAN IN OUR IMAGE, IN OUR LIKENESS, AND LET THEM RULE OVER THE FISH OF THE SEA AND THE BIRDS OF THE AIR, OVER THE LIVESTOCK, OVER ALL THE EARTH, AND OVER ALL THE CREATURES THAT MOVE ALONG THE GROUND." 27 SO GOD CREATED MAN IN HIS OWN IMAGE, IN THE IMAGE OF GOD HE CREATED HIM; MALE AND FEMALE HE CREATED THEM.

Is this accurate or did the translators falsify the text by adding words and twisting existing words to write the doctrine of the Trinity into the text?

I will prove the proper translation of this text from Hebrew to English is:

Genesis 1:26-27

THEN ELOHIM (*this is the last point of clear context, Yahuah* - *Genesis* 2:8) SAID, "LET MANKIND BE MADE IN THE IMAGE AND LIKENESS OF ELOHIM (*sons of God* - *Psalms* 82:6), AND LET MANKIND RULE OVER THE FISH OF THE SEA AND THE BIRDS OF THE AIR, OVER THE LIVESTOCK, OVER ALL THE EARTH, AND OVER ALL THE CREATURES THAT MOVE ALONG THE GROUND." 27 SO YAHUAH CREATED MAN IN HIS OWN IMAGE (*Genesis* 2:8, *Psalms* 82:6), IN THE IMAGE OF ELOHIM (*as sons*) HE (*singluar*) CREATED HIM; MALE AND FEMALE HE (*singluar*) CREATED THEM

I will prove textually and in the context that Yahuah singularly is the creator and that the plural nature of the word "elohim" used in this verse is referring to the family of Yahuah or "sons of God" or "mankind" NOT a plurality of creator gods.

The Hebrew Word "Elohim/elohim"

Elohim is in the Bible 2,598 times and 2,596 times it is translated as "God" referring to Yahuah or "gods" referring to the sons of

Yahuah or messengers (Angles).

Elohim can be singular or plural depending on the context. We indicate the singular use with a capital E and the plural use with a small e. So Yahuah is Elohim and His sons are elohim in English. Or God and gods in the Hellenized sense of the words.

The only two times Elohim is not translated as "God" or "sons of God".. is in Genesis 1:26 where all of a sudden Elohim is translated as "us" and "our"! A Clear red flag that the lying pen of the scribe has struck yet again to deceive!

Jeremiah 8:8
'"HOW CAN YOU SAY, "WE ARE WISE, FOR WE HAVE THE LAW OF YAHUAH," WHEN ACTUALLY THE LYING PEN OF THE SCRIBES HAS HANDLED IT FALSELY?

Now, when you look at the Hebrew Interlinear the words "us" and "our" were added by scribes (in error as I will prove).

Under the English words above that are actually in Hebrew, you see "Noun or Verb". The other words without a Hebrew word under them are scribal additions. The only English words are "said, God, make, man, image, likeness" in Hebrew.

Notice in the image there are only 6 words in Hebrew and 14

English words. 8 words were added by the translators. Now, I admit when going from Hebrew to English there is a need to add words, so that is not the issue. The issue is, did they do the text justice and follow the standard rules of translation? Or did they deviate from the rules of translation here to build in a false pagan doctrine?

Let "us" find out (pun intended).

First, we need to understand what those "rules" that govern proper translation are! The rules that govern translation ensure that the words we have to add in English are correct and in context. Context is what must be kept at all costs, contradictions resolved, tense of words kept in agreement. All violated this one verse!

We must keep the Textual Context, Historical Context, Scriptual Context, and Spiritual Context to properly understand in English was it said in Hebrew in any single verse. We must NEVER "sound bite" a verse out of context and build an entire doctrine out of context (basically all of Christianity falls into this category).

To keep "Textual Context" in translation, we look around the portion of scripture in question for the last point in the text around it where "context" is clearly established. Everything after that point is within THAT context until there is another point of clear context change.

First, let's read Genesis 1:26 as it would read in Hebrew using just the 6 Hebrew words in the original text. Those 6 Hebrew words are:

way·yō·mer...'ĕ·lō·hîm... na·'ă·śeh... 'ā·ḏām... bə·ṣal·mê·nū... kiḏ·mū·ṯê·nū

and literally, it reads *"said Elohim make man image likeness"* when transliterated into English. We (the translators) have to add

61

some words to make it make sense. To do that, we look for the last point of clear context... The context set above is that of "Elohim" with a capital "E" referring to Yahuah Elohim. This is clearly documented in context:

Genesis 2:7-8
NOW THE LORD GOD (*Yahuah Elohim*) HAD PLANTED A GARDEN IN THE EAST, IN EDEN; AND THERE HE PUT THE MAN HE HAD FORMED.

There was no "us" or "our" as there was NO OTHER GOD with Him at creation, he did all by himself.

Isaiah 44:24
24 "THIS IS WHAT YAHUAH SAYS— YOUR REDEEMER, WHO FORMED YOU IN THE WOMB: I AM YAHUAH, THE MAKER OF ALL THINGS, WHO STRETCHES OUT THE HEAVENS, WHO SPREADS OUT THE EARTH BY MYSELF.

Isaiah 45:5-18
5 I AM YAHUAH, AND THERE IS NO OTHER; APART FROM ME THERE IS NO GOD. 7 I FORM THE LIGHT AND CREATE DARKNESS, I BRING PROSPERITY AND CREATE DISASTER; I, YAHUAH, DO ALL THESE THINGS. 12 IT IS I WHO MADE THE EARTH AND CREATED MANKIND UPON IT. MY OWN HANDS STRETCHED OUT THE HEAVENS; I MARSHALED THEIR STARRY HOSTS. 18 FOR THIS IS WHAT YAHUAH SAYS— HE WHO CREATED THE HEAVENS, HE (ALONE) IS GOD; HE WHO FASHIONED AND MADE THE EARTH, HE FOUNDED IT; HE DID NOT CREATE IT TO BE EMPTY, BUT FORMED IT TO BE INHABITED— HE SAYS: "I AM YAHUAH, AND THERE IS NO OTHER (GOD)."

So Yahuah cleared that up with His declarations over and over (the above a just a sampling of many more) that He alone is God, He is singular, and created all things by Himself. That overturns the twisted translations of Genesis 1:26 that added "us" and "our" to the text!

So literally it should have been properly translated as:

___

Genesis 1:26-27
THEN YAHUAH (*Genesis* 2:8) SAID, "LET MANKIND BE MADE IMAGE LIKENESS,

___

Many "Hebrew experts" will point out that the word "elohim" in this verse is plural which is why they added "us" and "our" to the text to indicate the plurality of the term "elohim".

However, as I stated earlier", the word "elohim" can be singular or plural referring to Elohim (Yahuah) or elohim (sons of Yahuah). We read in Genesis 2:7 that it was Yahuah Elohim, singular, who created mankind.

Therefore, the plural nature of the word "elohim" in *Genesis* 1:26-27 refers to "mankind" which was mistranslated as singular "man" in error. It is MANKIND plural that was created in the image of elohim. Again, it was "I" singular who said "you/mankind" are elohim, sons of the Most High (singular).

___

Psalm 82:6
"I SAID, 'YOU ARE "GODS"; YOU ARE ALL SONS OF THE MOST HIGH.'

___

Given the clear context of Scripture, the declaration of Yahuah, and the actual Hebrew words and definitions below is the proper translation into English:

___

Genesis 1:26-27
THEN YAHUAH ELOHIM (*Genesis* 2:7-8) SAID, "LET MANKIND BE MADE IN THE IMAGE AND LIKENESS OF ELOHIM (*sons of God - Psalms* 82:6), AND LET MANKIND RULE OVER THE FISH OF THE SEA AND THE BIRDS OF THE AIR, OVER THE LIVESTOCK, OVER ALL THE EARTH, AND OVER ALL THE CREATURES THAT MOVE ALONG THE

GROUND." 27 So YAHUAH CREATED MAN IN HIS OWN IMAGE (*Genesis* 2:8, *Psalms* 82:6), IN THE IMAGE OF ELOHIM (*as sons*) HE (*singluar*) CREATED HIM; MALE AND FEMALE HE (*singluar*) CREATED THEM.

Tense Violation

The translators twisted the text in Genesis 1:26 to support their own pagan beliefs in a Trinitarian "Godhead". They ignored the clear context of "Elohim" which is the singular form referring to the MOST HIGH, Yahuah Elohim. They added the words "us" and "our" in error, ignoring the clear scriptural context that Yahuah alone created mankind confirmed in the original Hebrew and in the very next verse.

In doing so; they were able to "build into the text" the pagan doctrine of the Trinity and make Genesis contradict itself from one verse 26 to the very next verse 27 which clearly says He created man in His image! Confirmed in Psalms 82:6 that says "I" singular created man in the image of "elohim" plural meaning gods in the image of The Most High (singular).

So in verse 26, the tense of the Creator is said to be plural then in verse 27 the tense of the Creator is singular! They would not pass 3rd-grade English classes with that one!

The plural tense in verse 26 refers to lowercase elohim or "mankind" not the Creator. Verse 27 is accurate.

Genesis 1:26 is a case study of the errors inherent in transliteration from 4 dead languages (Biblical Hebrew into Latin, then Greek, then Old English) finally into modern English and modern Hebrew. Whew! I'm exhausted already.

Not only is the "word-for-word" transliteration not based on any provable fact as we are dealing with DEAD languages, but we can be 100% certain verse 26 is in grave error as it violates clear declarations from the Creator Yahuah Himself that HE ALONE created man all by Himself. And verse 26 "we" and "our" contradict the very next verse 27 which uses the singular pronoun "He created" which is in context and accurate to the rest of the Scriptures.

The question we must, if we are being honest, ask ourselves is this: *"Do we trust an impossible word-for-word transliteration or build our understanding on "intent and context"?*

Word-for-Word or In-Context Translation by Intent

Ok Sha'ul, so we don't know without a doubt what ancient Biblical Hebrew said in any one specific verse. At best, we have educated guesses by teams of modern intellectuals forcing a round peg (ancient Hebrew) into a square hole (modern Hebrew). How then are we to have any confidence in what the Scriptures say today vs what was actually written in ancient times?

Taking Scriptural "sound bites" and stringing them all together out of context to create an implied doctrine or simply taking one verse and claiming it is "word-for-word" is folly. These doctrines are always easy to identify because they violate clear explicit doctrine (sound doctrine). Anytime an implied doctrine is formulated that contradicts explicit Scriptures, we must reject that doctrine as our "understanding" is flawed.

I have put together my "rules of translating" the Scriptures to ensure there is NO contradiction and no sound-biting out of context while keeping the intent of the text throughout.

- Yahuah reveals His Word progressively over time through Prophets not "committees/teams" of human experts!

- Focus should be on the destination language, not the source language.

- The most important aspect of handling The Word of Yahuah is anointing.

- Never translate one language to the next word-for-word!

- The Bible is written in dead languages, no one speaks those languages today, therefore there are no "experts."

Progressive Revelation NOT "By Committee"

Wisdom and understanding of Yahuah's Word, Will, Purpose, and Plan come through His anointed men who teach... not committees of intellectual "experts".

Matthew 23:34
THEREFORE I AM SENDING YOU PROPHETS AND SAGES AND TEACHERS. SOME OF THEM YOU WILL KILL AND CRUCIFY; OTHERS YOU WILL FLOG IN YOUR SYNAGOGUES AND PURSUE FROM TOWN TO TOWN.

One of the major failures of all translation efforts in human history is they are done by "committee". A team of self-absorbed "experts" who are not Nazarenes and certainly not anointed by the Throne of Creation for the task.

Anytime you have a team of so-called "experts" every decision in translation is done by committee. The resulting translation is a severely compromised version required to come to a consensus among the experts. Compromises to get their approval bringing in their existing misconceptions, false doctrines, and so forth.

There should be one... only one anointed prophet of Yahuah, a true Nazarene at the heart of the effort qualified and gifted to bring the text from one language to another and honor the Nazarene authors of the originals. One anointed to understand The Mystery Language the Scriptures are written in and gifted in the destination language to make this language easily understood in the resulting translation. Trained by Yahuah over the course of a lifetime for this most important of all callings.

Daniel spoke of these "men of wisdom" to come at the end to fix "the Lying Pen of the Scribe"...

Daniel 11:33-34

33 THOSE WITH INSIGHT WILL INSTRUCT MANY, THOUGH FOR A TIME THEY WILL FALL BY SWORD OR FLAME, OR BE CAPTURED OR PLUNDERED. 34 NOW WHEN THEY FALL, THEY WILL BE GRANTED A LITTLE HELP, BUT MANY WILL JOIN THEM INSINCERELY. 35 SOME OF THE WISE WILL FALL, SO THAT THEY MAY BE REFINED, PURIFIED, AND MADE SPOTLESS UNTIL THE TIME OF THE END, FOR IT WILL STILL COME AT THE APPOINTED TIME

Focus Should be on the Destination Language

In every past translation effort, the focus is not on the destination language (which is the point of the effort) but on the original languages.

This is a major error in any translation effort. The "originals" are already written! What is being created is in the destination language. That is the focus of any good modern-day translation effort. The existing texts of the Scriptures are already written, and we have 2,000 years of "experts" explaining, exploring, and defining those texts and the structure of those languages.

We have reference material at our disposal that these past translators did not have, we have interlinear references to show the structure and how it was translated, dictionaries, commentaries, etc. Those are "the experts" required in the original languages.

I have more knowledge at the end of my mouse click (the Internet) than all the translators who ever worked on any translation over the past 2,000 years COMBINED...

Anointing the Main Qualification of the Translator

That is where the Truth is found. It should be done independent of any "commissioning organization" or any outside influence... by a singular anointed servant sent by Yahuah to restore The Word of His Testimony just like Yahuah has done throughout history called PROPHETS. Not "committees".

Never Translate One Language to the Next "Word-for-Word:

We have all purchased goods from Wal-Mart made in China. Opened them up to assemble them and the instructions made no sense whatsoever in English.

https://www.buzzfeed.com/nataliemorin/chinese-signs-that-got-seriously-lost-in-tranlsation?utm_term=.gfL9RbK8l#.lx5b0wGlQ

This is because the translators putting it into English did not speak English as their first language. Instead, they simply put together a word-for-word translation from Chinese into English... the result is confusing and sometimes ridiculous and the "intent and meaning" of the instructions are lost in translation.

Why do I bring this up? That is exactly what every translation team attempted for 2,000 years. They misunderstood "don't add to or subtract from" to mean "the words" and tried to just translate each word from Hebrew/Greek into a word in English.
This is a complete violation of the main principle in any translation effort.

The MOST IMPORTANT member of the translation team is the expert in the destination language. The sentence structure in one language never matches the sentence structure in another language, the words don't match up "one to one", and the figures of speech, idioms, metaphors, and so forth are not shared from one language/cultural matrix to the next.

When you simply translate word-for-word you get a confusing and many times misleading result.

This is what we have today in our English Bibles. The Hebraic flavor, figures of speech, meaning, and intent are lost as the translators put together a word-for-word translation and ignore the intent, context, and language/cultural matrix from one language to the next.

Old English a Dead Language

The Word was transliterated from Greek into "Old English" yet ANOTHER dead language long before Modern Hebrew came along. Ancient Hebrew is to Modern Hebrew what Old English is to Modern English! Let me illustrate.

> John Locke in a 1692 publication, wrote... *"I fear, that the jumbling of those good and plausible Words in your Head..might a little jargogle your Thoughts..."*'

Why do I mention this? Not one person reading that statement who speaks English knows what he just said. Speaking today's modern English is no help at all as "Old English" is a dead language. The words are no longer used and the way the sentences are structured makes no sense to us today.

From https://en.oxforddictionaries.com/usage/old-fashioned-language

> Some words that were common in the past are no longer in ordinary use but remain in our stock of words. Many dictionaries divide this type of vocabulary into two categories.

Archaic

Words and expressions described as archaic are those which haven't been in everyday use for a century or more. Some dictionaries describe such terms as 'old use', or 'old-fashioned use'. You are unlikely to hear anyone using these terms in everyday conversation or to come across them in modern writing, but you will encounter them in the literature of the past.

This category of vocabulary is sometimes used to give a deliberately old-fashioned effect, for example in historical novels. Some writers also use it to amuse people.

71

Examples:
- *bedroom / bedchamber*
- *frighten / affright*
- *perhaps / peradventure*
- *willing / fain*

Dated
Words and expressions described as dated may still be used occasionally, especially by older people, but they are no longer used by most English speakers. Here are some examples of dated words:

Examples:
- *boyfriend / beau*
- *educated / lettered*
- *hurry / make haste*
- *nonsense / bunkum*
- *your / thine*
- *you / thee*

Hmmm.... a little "jargogle" for thought from one of the "foundations of the English Bible" the original King James... Widely regarded as the "inerrant word of God"...

O YE CORINTHIANS, OUR MOUTH IS OPEN UNTO YOU, OUR HEART IS ENLARGED. YE ARE NOT STRAITENED IN US, BUT YE ARE STRAITENED IN YOUR OWN BOWELS. NOW FOR A RECOMPENSE IN THE SAME, (I SPEAK AS UNTO MY CHILDREN,) BE YE ALSO ENLARGED. (2 *Cor* 6:11-13, *KJV*)

HE RUNNETH UPON HIM, EVEN ON HIS NECK, UPON THE THICK BOSSES OF HIS BUCKLERS: BECAUSE HE COVERETH HIS FACE WITH HIS FATNESS, AND MAKETH COLLOPS OF FAT ON HIS FLANKS. (*Job* 15:26,27, *KJV*)

HE THAT IS SURETY FOR A STRANGER SHALL SMART FOR IT: AND HE THAT HATETH SURETISHIP IS SURE. (*Prov* 11:15, *KJV*)

IN MEASURE, WHEN IT SHOOTETH FORTH, THOU WILT DEBATE WITH IT: HE STAYETH HIS ROUGH WIND IN THE DAY OF THE EAST WIND. (*Isaiah* 27:8, *KJV*)

FOR THE LORD SHALL JUDGE HIS PEOPLE, AND REPENT HIMSELF FOR HIS SERVANTS, WHEN HE SEETH THAT THEIR POWER IS GONE, AND THERE IS NONE SHUT UP, OR LEFT. (*Deu* 32:36, *KJV*)

TAKE HIS GARMENT THAT IS SURETY FOR A STRANGER: AND TAKE A PLEDGE OF HIM FOR A STRANGE WOMAN. (*Prov* 20:16)

WHOSO PRIVILY SLANDERETH HIS NEIGHBOUR, HIM WILL I CUT OFF: HIM THAT HATH AN HIGH LOOK AND A PROUD HEART WILL NOT I SUFFER. (*Psa* 101:5)

OR IF THERE BE ANY FLESH, IN THE SKIN WHEREOF THERE IS A HOT BURNING, AND THE QUICK FLESH THAT BURNETH HAVE A WHITE BRIGHT SPOT, SOMEWHAT REDDISH, OR WHITE; (*Lev* 13:24)

AND ELISHA CAME AGAIN TO GILGAL: AND THERE WAS A DEARTH IN THE LAND; AND THE SONS OF THE PROPHETS WERE SITTING BEFORE HIM: AND HE SAID UNTO HIS SERVANT, SET ON THE GREAT POT, AND SEETHE POTTAGE FOR THE SONS OF THE PROPHETS. (2 *Ki* 4:38)

I "almost" rest my case with that bit of "jargogle".

To all those who say speaking modern Hebrew is the same language as Biblical Aramaic... wise up. The language spoken by the writers of the Bible is a DEAD language and not the same language as modern Hebrew the same thing for Greek/Latin... all DEAD. The character set is all that is similar, the words they used are obsolete and so are the sentence structures and the common knowledge they shared within that 2000-year-old language and cultural matrix!

Scholars have demonstrated all written texts have been altered over time by scribes. The New Testament comes under scrutiny by Judaism which claims it is a work of "fiction". They point out the following facts about the texts in what is called The New Testament:

- No original autographed copies

- No known authors assembled over time hundreds of years removed

- Additions and alterations by the scribes

- Miracles parallels of other pagan gods

- Contradictions

- New doctrines and truths – "Anything true in the NT isn't new and anything new isn't true"

In the next couple of chapters, we are going to hold the Tanakh to that same standard. Will it pass the test, or can the same criticism of the New Testament also apply to the Tanakh?

Chapter 2
Holding the Tanakh to the Same Standard as the New Testament

Chapter 2: Introduction

Rabbinical Judaism would have us believe you must speak modern Hebrew to understand the Scriptures. Is this true? Is Modern Hebrew the language of the Tanakh (OT) or even the writings of the Nazarenes (NT)?

The Jews, after the Babylonian exile, ended up adopting a Jewish Babylonian Aramaic dialect and the Hebrew language died out. Ancient Hebrew spoken by our forefathers in the Tanakh was succeeded by an intermediary form, Mishnaic Hebrew and Aramaic about the 3rd century BC. After 135 CE these intermediary languages became dead languages for nearly 1,500 years before Modern Hebrew was developed in the 19th and 20th centuries. Modern Hebrew was a relatively new language with little in common with the language of the Bible.

The Hebrew language spoken by our forefathers died out around 3 BC. The intermediary language of Aramaic spoken in the time of Yahusha and Ancient Hebrew are distinct from one another yet similar languages. They can be compared as distant relatives, just like English and Dutch. All, however, are dead languages today like Greek and Latin.

English is derived from Dutch and the two languages are the closest yet speaking English does not add any value in translating Dutch to English. If an expert in the English language heard another speaking Dutch, it would be foreign and not understood. The same is true of Biblical Hebrew and Modern Hebrew.

When the Romans destroyed the second Jewish Temple in 70 CE, the language of Babylonian Aramaic spoken in the language cultural matrix of the time Yahusha lived began to die out. It was essentially completely dead 65 years later in 135, after the failure of the Bar Kokhba Revolt, when Roman emperor Hadrian expelled, enslaved, or killed most of Israel's remaining Jews — the final native Hebrew speakers.

So, must we speak modern Hebrew to understand what was written in a language long since dead? Must we accept the modern-day Hebrew "language and cultural matrix" to understand that written in a language and cultural matrix that died out in 70 CE and ceased to exist after 135 CE?

No. Most of the Tanakh was written in Paleo Hebrew script that has been dead for over 2,000 years. Palaeo-Hebrew, Proto-Hebrew or Old Hebrew, is considered to be the script used to record the original texts of the Hebrew Bible. By the 5th century BCE, the Paleo-Hebrew alphabet had been mostly replaced by the Aramaic alphabet as officially used in the Achaemenid Empire. The "Jewish square script" of today is a stylized form of the Aramaic alphabet variant of today now known simply as the Hebrew alphabet. This modern Hebrew script evolved directly out of the Aramaic script by about the 3rd century BCE and was not standardized until the 1st century CE.

No "Jewish Rabbi" today speaks ancient Hebrew (a dead language) and speaking modern Hebrew does little to enlighten us. No longer under the pagan influence of the Christian Church, many trying to find a solution look to Judaism. Judaism is just as pagan as Christianity, both being Hellenized Religions.

In Judaism—Revelation of Moses Or Religion of Men? By P Neal we read:

> "Solomon Grayzel notes that Hellenism—as compared to the effects of exile in Babylon—was "more persistent and more subtle in its efforts to lure the Jews from their [Scripture-based] way of life" (A History of the Jews, pp. 41-42). Martin brings out that the Jews found it impossible to escape the omnipresence of Hellenistic thought. Greek quickly became the language of commerce and social intercourse, making it

necessary to acquire fluency in Greek (p. 77). In Story Without End, Solomon Landman writes that the Jews were "charmed by the customs and manners, by the very spirit of the Greeks" (p. 73). But as we will see, nowhere was this effect more pronounced than, ironically, among the leaders of the Jews—the chief priests."

As we will see, it was the corrupting influence of Hellenism on the Aaronic priesthood that led to their loss of favor among the People of the Land and the subsequent rise of the Hasidim, the progenitors of the Pharisees. With the aid of their scribal cohorts, the outcome would ultimately be today's Judaism.

We must overcome the Hellenistic Mindset of the current English translations and the influence of BOTH Christianity and Judaism if we are ever going to understand Scripture. Specifically, the Nazarene writings called "The New Testament".

The Greco-Roman mindset of Hellenized Jewish translators gave preference to the Greek over the Hebrew language, and played down the Hebrew terminology, to make everything more acceptable to the pagan culture of the unwashed, uneducated masses. They blended the Holy Scriptures with the worship of the Greek Pantheon (called syncretism) and that is the context in which modern-day religions of Christianity and Judaism were formed over time.

Hellenistic religion – Wikipedia

Hellenistic religion is any of the various systems of beliefs and practices of the people who lived under the influence of Ancient Greek culture during the Hellenistic period and the Roman Empire (c. 300 BCE to 300 CE). There was much continuity in Hellenistic religion: the Greek gods continued to be worshipped and the same rites were practiced as before.

We call this assimilation of Greek Hellenism, *to be Hellenized*. We know that the pagan Greek religions (Hellenism) overtook the Truth of Yahuah, as Rome won the Roman/Jewish wars. "Jews" looked to assimilate into Greek/Roman culture to avoid persecution and maintain their power over the people. It is through this process of Hellenism, that we have our modern English translations of Scripture from both Judaism and Christianity:

Hellenization – Wikipedia

The twentieth century witnessed a lively debate over the extent of Hellenization in the Eastern Mediterranean region and particularly among the Ancient Palestinian Jews that has continued until today. The Judaism of the diaspora was thought to have succumbed thoroughly to its influences. Bultmann thus argued that Christianity arose almost completely within those Hellenistic confines and should be read against that background as opposed to a more traditional (Palestinian) Jewish background.

In the book **Judaism— *Revelation of Moses Or Religion of Men? We read:***

As a reliable historical source, the extra-biblical book of II Maccabees informs us that under Jason's influence, "the Hellenizing process reached such a pitch that the priests ceased to show any interest in the services of the altar; scorning the Temple and neglecting the sacrifices, they would hurry to take part in [Greek activities] .... They disdained all that their ancestors had esteemed and set the highest value on Hellenic honors" (II Macc. 4:13-15; emphasis added).

The idea of a so-called "oral law" was most contrived (created or arranged in a way that seems artificial and unrealistic). In fact, with religious constraints cast off, new ideas found fertile ground among these Jewish scholars.

79

> *Thus, while outwardly supporting the Scriptures and resisting Hel-lenization, the scribes could justify virtually any doctrine by claiming that it was part of an esoteric oral tradition—hidden all along in the depths of the written Torah.*

The Jews lost their way in diaspora. Judaism of today is a result of the Jews assimilation. Gamaliel is the most influential Jewish Rabbi in history and mentor of Sha'ul the Apostle. Gamaliel was such a respected figure during the time of Yahusha, that he dictated the proceeding of the Sanhedrin. His authority was such, that he even rivaled the authority of the High Priest, as we read in Acts Chapter 5! The epigram that Rabbinic literature gives to him speaks of the respect with which Gamaliel was held:

When he died the honor [outward respect] of the Torah ceased, and purity and piety became extinct"(Sotah xv: 18).

Even the Jews admit that upon Gamaliel's death, the honor of the Torah ceased (succumbed to Hellenism) and purity and piety became extinct where it remains today, in the form of Rabbinical Judaism. From that point forward, history records that Judaism succumbed to Hellenization and paganism. So, the Jews recognize Gamaliel's' death as the defining moment when Judaism went astray.

This is the hotbed in which Modern Judaism arose and what Yahusha the Messiah pushed back against during his lifetime. The "Jews" tell us we cannot know the Father unless we know "their" Hebrew. However, that is a lie to maintain the influence and power of their priestly class of Rabbis. Biblical Hebrew is a DEAD language. Ancient Paleo (the language of the Torah) is deader still. Modern Hebrew is NOT Biblical Hebrew (Paleo - Aramaic).

In the same way, the Church of Rome tells us we cannot know their God (the Trinity) unless we know Latin, also a dead language. Again, like Rabbinical Jews, to maintain the influence and power of their priestly class.

Leaving us still with the burning question... "where is the Truth and how can we come to know it"? It is found in His Divine Counsel...

ISAIAH 48:11-15

[11] FOR MY OWN SAKE, FOR MY OWN SAKE I WILL DO IT; FOR HOW COULD DISHONOR COME TO MY NAME (Yahuah)? I WILL NOT GIVE MY GLORY (as Creator) TO ANOTHER (not even Yahusha, Yahuah ALONE sits on the Throne of Creation - Isaiah 44:24)! [12] LISTEN TO ME, JACOB AND ISRAEL, MY CALLED; I AM HE; I AM THE ALEPH, I ALSO AM THE TAV. [13] MY HAND HAS LAID THE FOUNDATION OF THE EARTH (by Himself Isaiah 44:24), AND MY RIGHT HAND HAS SPANNED (spread out like a tent) THE HEAVENLY SCROLL; WHEN I SUMMON THE SUN/STARS/CONSTELLATIONS TOGETHE THEY WILL MINISTER THE GOSPEL TOGETHER AS A DIVINE COUNSEL TO ALL MANKIND (DEUT. 4:19). [14] ALL OF YOU, GATHER YOURSELVES TOGETHER AND HEAR (what the Sun/stars/constellations Proclaim day after day, night after night - Psalm 19, Enoch 35:3)! WHO AMONG THEM HAS FORETOLD THESE THINGS IN THE HEAVENS/STARS?

Language Cultural Matrix

There is what is called a language and cultural matrix that exists at any time among a people. That Language and Cultural Matrix that existed 2,000 years ago does not exist today. It has long since died out consumed by Hellenism. Judaism today is NOT that matrix. To truly understand the Scriptures (from Genesis to Revelation as well as many Apocryphal books) we must put ourselves into a matrix that was woven together 2,000 years ago defined by a language that no longer exists and culture long since gone.

Can that be done? Yes. And that is what we will do together. We will go back and seek "the ancient path" they followed prior to 2,000 years ago in Israel.

This is not a "Jew bashing session" but important that we understand they are as opposed to their Messiah and their Scriptures manipulated (as I will prove) just as Christianity is worshiping a false one based on twisted Scripture.

Standard of Judgment

Below are the arguments used to discredit the writings of the Nazarenes called the New Testament:

- No original autographed copies

- No known authors and the New Testament was assembled over time hundreds of years removed

- Additions and alterations by the scribes

- Miracles were parallels of other pagan gods

- Contradictions

- New doctrines and truths – "Anything true in the NT isn't new and anything new isn't true"

Next, I am going to apply this same standard to the Tanakh (Torah). Is the Tanakh a work of Moses alone? Do we have autographed originals of any of the books in the Tanakh? Are the authors accurate? Are the miracles paralleled by other pagan myths? Have they been altered by scribes? Are they compilations of various writings assembled over time by a "redactor" or editor? It is said the forefathers never really existed they are just legends and myths of oral traditions.

In short, does the Tanakh fail the same tests used to discredit the New Testament? If so, then where to we look for His Word, Righteousness, and Truth?

No Originals

Now, let us hold up the Tanakh to the same standards of scrutiny used to discredit the NT.

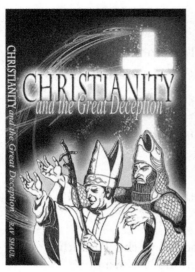

The NT is disregarded because there are no "surviving autographs" of the books. Just copies found mainly in Greek dating around 300 CE after the Council of Nicaea. You see, they were burnt by Constantine to hide the abomination he had created now known as Christianity. See my book ***Christianity and the Great Deception***.

But what about the Tanakh? Does it pass or fail this test?

We see by the time of Jeremiah (600 BC) the "word of Yahuah" had been so altered by scribes it was unrecognizable and "lost".

Jeremiah 8:7-8

7 BUT MY PEOPLE DO NOT KNOW THE ORDINANCE OF YAHUAH *(Eternally preserved in the stars - Psalm 119:89, Psalm 89:2)*. 8 HOW CAN YOU SAY, WE ARE WISE MEN *(h2450 chakam - 'astrologers')*, AND THE WORD OF YAHUAH'S TESTIMONY *(that Yahusha is The Branch foretold in The Heavenly Scroll)* IS WITH US? BUT BEHOLD, THE 'LYING PEN OF THE SCRIBES' HAS MADE MY WORD *(LOGOS / DABAR - 'Spoken Promise in the beginning' Eternally preserved in The Heavenly Scroll - Psalm 119:89)* INTO A LIE.

Again, in Jeremiah, we are told that our faith would be based on "nothing but lies". Not a "few lies", not "a little lie here or there", not "mostly lies", but TOTAL LIES... "Nothing but lies" there would be no truth in the twisted Scriptures we have had handed down to us since at least 600 BC.

Jeremiah 16:19

18 "I WILL FIRST DOUBLY REPAY THEIR INIQUITY AND THEIR SIN, BECAUSE THEY HAVE POLLUTED MY LAND; THEY HAVE FILLED MY INHERITANCE WITH THE CARCASSES OF THEIR DETESTABLE IDOLS AND WITH THEIR ABOMINATIONS." 19 O YAHUAH, MY STRENGTH AND MY STRONGHOLD, AND MY REFUGE IN THE DAY OF DISTRESS, TO YOU THE *(lost sheep among the)* NATIONS WILL COME FROM THE ENDS OF THE EARTH AND SAY, "*Our fathers have inherited nothing but LIES, Idols and worthless things of no profit.*" 20 CAN MAN MAKE GODS FOR HIMSELF? YET THEY ARE NOT GODS!

We don't have any extensive manuscripts of anything from much before 150 BC. We have a number of messages written on tablets, sherds of clay pot, walls and other durable objects. However, manuscripts created on parchment or papyrus are much more fragile.

Abraham lived almost 2000 years before the first messages, which were *discarded scribal notes,* are in the historical record of about 150 BC. Abraham lived in 1800 BC. Moses lived 1500 years before that in 1200 BC. The duration from the lost "originals" and when we first see any manuscripts is thousands of years longer than that of the NT. The NT "original" predates the first written manuscripts by a mere 70-300 years. So, there was a significant duration of time where the Tanakh was manipulated by the scribes compared to the NT by more than 1,000 years.

The more popular a document was, the shorter its life would be. A scroll of the Tanakh would have been used over and over, passed around, and used again. One of the reasons for the survival of some ancient Egyptian fragments is that they were transitory documents that no one would necessarily have wanted to refer to later called **Discarded Scribal Notes**.

Discarded Scribal Notes

What we do have are not copies of originals of the Tanakh but scribal discards! Discarded for a reason yet we use them as our source of the Tanakh. Reading a scroll is destructive to it. Scrolls in intensive use, such as the Torah, needed regular recopying, and we have extensive evidence that this took place on a mass-production scale. This process destroyed any written scrolls leaving only the small notes the scribes discarded. Not used like the Torah scrolls, the scribal notes, meant to be thrown in the trash, survived.

The Bible consists of a bunch of stories written down by dozens (NT) and hundreds of people (Tanakh) in different times of history, later collected and redacted, again and again, changed or removed if they did not conform to the doctrine of the time. Also, it was translated, and translations were translated again and again to result in the Bibles you usually can buy in a bookshop today. Manipulated by scribes working for specific classes in Israel (Rabbis, Priests, King's scribes, etc.) to increase their power and authority over the people and the other classes.

No Known Authors and Assembled Over Time

Those who have chosen to deny The Yahushaic Covenant point out the authors of the books of the NT cannot be verified. Evidence points to ghostwriters long after the first century (in most cases) and even assembled from various sources over time. That sounds like a great point as they fall back on The Tanakh and tell us how meticulously it was maintained.

The truth is that "authorship" of a writing was not typically provided prior to Hellenization. Simply not seen as important or even proper. Names of those who wrote the Tanakh are not given, they were "assigned" like the NT authors.

From Wikipedia: Authorship of the Bible:
> *"Authorship was not considered important by the society that produced the Hebrew Bible, and the Torah never names an author. It was only after c. 300 BCE, when Jews came into intense contact with author-centric Greek culture, that the Hellenized rabbis began to feel compelled to find authors for their books. They assigned authors the same way the NT books were... "educated guess".*
>
> *There is much disagreement within biblical scholarship today over the authorship of the Bible. The majority of scholars believe that most of the books of the Bible are the work of multiple authors, assembled over time and that all have been edited to produce the works known today.*
>
> *Today, the majority of scholars agree that the Torah does not have a single author and that its composition took place over centuries. This is known as the Documentary Hypothesis, which suggests that the first four books (Genesis, Exodus, Leviticus, Numbers) were created by*

87

combining four originally independent documents, written by what is known as the Jahwist, the Elohist, the Deuteronomist, and the Priestly sources. Each adding texts to increase the power and influence of their respective group.

Failure of the Priesthood

The role of ensuring the scribes had a standard by which they all used and guidelines of handling discarded or marginal notes and so forth primarily fell upon the Priesthood. However, the Priesthood fell into ruin and idol worship. So goes the Priests... so goes the scribes who work for them!

From: <u>FAILURE OF THE PRIESTHOOD</u>
<u>(victoriouslivingbiblestudy.com)</u>

"The Levites, the descendants of Aaron, were designated by Yahuah to perform the role of priests, as well as the care of the Tabernacle, referred to as the House of God. The priesthood failed to do its job of keeping the people's focus on Yahuah and worshipping Him. Thus the people strayed into idol worshipping which made Yahuah angry with them and having to deal with their rebellion. The failure was with the priesthood as God told the prophets Isaiah and Ezekiel."

Isaiah 56:10-11

HIS WATCHMAN (*scribes, priests, prophets, elders*) ARE BLIND: THEY ARE ALL IGNORANT, THEY ARE ALL DUMB DOGS, THEY CANNOT BARK (*proclaim the truth*); SLEEPING, LYING DOWN, DOWN, LOVING TO SLUMBER. YEA, THEY ARE GREEDY DOGS WHICH CAN NEVER HAVE ENOUGH, AND THEY ARE SHEPHERDS THAT CANNOT UNDERSTAND: **they all look to their own way, every one for his own gain, from his quarter**.

"Yahuah's Word to Isaiah says the spiritual leadership was self-indulgent and failed to look out for the spiritual well-being and development of their people. We read in Ezekiel how the priesthood had fallen into ruin."

EZEKIEL 22:26

ISRAEL'S PRIESTS HAVE VIOLATED MY LAW, AND HAVE PROFANED MINE HOLY THINGS: THEY HAVE PUT NO DIFFERENCE BETWEEN THE HOLY AND PROFANE, NEITHER HAVE THEY SHEWED DIFFERENCE BETWEEN THE UNCLEAN AND THE CLEAN, AND HAVE HID THEIR EYES FROM MY SABBATHS, AND I AM PROFANED AMONG THEM.

Additions and Altaration by the Scribes

Scholars today are concluding the Tanakh was not written by individual authors, but rather by scribes inserting oral traditions that cannot be backed up by any written source. The sources that form the basis for the modern written Torah are small fragments of scrolls pieced together by scribes over many centuries.

From Wikipedia: Documentary hypothesis

Wellhausen used the sources of the Torah as evidence of changes in the history of the Israelite religion as it moved from free, simple, and natural to fixed, formal, and institutional. Modern scholars of Israel's religion have become much more circumspect in how they use the Old Testament, not least because many have concluded that the Hebrew Bible is not a reliable witness to the religion of ancient Israel and Judah, representing instead the beliefs of small segments of the ancient Israelite community centered in Jerusalem and devoted to the exclusive worship of the god Yahweh (the Jahwist, the Elohist, the Deuteronomist, and the Priestly sources).

Source criticism is the search for the original sources that form the basis of biblical texts. In Old Testament studies, source criticism is generally focused on identifying sources of a single text. For example, the seventeenth-century French priest Richard Simon (1638–1712) was an early proponent of the theory that Moses could not have been the single source of the entire Pentateuch."

According to Simon, parts of the Old Testament were not written by individuals at all, but ***by scribes recording their community's oral tradition, shrowded in mystery*** *not having texts to back them up.*

The Newer Documentary Thesis inferred more sources, with increasing information about their extent and inter-relationship. The fragmentary theory was a later understanding of Wellhausen produced by form criticism. This theory argues that fragments of documents — rather than continuous, coherent documents — are the sources for the Torah.

Several portions of the Tanakh were passed down orally by a society in the process of becoming a nation, who at times were nomads, and at times were living among strangers in exile. Sacred texts were eventually recorded on separate scrolls over many centuries by different authors with varying agendas and styles to make their messages clear in their own contemporary societies.

Rabbinical Judaim's stranglehold on 'the Truth' cannot be justified. They would have us believe the Torah has been meticulously copied by THEIR scribes without error for thousands of years. However, the opposite is true.

Miracles Mirrored by Other Pagan God Myths

The NT comes under scrutiny because the miracles displayed by Yahusha have parallels performed by pagan gods. I agree but under further scrutiny these pagan legends do not predate the Messiah. Rather, miracles perfromed by Yahusha were incorporated into the pagan beliefs through syncretism as the Gospel spread into pagan lands.

But what about the Tanakh? How does it stand up to the same scrutiny? While there are many instances, let's look at just 7 (you cannot make an argument for 7 in the NT).

From 7 Bible Stories and Texts With Roots in Ancient Literature (thecollector.com)

The question may also be asked whether similarities, with turns and embellishments particular to each phase of human culture and times, are not based on historical events that affected their ancestors. Maybe there were events and wisdom in deep-seated human memory and genetics, which happened before people split into cultural groups after the tower of Babel.

Ref: 7 Bible Stories and Texts With Roots in Ancient Literature (thecollector.com)
Story of Noah and the Flood is paralleled by the pagan story of the Sumerian legend of Ziusudra (ca 2300 BC). In a later version in Old Babylonian ca 1646 BCE, he is called Atrahasis. Around the middle of the Old Babylonian Empire, he and the flood account are weaved into the Epic of Gilgamesh as Utnapishtim (also Pir-Napishtim). All these texts predate the Hebrew sacred texts, which would later become the Hebrew Bible.

93

Below are a few more of the "miracles" in the Tanakh which parallel pagan myths:

- *Moses and Sargon of Akkad*

- *Job and the Mesopotamian Righteous Sufferer*

- *Proverbs, Ecclesiastes, and Egyptian Teachings*

- *Psalm 104 and Akhenaten's Hymn to the Aten*

- *Song of Songs and Sumerian Literature*

It becomes obvious that Rabbinical Judaism is based on "**nothing but lies**" at the hand of the "**lying pen of the scribes**". History and Scripture stands as a witness against them (Jeremiah 8).

Jeremiah 8:7-8

7 BUT MY PEOPLE DO NOT KNOW THE ORDINANCE OF YAHUAH (*Eternally preserved in the stars - Psalm* 119:89, *Psalm* 89:2). 8 HOW CAN YOU SAY, WE ARE WISE MEN (*h2450 chakam - 'astrologers'*), AND THE WORD OF YAHUAH'S TESTIMONY (*that Yahusha is The Branch foretold in The Heavenly Scroll*) IS WITH US? BUT BEHOLD, THE 'LYING PEN OF THE SCRIBES' HAS MADE MY WORD (*LOGOS/DABAR - 'Spoken Promise in the beginning' Eternally preserved in The Heavenly Scroll - Psalm* 119:89) INTO A LIE.

Next, I will look at the claim *"Anything true in the NT isn't new and anything new isn't true"*! Does the Tanakh show a progression in revelation over time, new laws, new covenants, and additions to the previous covenants just like The Yahushaic Covenant?

94

New Doctrines and Truths Rejected

I was told that *"Anything true in the NT isn't new and anything new isn't true"*. But what of the OT? If the statement above is true, then almost all of the Tanakh is false because it is the story of a Spiritual Kingdom revealed progressively through Earthly covenants.

Regardless of how much Rabbinical Judaism wants us all back under the Mosaic Covenant as if that is the only covenant in the Tanakh, there are many covenants in the Tanakh. Each one added new aspects and truths to the previous one! Are we to reject all covenants after the Mosaic? Judaism would say 'Yes', if that is the standard for rejecting The Yahushaic Covenant because it has unique revelation (as do all covenants).

Progressive Revelation

Over time, through covenants, the Will of Yahuah to establish His Kingdom with His King was further revealed through 7 covenants. The first 6 were physical covenants which were shadows cast by The Heavenly Scroll. The final 7th is the revelation of the Spiritual Kingdom.

Each progressive covenant enforces, strengthens, *and adds to the one before it a very specific aspect of His Kingdom* through physical to Spiritual parallels. Ultimately all previous 6 physical covenants would be fulfilled in the 7th final covenant in the Spiritual realm. All the shadows cast by The Heavenly Scroll revealing the "complete plan" for the Spiritual Kingdom would be fulfilled "on Earth as it is written in The Heavenly Scroll".

Below are the 7 major covenants between The Creator and His "Chosen Few":

1. The Sabbath Covenant

2. The Edenic/Adamic Covenant

3. The Noahic Covenant

4. The Abrahamic Covenant

5. The Mosaic Covenant

6. The Davidic Covenant

7. The Yahushaic Covenant

Now let's go further into each one closely and we will see each covenant builds on the previous one with unique revelation. Further revealing His Kingdom on Earth through the line of the House of King David and the House of Zadok. Two lines of Kings and High Priests restored and fulfilled in Yahusha the Melchi (Royal) Tsedek (Righteous High Priest).

His Kingdom is not of this Earth. So, for us to understand a Kingdom we cannot see or touch Yahuah uses this physical realm to teach us of the Spiritual Realm. This is called physical to Spiritual parallels. The Bible is the story, from our human experience, of Yahuah fulfilling His Will on Earth as it was written in The Heavenly Scroll. The Tanakh and the N.T. must be understood in the context of The Heavenly Scroll. History and the future must be weighed against it!

A Tour of All 7 Covenants

Let's take a brief tour of the covenants in The Bible. Next, I summarize each covenant to demonstrate how each one progressively revealed vital aspects of the Kingdom of Yahuah (*this is a simple overview not intended to be an in-depth study of these covenants*):

The Sabbath Covenant

The Sabbath Covenant established Yahuah as The Creator. It is between Yahuah and His Creation and the basic revelation in that covenant was:

- The Sabbath Covenant was defined as 6 days then a Sabbath Rest on the 7th Day specifically. This 7-day portrait is a Physical to spiritual parallel that established the timeframe by which Yahuah would introduce His Kingdom through covenants and progressive revelation. The "days" are prophetic days where 1 day = 1 thousand years. So the Sabbath Covenant establishes a 6,000-year timeframe by which Yahuah would train His sons by putting them through a life on Earth. It is during this life that Yahuah would purchase their salvation to serve Him in His Kingdom. At the end of 6,000 years, Yahuah would establish His Kingdom on Earth and further train His sons to rule under the authority of Yahusha the Messiah. At the end of 7,000 years, His Kingdom would be complete, His sons trained to rule, and the Kingdom of Yahuah would then expand to govern all of His Creation for eternity... Yahuah blessed and sanctified the Sabbath (7th Day) and made it Holy.

- The Sabbath would serve as a "sign" between Yahuah and His chosen sons for eternity in all covenants and those who keep the Sabbath are set apart from His Creation with Him. It is the Sabbath that is "the Standard of the Kingdom of Yahuah". Keeping the Sabbath weekly is expressing faith and hope in the coming Kingdom of Yahuah.

The Edenic/Adamic Covenants

Yahuah reveals in these first covenants with man:

- He has given His sons the authority to rule creation.

- Yahuah discloses His intent to choose a human King/Messiah through the "seed of a woman" who would crush all those opposed to Yahuah's Authority.

- Yahuah establishes the "system of training" used to train His chosen. A system of "right" and "wrong" is defined as "obedience to Yahuah's commandments" known as the Law.

- It is the Law that is the foundation of and constitution of His Divine Government.

- The Law in the Edenic/Adamic Covenants was active but unknown to man as it was in the Mind of Yahuah. It was slowly being transposed from the Mind of Yahuah to man orally.

The Noahic Covenant

Yahuah renewed the two previous covenants with Noah after destroying the remnant seed of the Nephilim (Satan's sons from the seed of women) from the face of the earth. In this covenant:

- Yahuah made a promise not to destroy this planet again by flood. The rainbow is the sign of this promise.

- The Noahic Covenant is a continuation of the previous two covenants and all aspects of the Edenic/Adamic Covenants are still in effect nothing changed, it just needed to be renewed as mankind started over with Noah.

The Abrahamic Covenant

Yahuah reveals His chosen bloodline among the sons of men. In the Abrahamic Covenant Yahuah reveals:

- The bloodline would run through Abraham/Isaac/Jacob and be called "Israel".

- It is from within this bloodline that Yahuah would introduce His chosen family to His creation, train them through a life on Earth, and prepare them for His coming Kingdom.

- It is through this bloodline that Yahuah would bring forth "Yahuah's Salvation" which is what the name Yahusha means in Hebrew.

- Yahuah also reveals the physical-to-spiritual parallel of the Promised Land and His promises to His sons of inheritance.

- The Abrahamic Covenant contains all the terms and conditions of the previous 3 covenants with the addition of the chosen bloodline and promises to that bloodline.

- The Law of Yahuah was then fully transposed to Abraham orally and the Oral Law was passed down from generation to generation.

The Mosaic Covenant

The Mosaic Covenant builds on all the previous covenants as Yahuah:

- Transposed His Law from oral to written down in stone as He reveals the "Constitution of His Kingdom" in detail. The instructions to His sons on how to be righteous before Him are known as the Law of Yahuah.

- Yahuah firmly establishes in stone that His Kingdom is a kingdom of law.

- Yahuah establishes and defines various "cabinets/positions" within His Kingdom such as High Priests, Priests, Judges, Kings, etc.

- Yahuah chose specific bloodlines within "Israel" to serve Him as Priests (Levi) and High Priests (Aaron). These priesthoods served as physical examples of what Yahusha would do spiritually as Melchizedek.

- Yahuah reveals specific seasons i.e. Holy Days which were to serve as training aids (Physical to spiritual parallels) to help His chosen to know the Messiah when he came/comes again.

The Davidic Covenant

The Davidic Covenant builds on all previous covenants as Yahuah:

- Established a physical righteous King to serve as an example of the coming Spiritual King (Physical to spiritual parallels).

- It was established that the Throne of David would be the throne and bloodline through which the Messiah and King would come to govern His Kingdom for eternity.

- Yahuah established His Throne, Capital City, Temple, and Altar in detail physically as physical to spiritual parallels.

The Yahushaic Covenant

The Yahushaic Covenant builds on all previous covenants and "fulfills" them all by transposing them to their fullest spiritual application. The Yahushaic Covenant is "new" in that the Law is now written on our hearts. This is the final transposition of the Law which went from the mind of Yahuah, to orally passed down, to written in stone to written on our hearts.

The "intent" behind the "letters" supersedes the physical act. Up to this point, Yahuah had fully defined His coming Kingdom through physical to spiritual parallels so that we could understand the Yahushaic Covenant.

All previous 6 physical covenants are TRANSPOSED to Spiritual Reality in the Yahushaic Covenant:

- *Sabbath Covenant* – Yahusha fulfills the Sabbath Covenant when he returns to reign as King of the 7th Millennium and gives us "rest".

-

- *The Edenic Covenant* – Yahusha is given all authority over creation and trains the sons of Yahuah to rule creation. the Kingdom of Yahuah is set up on a smaller scale over the Earth during the 7th Millennium and "Eden" is restored.

- *The Adamic Covenant* - Established the system for training His sons to rule and foretold of His coming

101

Messiah/King that would crush all rebellion against Him —
Yahusha is that prophesied king who is born of a woman
and crushes the head of the enemy. As the firstborn of the
resurrection and first son to be TRANSPOSED to the
Kingdom of Yahuah; Yahusha is called "the Second Adam"
and "forefather of everlasting life"

- *The Mosaic Covenant* - Yahusha TRANSPOSES the Law
  from written in stone or "the letter" to the Spiritual intent
  of your heart. the Law is transposed from the Law of Sin
  and Death to the Law of the Spirit of Life as Yahusha's
  blood covers the decrees in the Law that demand our death
  for disobedience. The Priesthood is TRANSPOSED to the
  Spiritual Kingdom under a new eternal High Priest...
  Melchizedek. The law that defines the role of the priesthood
  is TRANSPOSED to the Spiritual Kingdom of Yahuah to
  give Yahusha authority to make the proper sacrifices and
  atonement as High Priest.

- **The Davidic Covenant** - Yahusha is the spiritually
  righteous King from the line of David and sits on the
  Throne of David for eternity. Yahusha TRANSPOSES the
  Temple, the Altar, and the Capital City to the Spiritual
  Kingdom of Yahuah. Yahuah's Temple is our body, His
  Altar is in our hearts, His Capital City is made up of all of
  the sons of Yahuah; Yahusha is the cornerstone. All the
  physical metaphors, examples, rehearsals, and shadow
  pictures find their fullest expression Spiritually as Yahusha
  "fulfills" them all and ushers them into the Kingdom of
  Yahuah.

As we can see with each new covenant the previous covenants are
still valid. Each covenant adds to the Law, defining new elements
of the Kingdom of Yahuah, and progressively disclosing new
physical shadows that parallel Spiritual Truths.

Summary

Yes, there are new aspects to The Yahushaic Covenant that further define and fulfill the previous 6 physical covenants. Just as each of the previous further defined and added new aspects to the ones before them. If we are to reject The Yahushaic Covenant because of this, then all covenants must be rejected as well.

Chapter 3
The Ancient Path

Chapter 3: A Journey Back in Time

To rediscover the Ancient Path, we must journey back in time at a time when the Ancient Path was "in existence". What does "ancient path" mean? What is ancient to us was not "ancient" at the time of Jeremiah. Ancient refers to anything past 2,000 years as the progression of the Ages revealed in The Heavenly Scroll. To us, the time prior to the Age of Pisces is considered ancient. To Jeremiah, anything before the Age of Taurus (4,000 years ago to us) was "ancient".

We see that Israel refused to walk in the Ancient Path and was told to "look at them all" and admit them. What is the Ancient Path that we can "see" throughout history that no longer exists? The English word **ancient** means:

> **Dictionary**
> an·cient1 - *belonging to the very distant past and no longer in existence.*

What is it that proclaims His Handiwork, His Will, and His Counsel that "is before our very eyes" where Yahusha is portrayed as crucified? That path that "is in the very distant past and is no more" and "no longer in existence"?

Jeremiah 6:16
THIS IS WHAT YAHUAH SAYS: "STAND AT THE CROSSROADS AND LOOK; ASK FOR THE ANCIENT PATHS, ASK WHERE THE GOOD WAY IS, AND WALK IN IT, AND YOU WILL FIND REST FOR YOUR SOULS. BUT YOU SAID, '*WE WILL NOT WALK IN IT*!'"

Isaiah 48:3-6
3 I FORETOLD THE FORMER THINGS LONG AGO, MY MOUTH ANNOUNCED THEM AND I MADE THEM KNOWN; THEN SUDDENLY I ACTED, AND THEY CAME TO PASS. 4 FOR I KNEW HOW STUBBORN YOU WERE; YOUR NECK MUSCLES WERE IRON; YOUR FOREHEAD WAS

BRONZE. 5 THEREFORE I TOLD YOU THESE THINGS LONG AGO; BEFORE THEY WERE FULFILLED, I ANNOUNCED THEM SO THAT YOU COULD NOT SAY, 'MY IMAGES BROUGHT THEM ABOUT; MY WOODEN IMAGE AND METAL GOD ORDAINED THEM.' 6 YOU HAVE HEARD THESE THINGS; LOOK AT ALL THEN ALL. *WILL YOU NOT ADMIT THEM*?

Galatians 3:1

YOU FOOLISH GALATIANS! WHO HAS BEWITCHED YOU? *BEFORE YOUR VERY EYES, YAHUSHA THE MESSIAH WAS CLEARLY PORTRAYED AS CRUCIFIED.*

It is in the stars/constellations where the Ancient Path is found called The Heavenly Scroll. Yahuah's Will was written into His Creation that testifies to Yahusha being the Messiah before the foundation of the world. This was the faith of the Nazarenes:

1 Corinthians 2:7

NO, WE SPEAK OF THE MYSTERIOUS AND HIDDEN WISDOM OF GOD, WHICH HE DESTINED FOR OUR GLORY BEFORE TIME BEGAN.

Titus 1:2

IN THE HOPE OF ETERNAL LIFE, WHICH GOD, WHO CANNOT LIE, PROMISED BEFORE TIME BEGAN.

Revelation 13:8

THE LAMB WHO WAS SLAIN FROM THE CREATION OF THE WORLD.

Matthew 25:34

THEN THE KING WILL SAY TO THOSE ON HIS RIGHT, 'COME, YOU WHO ARE BLESSED BY MY FATHER, INHERIT THE KINGDOM PREPARED FOR YOU FROM THE FOUNDATION OF THE WORLD.

1 Peter 1:20

HE WAS KNOWN BEFORE THE FOUNDATION OF THE WORLD, BUT WAS REVEALED IN THE LAST TIMES FOR YOUR SAKE.

Ephesians 1:4

ACCORDING AS HE HATH CHOSEN US IN HIM BEFORE THE FOUNDATION OF THE WORLD, THAT WE SHOULD BE HOLY AND WITHOUT BLAME BEFORE HIM IN LOVE:

To know the Word of Yahuah we must go back to "before the foundation of the world" and see if we can recount the meaning of the stars/constellations as Abraham did in Genesis 15:5.

Days of Old vs Ancient

Below, Isaiah mentions the days of Joshua as "days of old" when they came into the land. Isaiah lived around 700 BCE.

Isaiah 51:9
9 AWAKE, AWAKE, PUT ON STRENGTH, O ARM OF YAHUAH; AWAKE AS IN THE DAYS OF OLD, THE GENERATIONS OF LONG AGO. WAS IT NOT YOU WHO CUT RAHAB IN PIECES, WHO PIERCED THE DRAGON?

In Isaiah's case "**_long ago_**" can also be "**_ancient_**" h6924 - **Qedem**. The translators understood "*ancient*" implies "*very long ago, no longer in existence*" and most translations preferred "*long ago*" in translation as Rahab and Joshua were less than 1,000 years before Isaiah. The definition of ancient is "*no longer in existence belonging to the VERY distant past.*" Since the Mosaic Covenant was still very much active and "in existence" it does not qualify as "ancient" but "long ago" in Isaiah.

However, we are focusing on Jeremiah's prophecy of the lying pen of the scribe. Ancient in Jeremiah 6:16 is

> h5769 - **Olam** which means "*antiquity, long duration, no longer, not anymore*" and is translated as "**_ancient_**" not "**_long ago_**".

Ancient to Jeremiah who lived around 500 BCE would then be around the time before Abraham (Age of Taurus). Jeremiah lived 900 years after Moses which is not "ancient" to his day and within the same Age (of Aries).

Abraham lived in the 18th century BCE. Dating back from Abraham to Creation would all be considered "ancient" to all mankind including Jeremiah.

When looking for "the way" or the "ancient path" we refuse to walk and the "word that can be seen" that we refuse to admit we must look past the Age of Aries into the Age of Taurus which was "ancient" to Jeremiah.

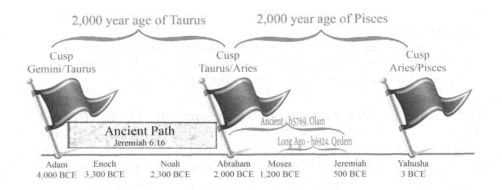

The book of Ezra provides an account of the Jews' regathering, their struggle to survive, and to rebuild what had been destroyed during the Babylonian captivity. We see concerning the prophet Ezra/Esdras:

Ezra 7:6

THIS EZRA CAME UP FROM BABEL. AND HE WAS A SCRIBE, SKILLED IN THE TORAH OF MOSHEH, WHICH יהוה ELOHIM OF YISRA'ĔL HAD GIVEN. AND THE SOVEREIGN GAVE HIM ALL HE ASKED, ACCORDING TO THE HAND OF יהוה HIS ELOHIM UPON HIM.

FURTHER ELABORATED IN THE BOOK OF II ESDRAS OF EZRA:

II Esdras 14:20

20 THE WORLD IS IN DARKNESS. THOSE WHO LIVE IN IT HAVE NO LIGHT, 21 BECAUSE YOUR LAW HAS BEEN BURNED, AND SO NO ONE KNOWS WHAT THINGS YOU HAVE DONE OR WHAT WORKS ARE ABOUT TO COME TO PASS. 22 IF THEN I HAVE FOUND FAVOR BEFORE YOU, SEND A HOLY SPIRIT INTO ME, AND I WILL WRITE EVERYTHING THAT HAS

110

HAPPENED IN THE WORLD FROM THE BEGINNING, THE THINGS THAT WERE WRITTEN IN YOUR LAW, SO THAT HUMAN BEINGS CAN FIND THE PATH, AND THOSE WHO WANT TO LIVE IN THE LAST DAYS MAY LIVE." 23 HE REPLIED TO ME: "GO, GATHER THE PEOPLE AND SAY TO THEM THAT THEY SHOULDN'T SEEK YOU FOR FORTY DAYS. 24 GATHER UP MANY WRITING TABLETS, AND TAKE WITH YOU SAREA, DABRIA, SELEMIA, ETHANUS, AND ASIEL, THESE FIVE, WHO ARE TRAINED TO WRITE FAST. 25 COME HERE, AND I WILL LIGHT IN YOUR HEART THE LAMP OF UNDERSTANDING. IT WON'T BE EXTINGUISHED UNTIL YOU HAVE WRITTEN EVERYTHING DOWN. 26 WHEN YOU ARE FINISHED, YOU WILL MAKE SOME THINGS PUBLIC, **OTHERS YOU WILL TRANSMIT SECRETLY TO THE WISE**. YOU WILL BEGIN TO WRITE TOMORROW AT THIS TIME."

We see above that the "Ancient Path", now including Moses, was lost in Babylonian captivity. The world was in total darkness and the "light" no longer shined. Every word had to be restored and much was still "transmitted secretly to the wise". Who are the "wise men" in the Bible? Astrologers! h2450 - chakam. This is why the only ones to find Yahusha when he was born were astrologers translated "wise men"!

111

Israel Refused to Admit the Ancient Path

ISAIAH 48:3-6

3 I FORETOLD THE FORMER THINGS LONG AGO (written in the stars on Day 4 of Creation), MY MOUTH ANNOUNCED THEM (to My Prophets who all read The Heavenly Scroll) AND I MADE THEM KNOWN (to all mankind - Deuteronomy 4:19); THEN SUDDENLY I ACTED, AND THE MESSAGE PROCLAIMED BY THE STARS/CONSTELLATIONS CAME TO PASS. 4 FOR I KNEW HOW STUBBORN YOU WERE; YOUR NECK MUSCLES WERE IRON; YOUR FOREHEAD WAS BRONZE. 5 THEREFORE I TOLD YOU THESE THINGS (in The Heavenly Scroll) LONG AGO (at Creation); BEFORE THEY WERE FULFILLED I ANNOUNCED THE PLAN OF SALVATION TO YOU (in The Heavenly Scroll Psalm 19) SO THAT YOU COULD NOT SAY, 'MY IMAGES BROUGHT THEM ABOUT; MY WOODEN IMAGE AND METAL GOD ORDAINED THEM.' 6 YOU HAVE HEARD THESE THINGS (that the stars Proclaim day after day, night after night to all mankind as a witness Psalm 19); LOOK AT ALL THE STARS/CONSTELLATION (in The Heavenly Scroll). WILL YOU NOT ADMIT THEM?

Israel started down the path to two Hellenized religions (Judaism and Christianity) then refused to admit or walk the Ancient Path. The Heavenly Scroll was lost. Israel and its priesthood fell into pagan worship. Therefore so did the scribes who elaborated on the Torah, which was faithfully transmitted to Ezra and his scribes, with unproven often made-up "oral traditions". This was the state of the "word" in Yahusha's day, which he pushed back against.

Mark 7:13

THUS YOU NULLIFY THE WORD OF YAHUAH BY YOUR TRADITION THAT YOU HAVE HANDED DOWN (*orally*). AND YOU DO MANY THINGS LIKE THAT."

When did the Israelites worship other gods? It was only during the Babylonian Exile (about 586 B.C.E. to 500 B.C.E) and then followed in the Second Temple period (500 B.C.E. to 70 C.E.). From that point on... Rabbinical Judaism took over and totally corrupted the Torah and Prophets with oral traditions called the Talmud.

Oldest Torah Scroll

The Bologna Torah Scroll (1155–1225 CE) is the world's oldest complete surviving Torah scroll. The scroll contains the full text of the five Books of Moses in Hebrew. Concrete archaeological evidence bearing on the dating of the Torah is found in early manuscript fragments, such as those found among the Dead Sea Scrolls. The earliest manuscript fragments of the Torah date to the late third or early second centuries BCE.

Chapter 4
The Torah Controversy

Chapter 4: Masoretic Torah

If you Google "Torah controversy" you will find many to choose from. I am going to address the Rabbinical version of the Torah written by the Masoretes versus the Torah of the Samaritans.

The issues at hand are:

- Who are the Masoretes and what is the origin of their Torah?

- Who are the Samaritans and what is the origin of their Torah?

- Where to offer sacrifices on an altar to Yahuah?

- What about the Dead Sea Scrolls?

- • Did the Essenes follow the Rabbinical or Samaritan Torah?

- What is the relationship between the Essenes and Samaritans?

- Was John the Baptist a Samaritan?

- Who were the Nazarenes?

- Did Yahusha frequent Mount Gerizim? If so, could this explain his absence in the Temple at Jerusalem?

- What would Yahusha be doing with the Samaritans on Mount Gerizim?

Once I address the above topics, what do we conclude from the evidence? What, as Nazarenes, do we put our faith in?

115

Who are the Masoretes and the Masoretic Torah?

The Masoretes Torah combined with oral traditions resulted in Rabbinical Judaism. Rabbinical Judaism is the evolution of the cult of Pharisees of the first century who were distinguished from other major cults (Nazarenes, Sadducees, and Essenes) in that they combined oral and written traditions "of the elders" into their text. This continued outside the Masoretic Torah in other written texts they considered almost equal to their Torah (the Talmud for example).

Masoretic Text - Wikipedia

The Masoretic Torah was primarily copied, edited, and distributed by a group of Jews known as the Masoretes between the 7th and 10th centuries of the Common Era (CE). The oldest known complete copy, the Leningrad Codex, dates only to the 11th century CE.

The fact that they combined oral traditions with written texts is brought out in the meaning of the name they were known by:

Masoretes which means "*Masters of Tradition*". The Masoretic Text means "*text of the Tradition*" as compiled by Masoretic Scribes.

MARK 7:13

THUS YOU NULLIFY THE WORD OF GOD BY YOUR TRADITION THAT YOU HAVE HANDED DOWN. AND YOU DO MANY THINGS LIKE THAT."

If what we consider "most accurate" is determined by age, that which is older is the source of edited newer versions, then which Torah is most accurate? The Masoretes Torah or the Samaritan Torah?

Who are the Samaritans and the Samaritan Torah?

The Samaritan Torah is much older than the Mosoretes Torah. It is written in Paleo Hebrew not Aramaic. It is the Torah found to be used by the Nazarenes at Qumran. But before we get to that, we need to dive deeper into the Samaritans. The Samaritans were from the line of Zadok Priests.

Samaritans - Wikipedia

> "The Samaritans were a group of Zadokite Priests who rebelled against the fallen priesthood and temple in Jerusalem. "Samaritan" means "Guardians/Keepers of the Torah"; They are known as Israelite Samaritans, and are an ethnoreligious group who originate from the ancient Israelites. They are native to the Levant and adhere to Samaritanism, an Abrahamic and ethnic religion similar to Judaism, but differing in several important aspects.

> Samaritan tradition claims the group descended from the northern Israelite tribes who were not deported by the Neo-Assyrian Empire after the destruction of the Kingdom of Israel. They consider Samaritanism to be the true religion of the ancient Israelites and regard modern mainstream Judaism as a closely related but altered religion. Samaritans also regard Mount Gerizim (near both Nablus and biblical Shechem), and not the Temple Mount in Jerusalem, to be the holiest place on Earth. They believe that the schism between them and the Jews originated from Eli's establishment of a competing shrine at Shiloh, in opposition to Mount Gerizim.

Disputes Among the Three Parties

	Sadducees	Pharisees	Essenes
Social Class	Priests, aristocrats	Common people	[Unknown]
Authority	Priests	"Disciples of the Wise"	"Teacher of Righteousness"
Practices	Emphasis on priestly obligations	Application of priestly laws to non-priests	"Inspired Exegesis"
Calendar	Luni-solar	Luni-solar	Solar
Attitude Toward:			
Hellenism	For	Selective	Against
Hasmoneans	Opposed usurpation of priesthood by non-Zadokites	Opposed usurpation of monarchy	Personally opposed to Jonathan
Free will	Yes	Mostly	No
Afterlife	None	Resurrection	Spiritual Survival
Bible	Literalist	Sophisticated scholarly interpretations	"Inspired Exegesis"
Oral Torah	No such thing	Equal to Written Torah	"Inspired Exegesis"

https://whc.unesco.org/en/tentativelists/5706/

"The Samaritans on Mount Gerizim represent the smallest, most ancient, living ethnic community in the world, bound together by a profound and rigid religious belief. Central to it is the sanctity of a particular mountain as decreed by Moses and on which, nearly four thousand years ago, Abraham may have nearly sacrificed Isaac.

The Samaritans believe that, since more than 3600 years ago, they came to live on Mount Gerizim because Moses, in his tenth commandment, ordered them to protect it as a sacred mountain and worship on it by making pilgrimages to it three times a year. These beliefs and traditions have been kept alive by Samaritans since then. This sanctity and longevity, through to the present day, make this sacred mountain a place of outstanding universal value going far beyond the beliefs of a few hundred people."

Excavations at the site at Mount Gerizim were initiated in 1983 and continued until 2006 and yielded tens of thousands of finds. Remnants found there identified that a Samaritan temple existed atop Mount Gerizim by the mid-5th century BC, and that it was eventually destroyed and rebuilt in the early 2nd century BC, only to be destroyed

118

again in 111–110 CE by Jewish forces under the orders of the Hasmonean leader John Hyrcanus.

<u>Samaritan Hebrew is written in the Samaritan alphabet, a direct descendant of the Paleo-Hebrew alphabet,</u> which in turn is a variant of the earlier Proto-Sinaitic script dating to the time of Abraham."

Samaritan Script

Samaritan Script - Wikipedia

https://en.wikipedia.org/wiki/Samaritan_Hebrew

The Samaritan alphabet is close to the script that appears on many Ancient Hebrew coins and inscriptions. By contrast, all other varieties of Hebrew, as written by Jews, employ the later square Hebrew alphabet, which is in fact a variation of the Aramaic alphabet that Jews began using in the Babylonian captivity following the exile of the Kingdom of Judah in the 6th century BCE. During the 3rd century BCE, Jews began to use this stylized "square" form of the script used by the Achaemenid Empire for Imperial Aramaic, its chancellery script while **the Samaritans continued to use the Paleo-Hebrew alphabet***, which evolved into the Samaritan alphabet.*

Scribal Changes/Additions to the Masoretic Torah

As I stated earlier, Judaism would have us believe THEIR Torah was faithfully maintained dating back to Moses. In reality, it only dates back to the Mesoretes. We are told there were no scribal errors or additions. We are not told of the competitive atmosphere among the royal scribes, the priestly scribes, the temple scribes, and the synagogue scribes. Each adding and twisting the text to their advantage.

From Masoretic Text: Wikipedia
Early rabbinic sources, from around 200 CE, mention several passages of Scripture in which the conclusion is inevitable that the ancient reading (Samaritan Torah) must have differed from that of the present text (Masoretic Torah). The explanation of this phenomenon is given in the expression "Scripture has used euphemistic language", i.e. to avoid anthropomorphism and anthropopathism (redefine the Mystery Language).

Rabbi Simon ben Pazzi (3rd century) calls these readings "emendations of the Scribes" rather than edits/additions to the oldest Samaritan Torah. This view was adopted by the later Midrash and by the majority of Masoretes. In Masoretic works these changes are ascribed to Ezra; to Ezra and Nehemiah; to Ezra and the Soferim; or to Ezra, Nehemiah, Zechariah, Haggai, and Baruch. All these ascriptions mean one and the same thing: that the changes were assumed to have been made by the Men of the Great Synagogue.

The emendations (additions/changes) are of four general types:

- *Removal of unseemly expressions used in reference to God; e.g., the substitution of ("to bless") for ("to curse") in certain passages.*

120

- *Safeguarding of the Tetragrammaton; e.g. substitution of "Elohim" or "Adonai" for "YHWH" in some passages.*

- *Removal of application of the names of pagan gods, e.g. the change of the name "Ishbaal" to "Ish-bosheth".*

- ***Safeguarding the unity of divine worship at Jerusalem.***

It is this last point of scribal alterations I want to address. ***"Safeguarding the unity of divine worship at Jerusalem."*** Why would this be necessary?

Where to Offer Sacrifices on the Altar to Yahuah?

In the Masoretic Torah, the scribes altered the ancient Torah to *"Safeguarding the unity of divine worship at Jerusalem."*. Why would this need to be done if the Scriptures clearly declared the worship of Yahuah is to be conducted on Mount Mariah? Because Scripture does not support moving the sacrifices from Mount Gerizim to Mount Mariah.

From: Mount Gerizim Wikipedia
> *The Masoretic Text says that Moses had also commanded the Israelites to build an altar on Mount Ebal, constructed from natural (rather than cut) stones, to place stones there and whiten them with lime, to make sacrificial offerings on the altar, eat there, and write the Mosaic Law in stones there. The Samaritan Pentateuch, as well as an ancient manuscript of the biblical text found in Qumran, both bring the same excerpt as the Masoretic Text, with the only difference being the name "Gerizim", instead of "Ebal", therefore stating that Moses commanded the building of the altar on Mount Gerizim. Recent work on the Dead Sea Scrolls, which include the oldest surviving manuscripts of the biblical text, further supports the accuracy of the Samaritan Pentateuch's designation of Mount Gerizim, rather than Mount Ebal, as the first location in the Promised Land where Moses commanded an altar to be built.*

The Pharisees needed "proof" in scripture to move the temple/altar from Mount Gerizim to Mount Mariah to ensure their power and authority. They created Scriptural support by doctoring up the Scriptures (much like Christianity did)! Giving us "the Torah" we have all been taught while hiding the truth found in the ancient Scriptures.

https://www.ifcj.org/news/stand-for-israel-blog/on-this-mountain-the-biblical-mount-gerizim

"In the Old Testament, the Israelites were told, "When the LORD your God has brought you into the land you are entering to possess, you are to proclaim on Mount Gerizim the blessings" (Deuteronomy 11:29), while they were to proclaim curses on nearby Mount Ebal.

Even after entering the Promised Land, Joshua and the Israelites renewed their covenant with God atop the biblical mountain, as He had told them: "Half the people stood in front of Mount Gerizim and half of them in front of Mount Ebal, as Moses the servant of the LORD had formerly commanded when he gave instructions to bless the people of Israel" (Joshua 8:33).

And in the Christian Bible, Mount Gerizim is where Yahusha met the woman at the well, telling her, "a time is coming when you will worship the Father neither on this mountain nor in Jerusalem" (John 4:23)."

Samaritans the True Zadokite Priesthood?

In the paper "**ESSENE SECTARIANISM AS A JUDAIC ALTERNATIVE TO PHARISAISM AND SADDUCEANISM BY P.D. BOTHA** we read":

> "*Nehemiah 8 describes how Ezra convoked a great assembly of all the Jews and read to them "...the Book of the Law of Moses which Yahweh had prescribed for Israel". (Neh.8:1) Anderson (1984:95-6) agrees that this event describes the promulgation of the Torah in the form that it exists in the present day. Although Jewish tradition insists that the Torah dates from the time of Moses, the fact that the people wept in agitation upon hearing Ezra read about certain ritual requirements indicates that at least some portions of the text were new. Other evidence that the Torah as such dates from the time of Ezra is provided by the Samaritan version of the Torah, which made its appearance at about the same time. If the Torah had actually been produced by Moses and known to all Israel for over seven hundred years, the Samaritans would not have been able to present an alternative version and claim that it, and not the Israelite one, was genuine.*
>
> *In Talmudic circles opinions concerning the Samaritans were not always the same. The great disputes occurred when both Samaritan and Jewish temples existed at the same time. Later, the opinion prevailed that the Samaritans were true converts and according to Rabbi Simeon ben Gamaliel, a Samaritan was the equal of a Jew in every respect. Other scholars were milder in their attitude and permitted the Samaritan priesthood was a collateral branch of the Zadokite priesthood in Jerusalem. The Zadokite priesthood had failed in Jerusalem and the accession to the high-priestly office by the Hasmoneans was viewed by many*

Jews as an illegitimate usurpation. The Samaritans could have strengthened their own position by forwarding the claim (which was probably true) that their priesthood was derived from the Zadokites in Jerusalem."

So, the Samaritans not the Pharisees, not the Sadducees, and not the Maserites were the true Zadokite Priesthood. And it is the Zadokite Priesthood that carried foreward the responsibity of sacrifices.The Samaritan Torah is the most ancient and written in Abrahamic Script NOT the Rabbinical Torah force-fed to us as "authentic and authoritative".

From holylandsite.com/shechem

Shechem lies between the two famous mountains of Gerizim and Ebal. It was in the Samaria region of Israel in the territory of Ephraim during Bible times.

About Shechem (Mount Gerizim):

1. *Shechem had a significant role in the Bible and is mentioned 58 times.*

2. *God first appeared to Abraham in Shechem and gave him the promise that he would inherit the land.*

3. *Abraham and Jacob lived here.*

4. *Jacob lived here and built a well.*

5. *Joseph's bones are buried here.*

6. *The blessings and curses given on Mount Gerizim and Mount Ebal took place here.*

7. *Joshua rallied all Israel and made a covenant with them in Shechem.*

8. *Abimelech, son of Gideon, reigned wickedly over Shechem for three years. It was he who burned down the fortress temple here called "El-Berith," and killed 1,000 people who had taken refuge in it. Later, he was killed by a woman who threw a millstone down on his head.*

9. *The nation of Israel became divided in Sheche.*

10. *Shechem became the capital of the northern tribes of Israel under King Jeroboam's rule.*

11. *The Samaritans worshiped on top of Mount Gerizim and there are substantial ruins there today.*

The Samaritans first built a temple here for worship in the 5th century. Later, in the 2nd century, they built walls around the temple to protect it.

In the latter part of the 2nd century, the Hasmoneans (Jewish rule from 165–63 BC) destroyed the Samaritan's temple on Mount Gerizim and the city at the base of the mountain (ancient Shechem).

During the Roman occupation of Israel, the Samaritans were given permission by the Romans to rebuild their temple and city.

In 475 AD, under Byzantine rule, the Samaritan temple was destroyed, and a Byzantine church was erected. Later, a monastery was built as well.

12. *Yahusha met with a Samaritan woman (John 4) at Jacob's Well in Shechem. Today, this well is located in a Greek Orthodox church called "The Church of Jacob's Well."*

13. *The Samaritans were a small group of unfaithful Israelites who remained in the land of Israel and intermarried with*

foreign unbelievers after the deportation of Israel by the Assyrians in 722 BC. They established their own religion at Mount Gerizim and built their own temple. They were despised and rejected by the Jews and considered unclean. The Samaritans, likewise, despised the Jews and had few dealings with them. The Samaritans only believe in the Torah (the first 5 books of the Old Testament).

Speculation and Debate Among Scholars

Moriah – Wikipedia

Whereas the mention of Moriah in Genesis could be referring to any mountainous region, the book of Chronicles says that the location of Araunah's threshing floor is on "Mount Moriah" and that the Temple of Solomon was built over Araunah's threshing floor. This has led to the classical rabbinical supposition that the Moriah region mentioned in Genesis as the place where Abraham almost sacrificed Isaac was in Jerusalem.

In consequence of these traditions, Classical Rabbinical Literature theorised that the name was a (linguistically corrupted) reference to the Temple, suggesting translations like the teaching-place (referring to the Sanhedrin that met there), the place of fear (referring to the supposed fear that non-Israelites would have at the Temple), the place of myrrh (referring to the spices burnt as incense).

On the other hand, some interpretations of a biblical passage concerning the king of Salem, would indicate Jerusalem was already a city with a priest at the time of Abraham, and thus is unlikely to have been founded on the lonely spot where Abraham tried to sacrifice Isaac.

There is also debate as to whether the two references to Moriyya/Moriah (Genesis 22:2 and 2 Chronicles 3:1) are correctly understood as the same name. Ancient translators seem to have interpreted them differently: whereas all ancient translations simply transliterated the name in Chronicles, in Genesis they tended to try to understand the literal meaning of the name and to translate it. For example, in the Greek Septuagint translation, these verses are translated as:

Genesis 22:2

"And he said, Take thy son, the beloved one, whom thou hast loved—Isaac, and go into the high land (Koine Greek: εἰς τὴν γῆν τὴν ὑψηλὴν), and offer him there for a whole-burnt-offering on one of the mountains which I will tell thee of."

2 Chronicles 3:1

"And Solomon began to build the house of the Lord in Jerusalem in the mount of Amoria, where the Lord appeared to his father David, in the place which David had prepared in the threshing-floor of Ornan the Jebusite."

Moreover, other ancient translations interpret the instance in Genesis in different ways from the Septuagint:

* The Samaritan Pentateuch disagree with the Jewish view that the binding of Isaac took place in the Temple Mount in Jerusalem, claiming instead that it happened in Mount Gerizim in the West Bank.

* Some modern biblical scholars, however, regard the name as a reference to the Amorites, having lost the initial a via aphesis; the name is thus interpreted as meaning land of the Amorites. This agrees with the Septuagint, where, for example, 2 Chronicles 3:1 refers to the location as Ἀμωρία. Some scholars also identify it with Moreh, the location near Shechem at which Abraham built an altar, according to Genesis 12:6.

Hence a number of scholars believe that the "מוריה" mentioned in Genesis actually refers to a hill near

***Shechem**, supporting the Samaritan belief that the near-sacrifice of Isaac occurred on Mount Gerizim — a location near Shechem.*

Summary and Conclusions

Allow me to summarize and then draw a conclusion not from the tradition of the Pharisees but from historical evidence.

Mount Gerizim – Wikipedia

"*The Masoretic Text says that Moses had also commanded the Israelites to build an altar on Mount Ebal, constructed from natural (rather than cut) stones, to place stones there and whiten them with lime, to make sacrificial offerings on the altar, eat there, and write the Mosaic Law in stones there.* **Samaritan Pentateuch, as well as an ancient manuscript of the biblical text found in Qumran, both bring the same excerpt as the Masoretic Text, with the only difference being the name "Gerizim", instead of "Ebal", therefore stating that Moses commanded the building of the altar on Mount Gerizim.**

Recent work on the Dead Sea Scrolls, which include the oldest surviving manuscripts of the biblical text, further supports the accuracy of the Samaritan Pentateuch's designation of Mount Gerizim, rather than Mount Ebal, as the first location in the Promised Land where Moses commanded an altar to be built.

All versions of the biblical text then have Moses' specifying how the Israelites should split between the two groups that were to pronounce blessings from Mount Gerizim and to pronounce curses from Mount Ebal. The tribes of Simeon, Levi, Judah, Issachar, Joseph, and Benjamin were to be sent to Gerizim, while those of Reuben, Gad, Asher, Zebulun, Dan, and Naphtali were to remain on Ebal.

The altar to God is again mentioned in the Book of Joshua, when, after the Battle of Ai, Joshua built an altar of unhewn stones, the Israelites made peace offerings on it, the law of

131

Moses was written onto the stones, and the Israelites split into the two groups specified in Deuteronomy and pronounced blessings on Mount Gerizim and curses on Mount Ebal, as instructed in the law of Moses.

Biblical scholars believe that the sources of the book of Joshua predate those of Deuteronomy, and hence that the order to build the altar and make the inscriptions is likely based on these actions in the sources of Joshua at Mount Gerizim, rather than the other way around on Mount Mariah. **Hence a number of scholars believe that the "מוריה" mentioned in Genesis actually refers to a hill near Shechem, supporting the Samaritan belief that the near-sacrifice of Isaac occurred on Mount Gerizim – a location near Shechem.**

When Joshua was old and dying, he gathered the people together at Shechem (present-day Nablus near Mount Gerizim) and gave a farewell speech, and set up "a stone as a witness", placing it "next to the sanctuary of Yahweh, under the oak tree", which indicates that a sanctuary to God existed on Mount Gerizim.

In the Book of John in the New Testament, in his discussion with the Samaritan woman at the well, Yahusha reveals his feelings about worshipping in either Mount Gerizim (as the Samaritans did) or Jerusalem (as the Sadducees and the Jews did): Yahusha said to her,

John 4:21–24
"WOMAN, BELIEVE ME, THE HOUR IS COMING WHEN YOU WILL WORSHIP THE FATHER NEITHER ON THIS MOUNTAIN NOR IN JERUSALEM. YOU WORSHIP WHAT YOU DO NOT KNOW; WE WORSHIP WHAT WE KNOW, FOR SALVATION COMES FROM THE LINE OF JUDAH. BUT THE HOUR IS COMING, AND IS NOW HERE, WHEN THE TRUE WORSHIPERS WILL WORSHIP THE FATHER IN SPIRIT AND TRUTH, FOR

THE FATHER SEEKS SUCH AS THESE TO WORSHIP HIM. YAHUAH IS SPIRIT, AND THOSE WHO WORSHIP HIM MUST WORSHIP IN SPIRIT AND TRUTH."

There is more "between the lines" of this story. If Yahusha was simply there as some unknown visitor to gather water from the well, there would have been no reason for the Samaritan woman's question. However, if Yahusha was there as the legit Zadok High Priest of Israel that would have explained what motivated her question. And beg the question today "What was Yahusha doing there as High Priest?"

The answer is obvious in light of the historical finds in the Dead Sea Scrolls. Yahusha was trained as a High Priest by John the Baptist at a temporary Temple in the wilderness at Qumran. Recent work on the Dead Sea Scrolls, which include the oldest surviving manuscripts of the biblical text, further supports the accuracy of the Samaritan Pentateuch's designation of Mount Gerizim, rather than Mount Ebal, as the first location in the Promised Land where Moses commanded an altar to be built.

This would explain why Yahusha's visit to the Temple in Jerusalem was to condemn it.

Matthew 21:12-13
12 THEN YAHUSHA ENTERED THE TEMPLE COURTS AND DROVE OUT ALL WHO WERE BUYING AND SELLING THERE. HE OVERTURNED THE TABLES OF THE MONEY CHANGERS AND THE SEATS OF THOSE SELLING DOVES. 13 AND HE DECLARED TO THEM, "IT IS WRITTEN: 'MY HOUSE WILL BE CALLED A HOUSE OF PRAYER.' BUT YOU ARE MAKING IT 'A DEN OF ROBBERS.'"

The Essenes were a group who separated from the Samaritans in expectation of the coming Messiah. As a Zadokite High Priest trained by Essenes Yahusha would have frequented Mount Gerizim to offer the Passover Sacrifice and celebrate the Feasts.

Evidence proves the Masoretic Text was altered by their scribes to *"Safeguarding the unity of divine worship at Jerusalem"* to bolster their control and authority away from the Samaritan Torah (the oldest version of the Torah written in Paleo-Hebrew the language of Moses) which gave the line of Zadok High Priests their rightful authority at Mount Gerizim! These edits/additions to the Jewish Torah vs the age of the Samaritan Torah support the understanding that the Samaritans were "keepers of the Torah".

So which Torah do we trust, the oldest version written in Paleo-Hebrew kept by the Samaritans which means "keeper of the Torah" that exists all the way back to before Ezra? Or the Rabbinical Torah written by the Masoretes which means *"Masters of Tradition"* whose version only dates back to the 11th century CE?

It comes down to the "written Torah" vs the "Torah of Tradition". Where do we as Nazarenes put our trust?

Mark 7:5
SO THE PHARISEES AND SCRIBES QUESTIONED YAHUSHA: "WHY DO YOUR DISCIPLES NOT WALK ACCORDING TO THE TRADITION OF THE ELDERS?

We see that the Nazarenes did not keep "the traditions of the elders". Why was Sha'ul called by Yahusha? Because it would take a Pharisee to overcome the oral traditions of the elders with the written Truth.

Galatians 1:14
I WAS ADVANCING IN JUDAISM BEYOND MANY OF MY CONTEMPORARIES AND WAS EXTREMELY ZEALOUS FOR THE TRADITIONS OF MY FATHERS.

Next, I will continue to address the controversy with the Torah:

134

- *Where did Abraham Sacrifice Isaac?*

- *The Essenes/Nazarenes an Offshoot of the Samaritan Priesthood*

- *Samarians accept the Gospel*

- *Yahusha a Samaritan?*

- *Steven a Samaritan?*

- *John a Samaritan?*

- *John the Baptist - The Teacher of Righteousness*

- *The Way - The Enochian Path*

- *Enochian Essenes · Ancient Priesthood*

- *Passing on "Secret Knowledge"*

- *What about the Dead Sea Scrolls? Did the Essenes follow the Rabbinical or Samaritan Torah?*

Once I finish the discussion above, we will begin laying a firm foundation to reveal the "secret knowledge" passed down through the Zadokite Priesthood.

I will begin rebuilding our trust and faith in The Truth and establish a baseline for understanding the Torah and Prophets.

Where did Abraham Sacrifice Isaac?

Jacob's Well and Joseph's Tomb are both at Mount Gerizim. This means Isaac's son and grandson and future generations would inhabit that area of land called Shechem in the Bible.

We see that land was given to Jacob and is where an altar was built:

Genesis 33:18-20
18 AFTER JACOB HAD COME FROM PADDAN-ARAM, HE ARRIVED SAFELY AT THE CITY OF SHECHEM IN THE LAND OF CANAAN, AND HE CAMPED JUST OUTSIDE THE CITY. 19 AND THE PLOT OF GROUND WHERE HE PITCHED HIS TENT, HE PURCHASED FROM THE SONS OF HAMOR, SHECHEM'S FATHER, FOR A HUNDRED PIECES OF SILVER. 20 THERE HE SET UP AN ALTAR AND CALLED IT EL-ELOHE-ISRAEL.

It is recorded that Abraham's descendants settled Shechem where Mount Gerizim is located. This is very strong evidence that Mount Gerizim is where Abraham attempted to sacrifice Isaac, not Mount Mariah.

Mount Gerizim is specifically mentioned in Scripture as the location of the Altar and sacrifices, meaning Mount Gerizim would have been the righteous location of the attempted sacrifice of Isaac:

Deuteronomy 11:29
WHEN THE YAHUAH YOUR GOD HAS BROUGHT YOU INTO THE LAND YOU ARE ENTERING TO POSSESS, YOU ARE TO PROCLAIM ON *Mount Gerizim* THE BLESSINGS, AND ON MOUNT EBAL THE CURSES.

Deuteronomy 27:12

"WHEN YOU HAVE CROSSED THE JORDAN, THESE TRIBES SHALL STAND ON *Mount Gerizim* TO BLESS THE PEOPLE: SIMEON, LEVI, JUDAH, ISSACHAR, JOSEPH, AND BENJAMIN.

Joshua 8:33
ALL ISRAEL, FOREIGNERS AND CITIZENS ALIKE, WITH THEIR ELDERS, OFFICERS, AND JUDGES, STOOD ON BOTH SIDES OF THE ARK OF THE COVENANT OF YAHUAH FACING THE LEVITICAL PRIESTS WHO CARRIED IT. HALF OF THE PEOPLE STOOD IN FRONT OF *Mount Gerizim* AND HALF OF THEM IN FRONT OF MOUNT EBAL, AS MOSES THE SERVANT OF THE LORD HAD COMMANDED EARLIER, TO BLESS THE PEOPLE OF ISRAEL.

Judges 9:7
WHEN THIS WAS REPORTED TO JOTHAM, HE CLIMBED TO THE TOP OF *Mount Gerizim*, RAISED HIS VOICE, AND CRIED OUT: "LISTEN TO ME, O LEADERS OF SHECHEM, AND MAY GOD LISTEN TO YOU.

Moriah – Wikipedia
Whereas the mention of Moriah in Genesis could be referring to any mountainous region, the book of Chronicles says that the location of Araunah's threshing floor is on "Mount Moriah" and that the Temple of Solomon was built over Araunah's threshing floor. This has led to the classical rabbinical supposition that the Moriah region mentioned in Genesis as the place where Abraham almost sacrificed Isaac was in Jerusalem.

In consequence of these traditions, Classical Rabbinical Literature theorised that the name was a (linguistically corrupted) reference to the Temple, suggesting translations like the teaching-place (referring to the Sanhedrin that met there), the place of fear (referring to the supposed fear that non-Israelites would have at the Temple), the place of myrrh (referring to the spices burnt as incense).

On the other hand, some interpretations of a biblical passage concerning the king of Salem, would indicate Jerusalem was already a city with a priest at the time of Abraham, and thus is unlikely to have been founded on the lonely spot where Abraham tried to sacrifice Isaac.

There is also debate as to whether the two references to Moriyya/Moriah (Genesis 22:2 and 2 Chronicles 3:1) are correctly understood as the same name. Ancient translators seem to have interpreted them differently: whereas all ancient translations simply transliterated the name in Chronicles, in Genesis they tended to try to understand the literal meaning of the name and to translate it. For **Hence a number of scholars believe that the "מוריה" mentioned in Genesis actually refers to a hill near Shechem, supporting the Samaritan belief that the near-sacrifice of Isaac occurred on Mount Gerizim – a location near Shechem**.

The Essenes/Nazarenes; A Remnant of the Samaritan Priesthood

The Essenes were an offshoot of the sect of Zadokite High Priests in Samaria (Biblical Shechem). John the Baptist, the Great Notsri, was an Essene. Those who followed John came to be known as Nazarenes. Ultimately the Nazarenes followed Yahusha (after John declared him the Lamb of God).

Below is more information on John the Essene and what the Essene's believed:

From: John the Baptist - Wikipedia
> "*Scholars maintain that John belonged to the Essenes, a semi-ascetic Jewish sect who expected a messiah and practiced ritual baptism. John used baptism as the central symbol or sacrament of his pre-messianic movement.*"

From: https://www.britannica.com/biography/Saint-John-the-Baptist/Possible-relationship-with-the-Essenes
> "*The discovery of the Dead Sea Scrolls drew attention to the numerous parallels between John's mission and that of the Essenes, with whom John may have received some of his religious training. Both were priestly in origin, were ascetic, and had intense and, in many respects, similar expectations about the end of the world.*"

https://www.jewishvirtuallibrary.org/pharisees-sadducees-and-essenes
> *The Essenes are said to have believed in absolute predestination. Probably related to this doctrine was their gift of prophecy. Josephus asserts that the Essenes seldom*

139

erred in their predictions. The name of Moses was held in high esteem, and the Essenes saw blasphemy as a capital crime.

*They studied the Torah and its ethics **and interpreted the scriptures allegorically**. They were extremely strict in observing the Sabbath. Their teachings were recorded in books that the members were required to pass on with great care. The Essenes were experts in medicinal roots and the properties of stones, the healing powers of which they claimed to have derived from ancient writings.*

Most notable among the doctrines of the Essenes was their belief in the immortality of the soul. According to Josephus, they believed that only the soul survived after death and rejected a bodily resurrection.

Samaritans were Among the First to Accept the Gospel

We learn in the Acts of the Apostles that those in Samaria were the first major sect to accept the news that Yahusha (their High Priest) had fulfilled The Heavenly Scroll. This should be expected as the Nazarenes were first Samaritans then Essenes, and finally Nazarenes.

ACTS 8:14-17
NOW WHEN THE APOSTLES AT JERUSALEM HEARD THAT SAMARIA HAD ACCEPTED THE WORD OF GOD, THEY SENT PETER AND JOHN TO THEM. THE TWO WENT DOWN AND PRAYED FOR THEM THAT THEY MIGHT RECEIVE THE HOLY SPIRIT (FOR AS YET THE SPIRIT HAD NOT COME UPON ANY OF THEM; THEY HAD ONLY BEEN BAPTIZED IN THE NAME OF THE KING YAHUSHA. THEN PETER AND JOHN LAID THEIR HANDS ON THEM, AND THEY RECEIVED THE HOLY SPIRIT.

Steven a Samaritan?

There are many clues to Steven's affiliation. It becomes clear in the way and content of his teaching which depends upon the Samaritan Torah not the Jewish Torah.

From: https://www.galaxie.com/article/wtj34-1-01
> In his Article: *Acts 7: Jewish or Samaritan in Character?*, author: W. Harold Mare proves the tradition that Stephen was a Samaritan. He quotes Abram Spiro in the volume on The Acts in the Anchor Bible that raises the question by stating: "Stephen was a Samaritan according to the native tradition preserved by Abul-Fath (Vilmar edition, 1865, p. 159). *Acts 7:2–50 confirms this, for it depends on the Samaritan Pentateuch and reflects Samaritan views of Old Testament history.*"

Yahusha a Samaritan?

When asked if he was a Samaritan with a demon, Yahusha did not correct them about being a Samaritan, just that he was not demon possessed. Why would they make this statement *"Are we not right to say that you are a Samaritan?"*

John 8:48-49
48 THE JEWS ANSWERED HIM, "ARE WE NOT RIGHT TO SAY THAT YOU ARE A SAMARITAN AND YOU HAVE A DEMON?" 49 "I DO NOT HAVE A DEMON," YAHUSHA REPLIED, "BUT I HONOR MY FATHER, AND YOU DISHONOR ME.

John a Samaritan

In his paper *"Did John Write His Gospel Partly to Win Samaritan Converts?"*, author Edwin D. Freed demonstrates the Gospel of John to be written from a Samaritan point of view to win Samaritans.

John the Baptist – The Essene Teacher of Righteousness

According to their own belief, the sect was founded by an individual referred to as the Teacher of Righteousness, a priest of Zadokite affiliation. While this teacher is not named and scholars offer other options as the "Teacher of Righteousness", we can confidently eliminate every contender as Yahusha believed John to be that teacher.

Matthew 11:11-12
10 *This is the one about whom it is written: 'Behold, I will send My messenger ahead of You, who will prepare Your way before You.' 11 Truly I tell you, among those born of women there has risen no one greater than John the Baptist.*

A further split occurred which saw the Teacher of Righteousness and his followers retreat to the wilderness at Qumran to prepare for the coming of the Messiah.

There the community immersed themselves in the development of a Judaic cult based on writings already in use by the group prior to the internal split. This viewpoint is reiterated by Davies (1987: 19-30) who is of the opinion that a clear distinction existed between the Essenes and the Qumran-Essenes, the latter being basically a messianic break-away. The texts found at Qumran reveal **the Qumran Essenes were excessively priestly in orientation**.

Source: https://www.jpost.com/jerusalem-report/article-705913
> *Most people would say it begins with Jesus. But Jesus and at least some of his disciples were influenced by, or followers of, people who called themselves "the sons of light." Others called them the Essenes – an extremely ascetic Jewish sect, who lived in Jerusalem and in the desert near the Dead Sea. Literary elites, they copied, collected and wrote scrolls, both biblical and secular texts, which have been dated from the beginning of the second century BCE until 70 CE, when the*

*Temple and their community were destroyed. **<u>The key figure for our inquiry was John the Baptist, apparently an Essene</u>**.*

The Samaritans, Essenes, and Nazarenes followed the Ancient Path

The Ancient Path or "the Good Way" came to be known as *The Way* by the Nazarenes and defined their faith.

JEREMIAH 6:16
THIS IS WHAT YAHUAH SAYS: "STAND AT THE CROSSROADS AND LOOK; ASK FOR THE ANCIENT (*Enochian*) PATHS (*The Heavenly Scroll, The Way*), ASK WHERE THE GOOD WAY IS, AND WALK IN IT (*AQUARIUS, Jeremiah 31, Ezekiel 36*), AND YOU WILL FIND REST FOR YOUR SOULS (*in the Age of AQUARIUS*). BUT YOU SAID, 'WE WILL NOT WALK IN IT.'

The Dead Sea Scrolls reveal the Essenes under John the Baptist, the Teacher of Righteousness, used the Book of Enoch extensively and followed the 364-day solar calendar given to Enoch.

From: The Essenes - The Way Missions.Org
The Enochian and Nazarene Essenes held more visionary and mystical views, especially that a Messiah was necessary (not just arriving). *They were followers of the "ancient path" dating back to Enoch. I will explain more later.*

As for the Sadducees who served in the Temple, they did not see a need for Messiah, as they thought the Torah was complete and that man needed only to adhere to it.

If there was one single factor that unified Pharisaism and Sadduceanism into one Judaic religion it was both groups' endorsement of the same Mosaic Torah. It has already been discussed above that one of the main factors that caused a rift between mainstream Judaism and Samaritanism was the sectarian Book of Law of the Samaritans which differed

144

with the Judaic Torah with regard to the authentic site of the Temple. That a discrepant version of the Torah also seemed to have been the motivating force behind the Qumran community's split from mainstream Judaism is clear from the Damascus Document (Col. V:2-5, VI:5-12).

The First Book of Enoch, also known as the Ethiopic Book of Enoch, is a sacred text found among the Dead Sea Scrolls in 1947. Initially accepted by the Jewish and Christian communities as a viable book of scripture, **it is very possible that the original library of Enochite material had an Essene origin**. Even if not, it would still be probable that whatever the real origin of the Book of Enoch, the Qumran community held it to be of paramount importance and used it extensively.

Enochian Essenes

From: The Essenes - The Way Missions.Org
The Enochian adherent believed there would be an end time and everyone must be prepared. The Nazarenes and the Osseaens held a similar belief. The idea of a designated group, including those who join them, is indicated or stated throughout the Book of Enoch.

The Enochians believed a Messiah would be needed to administer the final teachings of the Law and the Prophets. Enoch chapters 38–40: "The first is the merciful, the patient, the holy Michael," 40.8. The Enochian spiritual emphasis would be the Book of Enoch (Enoch), but otherwise very little is known about them.

However, the text of Enoch became a continued influence within the Hebrew Bible and probably has much to do with the Enochian sect's viability. Also, the Book of Enoch is represented in the New Testament. Revelations 1.13-14 references the Ancient of Days, "His head and his hairs were *like wool, as white as snow," with Enoch's 46.1-3, "...whose head was like white wool."*

Enoch 48.2-5, "In that hour the Son of man invoked before the Lord of spirits, and his name in the presence of the Ancient of Days. Before the sun and the signs were created, before the stars of heaven were formed, his name was invoked," compared with John 1.1-2, "In the beginning was the Word, and the Word was with God, and the Word was God. The same was in the beginning with God." Both scriptures would lead one to believe that the disciples John and John of Patmos must have had familiarity with Enochic beliefs, even though both were many generations removed from Enoch.

The above scriptures require time, acceptance, refinement, and a continued and organized effort that forms an extended theology. This would infer the Enochic vision as ongoing, a root of Judaism almost from the beginning, perhaps as early as the times of Enoch himself.

Ancient Priesthood

We read in the Tanakh that it is the lineage of the Zadok Priesthood that would carry forth the Covenant of Peace and the exclusive right to make atonement sacrifices.

NUMBERS 25:12-13
12"THEREFORE SAY, 'BEHOLD, I GIVE HIM MY COVENANT OF PEACE; 13AND IT SHALL BE FOR HIM AND HIS DESCENDANTS AFTER HIM, A COVENANT OF A PERPETUAL PRIESTHOOD, BECAUSE HE WAS JEALOUS FOR HIS GOD AND MADE ATONEMENT FOR THE SONS OF ISRAEL.'

This ancient priesthood was centered in the area of Samaria and those of that priesthood were known as Samaritans. Only once we admit the true nature of the Samaritans can we understand the animosity with other sects such as the Pharisees.

From: The Essenes - The Way Missions.Org

What later is designated as the Zadokite Priesthood is thought to have its roots in earlier priesthoods. The traditions observed within the books of Samuel indicate a true prophet led of the Spirit, for it is he who designates David. But earlier traditions show evidence as well, most prominently Melchizedek, the King of Salem, a priest-king; also, Brothers of the Righteous are mentioned in Enoch, also indicating much earlier priesthoods...

All Essene would consider themselves the Sons of Zadok, or Zadokites. "The Priests are the converts of Israel who departed from the land of Judah, and those (those of the Levitical priesthood) who joined them. The Sons of Zadok are the elect of Israel, the men called by name who shall stand at the end of days..." from the Damascus Document IV, Dead Sea Scrolls (also taken from Ezekiel 44.15-17). The Sons of Zadok were the most knowledgeable of the Zadokite

147

priesthood.

The Essenes teachings remained uncluttered by the legalistic approach, later described as spiritual or enlightened (Nazarenes). As Yahusha will demonstrate, the spirit of the law is more important than the written law itself. <u>*Early followers of Yahusha were usually referred* to as Nazaoreans, or those who practice in "the Way"</u>

We see in Acts, Sha'ul, the leader of the sect of Nazarenes, declare The Way was the foundation of their faith.

ACTS 24:14
HOWEVER, I ADMIT THAT I WORSHIP THE GOD OF OUR ANCESTORS AS A FOLLOWER OF THE WAY, WHICH THEY CALL A SECT. I BELIEVE EVERYTHING THAT IS IN ACCORDANCE WITH THE LAW AND THAT IS WRITTEN IN THE PROPHETS

Passing on "Secret Knowledge"

II Esdras 14:25
25 COME HERE, AND I WILL LIGHT IN YOUR HEART THE LAMP OF UNDERSTANDING. IT WON'T BE EXTINGUISHED UNTIL YOU HAVE WRITTEN EVERYTHING DOWN. 26 WHEN YOU ARE FINISHED, YOU WILL MAKE SOME THINGS PUBLIC, **others you will transmit secretly to the wise**. YOU WILL BEGIN TO WRITE TOMORROW AT THIS TIME."

This was a theme among the writings of the Nazarenes.

Matthew 13:35
I WILL OPEN MY MOUTH IN PARABLES; I WILL UTTER THINGS WHICH HAVE BEEN KEPT SECRET FROM THE FOUNDATION OF THE WORLD.

1 Corinthians 2:4-8

4 AND MY MESSAGE AND MY PREACHING WERE NOT IN PERSUASIVE WORDS OF WISDOM, BUT IN DEMONSTRATION OF THE SPIRIT AND OF POWER, 5 SO THAT YOUR FAITH WOULD NOT REST ON THE WISDOM OF MEN, BUT ON THE POWER OF GOD. 6 YET WE DO SPEAK WISDOM AMONG THOSE WHO ARE MATURE; A WISDOM, HOWEVER, NOT OF THIS AGE NOR OF THE RULERS OF THIS AGE, WHO ARE PASSING AWAY; 7 **but we speak God's wisdom in a mystery, the hidden wisdom which God predestined before the ages to our glory** (*in The Heavenly Scroll*); 8 THE WISDOM WHICH NONE OF THE RULERS OF THIS AGE HAS UNDERSTOOD.

This "secret knowledge" was passed down to the "wise" via the Zadok Priesthood.

Daniel 2

20 DANIEL ANSWERED AND SAID, BLESSED BE THE NAME OF GOD (*YAHUAH*) FOR EVER AND EVER: FOR WISDOM AND MIGHT ARE HIS: 21 AND HE CHANGES THE TIMES AND THE SEASONS: HE REMOVES KINGS, AND SETS UP KINGS: HE GIVES (*SPIRITUAL*) WISDOM UNTO THE (*Chosen*) WISE, AND KNOWLEDGE TO THEM THAT KNOW (*Spiritual*) UNDERSTANDING: 22 HE REVEALS THE DEEP AND SECRET THINGS!

These deep and secret things were not revealed to the average Israelite as the information was not relative to them. It was passed down to be given to those who live at the end.

Daniel 12:9-10

9 HE REPLIED, "GO YOUR WAY, DANIEL, BECAUSE THE WORDS ARE ROLLED UP AND SEALED UNTIL THE TIME OF THE END. 10 MANY (*chosen by Yahuah to teach*) WILL BE PURIFIED, MADE SPOTLESS AND REFINED, BUT THE WICKED WILL CONTINUE TO BE WICKED. NONE OF THE WICKED WILL UNDERSTAND, BUT THOSE WHO (*chosen by Yahuah*) ARE WISE WILL UNDERSTAND.

149

Summary

Today, living at the end of the Age of Pisces, we are at the end of the 6,000-year mark. We have thousands of years of research, archeology, and expert testimony from independent scholars regarding who the first-century Nazarenes were and what they believed. As a branch of the Essenes at Qumran, which was an offshoot of the Samaritans, we can draw the following conclusions:

- Abraham attempted to sacrifice Isaac on Mount Gerizim

- John the Baptist was The Teacher of Righteousness of the Essenes

- John was trained by the Zadokite High Priests of the Samaritans

- John and Yahusha performed duties as High Priest on Mount Gerizim

- Samaritans accepted The Yahushaic Covenant

- Steven was a Samaritan.

- John authored the Gospel of John to win the Samaritans.

- The Essenes/Nazarenes followed "the Ancient Path" of Enoch

- The Essenes/Nazarenes followed the solar Enoch Calendar

- The Samaritans were an ancient order of priesthood eventually becoming Zadok High Priests

- The Zadok Priesthood passed on "secret knowledge."

- The Samaritan Torah dates back to before Ezra in 500 BC

- The Samaritan Torah was the version of the Samaritan, Essenes, and Nazarenes.

- The Jewish Torah dates back to 1000 CE making the Samaritan Torah over 1,500 years older.

- Samaritan Torah written in Paleo Hebrew vs Jewish Torah written by Mesorites.

- The Jewish Torah is a compilation of ancient written Torah (the Samaritan Torah) and oral tradition.

- The Jewish scribes altered the text to justify worship on Mount Mariah and the Temple Mount.

Next, I am going to begin laying a firm foundation in righteousness and truth.

Chapter 5
Establishing Truth and Righteousness

Chapter 5: Abraham the Forfather of Astrology

Important Note: Biblical "Astrology" is faith in the message contained in The Heavenly Scroll. Horoscopes, fortune telling, etc. are the ABUSE of it.

Abraham is the forefather of faith for all major monotheistic religions. We are to have the same faith as Abraham, the father of our faith. But what exactly is the faith of Abraham and how did he obtain a state of righteousness?

We are told to look to Abraham that Yahuah established an everlasting covenant with Abraham which "the word" of this promise was commanded to a thousand generations.

Isaiah 51:1-8
"LISTEN TO ME, YOU WHO PURSUE RIGHTEOUSNESS, WHO SEEK YAHUAH: LOOK TO THE ROCK FROM WHICH YOU WERE HEWN, AND TO THE QUARRY FROM WHICH YOU WERE DUG. LOOK TO ABRAHAM YOUR FATHER, AND TO SARAH WHO GAVE BIRTH TO YOU IN PAIN;

Psalm 105:4-15
SEEK YAHUAH AND HIS STRENGTH; SEEK HIS FACE CONTINUALLY. REMEMBER HIS WONDERS WHICH HE HAS DONE, HIS MARVELS, AND THE JUDGMENTS UTTERED BY HIS MOUTH, O SEED OF ABRAHAM, HIS SERVANT, O SONS OF JACOB, HIS CHOSEN ONES! HE IS YAHUAH OUR GOD; HIS JUDGMENTS ARE IN ALL THE EARTH. *He has remembered His covenant forever, The word which He commanded to a thousand generations, The covenant which He made with Abraham, And His oath to Isaac.*"

Abraham was shown The Heavenly Scroll which is the Ancient Path and the promise of salvation. It is his faith in what he was shown that was the definition of righteousness long before the Law

153

was given to Moses. Abraham confirmed his faith in "the ancient path" called The Way.

Genesis 15:4-6

4 THEN THE WORD OF YAHUAH CAME TO ABRAM, SAYING, "THIS ONE WILL NOT BE YOUR HEIR, BUT ONE WHO COMES FROM YOUR OWN BODY WILL BE YOUR HEIR." 5 AND YAHUAH TOOK HIM OUTSIDE AND SAID, "NOW LOOK TO THE HEAVENLY SCROLL AND COUNT (*h5608 "recount or relate" the meaning of*) THE STARS, IF YOU ARE ABLE." THEN HE TOLD HIM, "SO SHALL YOUR SEED BE." 6 ABRAM BELIEVED YAHUAH (*what the stars recount*), AND IT (*his faith in The Heavenly Scroll*) WAS CREDITED TO HIM AS RIGHTEOUSNESS.

The word translated "count" above is more accurately "recount or relate".

◀ 5608. saphar ▶

Strong's Concordance

saphar: to count, recount, relate

Original Word: ספר

Part of Speech: verb; noun masculine

Transliteration: saphar

Phonetic Spelling: (saw-far')

Definition: to count, recount, relate

NAS Exhaustive Concordance

Word Origin

denominative verb from sepher

Definition

to count, recount, relate

NASB Translation

assigned (1), count (17), counted (6), counts (2), declare (6), declared (2), elapse (1), measuring (1), number (3), numbered (5), proclaim (1), recount (1), recounted (3), relate (3), related (9), relating (2), speak (1), state (1), surely (1), taken (1), taken account (1), talk (1), tell (23), telling (1), told (15), utter (1).

154

Abraham was told to "recount" or "relate" the meaning of The Heavenly Scroll which tells the life of the seed of Abraham that would not come until the end of the Age of Aries the "lamb". That is why Abraham was supplied with a male lamb (ram) to sacrifice as a standing annual reminder or rehearsal.

We see that it was Abraham's faith in what the stars recount or proclaim that was counted as Righteousness. It is in The Heavenly Scroll that Yahuah's will, and glory is proclaimed.

Psalm 19:1-6

1 THE HEAVENS (*Shamayim... the place in the sky where the stars are located*) ARE TELLING OF THE GLORY OF YAHUAH (*the Glory of Yahuah is Yahusha! - 2 Corinthians 4:6*); AND THEIR (*Stars and Constellatins*) EXPANSE IS DECLARING THE WORK OF HIS HANDS (*His Will*).

Daniel 4:35

35 "ALL THE INHABITANTS OF THE EARTH ARE ACCOUNTED AS NOTHING, BUT HE DOES ACCORDING TO HIS WILL WRITTEN IN THE HOSTS (*constellations*) OF HEAVEN.

This promise was shown to Abraham; that it was his "seed" (singular) that Yahuah would fulfill in the coming Messiah.

Ephesians 1:9-10

9 HE MADE KNOWN TO US THE MYSTERY OF HIS WILL ACCORDING TO HIS GOOD PLEASURE, WRITTEN IN THE HEAVENLY SCROLL WHICH HE PURPOSED TO FULFILL IN THE YAHUSHAIC COVENANT (*Daniel 4:35*), 10 TO BE PUT INTO EFFECT WHEN THE AGES REACH THEIR FULFILLMENT (*Age of Aquarius*) —

Yahusha stands alone as the fulfillment of The Heavenly Scroll.

Hebrews 10:7

7 THEN I SAID, 'HERE I AM—IT IS WRITTEN ABOUT ME IN THE HEAVENLY

Scroll- I HAVE COME TO DO YOUR WILL, MY ELOHIM! (*Matthew*
6:10)

Matthew 6:10
10 YOUR KINGDOM (*declared in heaven - Matthew* 4:17) COME,
YOUR WILL BE DONE, ON EARTH AS IT IS WRITTEN IN THE HEAVENLY
SCROLL (*Psalm* 19, *Daniel* 4:35).

Yahuah's Will and "spoken promise" in the beginning is the
everlasting covenant Yahuah later confirmed with Abraham. This
was "the word" that was commanded to a thousand generations as
we read in **Psalm** 105:4-15.

We see as far back as 200 years BC, it was understood that
Abraham was a Chaldean Astrologer. He was most probably the
founder of the Chaldean School of Astrology. Daniel too was of the
Chaldean school of Astrologers as I will show later.

From: **Out from Your Sign"- Rash**
Astrological Primary Direction -Its Background in Rabbinic
Literature and Parallels in Abraham bar Hiyya A- BRA(HA)M
THE ASTROLOGER IN JEWISH LITERARY TRADITION.
> *From early in the Jewish exegetical tradition, there has been*
> *a tendency to interpret Genesis 15:5 and its stargazing as*
> *some sort of reference to astral divination, specifically to*
> *astrology. In contrast to how some exponents of critical*
> *biblical study, for example, von Rad, view the beginning of*
> *chapter 15 as derived from a cultic setting (divine*
> *revelation, followed by a salvation oracle and an*
> *acknowledgment of sedäqä), <u>early Jewish exegesis clearly</u>*
> *<u>seems to have seen Abram here as a "wise man of</u>*
> *<u>Chaldea," so to speak, well-versed in astral divination. A</u>*
> *<u>tradition about Abraham as an astrologer can be found</u>*
> *<u>already in Josephus</u> (Ant. Iud. I 7.1.2, attributing the idea*
> *to Berossus), and another early reference (attributed to the*
> *possibly Samaritan writer Pseudo-Eupolemus) can be found*

156

in Eusebius of Caesarea (Praep. Evang. IX 17).6 Philo mentions Abraham as a knower of the stars (De Abrahamo 69-71), and Pseudo-Philo makes such a connection in his work Biblical Antiquities (18:5).

Qumran Scrolls

Interestingly, the Qumran text Pseudo-Jubilees appears to allude to a similar astrological connection to the promise of descendants to Abraham (4Q225 2 I 3-8).7 It is notable that this tradition seems to have extended to non-Jewish sources as well. **The second century CE astrological writer Vettius Valens mentions Abraham as an astrologer of repute** *(Anthologiae 28-29),* **as does the fourth century Firmicus Maternus, who lists him along other semi-mythical icons of astrology** *such as Nechepso-Petosiris (Mathesis 4. Proem. 5; 4.17.2, 5; 4.18.1).8*

The Talmud

Moving on to Rabbinic sources, **the Talmudic passage Bava Batra states that Abra(ha)m was a highly skilled astrologer whom the kings of the east and the west would come to consult,** *and it is quite likely that this idea emanates to a great deal from an early exegesis of Genesis 15:5. Such an analysis occurs already in the Genesis Rabbah (44:10, dealing with the somewhat earlier Gen 15:3):10*

From: **Abraham - Chabad.org**

Abraham was a great philosopher and astrologer. The Talmud teaches that, "Abraham held great astrology in his heart, and all the kings of the east and west arose early at his door". *... It is in the Holy Land where he met Malki Tzedek, King of Shalem, who was a priest to G d, the Most High (Genesis 14:18). Our Sages identify Malki Tzedek as Shem the son of Noah.* **There is evidence that the mystical tradition was taught to Abraham by Shem.**

The Talmud states that Abraham, Isaac, and Jacob all studied in the academies of Shem and Eber.

From the Dead Sea Scroll – brill.com

> *The Astrologer at Qumran? The description of this promise in 4Q225 2 i 3-8 is built on the three biblical formulations of the promise in Genesis (13:16; 15:2-6; 22:17), but the particularities of their reworking imply the view that* <u>**Abraham was versed in astrology**</u>.

From: **Abraham: Father of Nations—and a Scientist, Mathematician and Astronomer | ArmstrongInstitute.org**

> *Consider the record of third-century B.C.E. Babylonian historian Berossus: "In the 10th generation after the Flood, there was among the Chaldeans a man righteous and great, and skillful in the celestial science". While Berossus doesn't give this great scientist a name, first-century Jewish historian Josephus tells us that Berossus was writing about Abraham.... <u>**What many historians are unwilling to admit is that Abraham possessed advanced astronomical knowledge that would not be rediscovered for thousands of years. Josephus further records that Abraham wasn't the first astronomer in his family. The study of astronomy originated with Seth, the third son of Adam**</u>. He wrote that "God gave [those who lived before the Flood] such long life that they might perfect those things which they had invented in astronomy" (Antiquities, 1.3.9).*

From: **Lives of Abraham: Seeing Abraham through the Eyes of Second-Temple Jews | The Interpreter Foundation**

> ***Artapanus***
>
> *One of the earliest "biographies" of Abraham is found in the fragmentary writings of a Jewish author named Artapanus, as preserved in the writings of Christian fathers Eusebius*

and Clement. Dates for the writing have proposed between 250 BC and 50 BC, though some scholars suggest a tenable date of 200 BC. Artapanus claims that Abraham "came to Egypt with all his household to the Egyptian king Pharethothes, and taught him astrology, that he remained there twenty years and then departed again for the regions of Syria." In this short fragment, key additional details beyond the original biblical story give us an interval for Abraham's Egyptian sojourn as well as testimony that Abraham brought culture in the form of astrology to Egypt.

Conclusion

Abraham was a master astrologer. If you ask some scholars Abraham was taught "secret knowledge" passed down from Adam and the founder of astrology. This becomes obvious from all the evidence of scholars and scripture.

But what does that mean to us today? What was it that Yahuah showed Abraham via the witness of the stars? It was the Mazzaroth.

https://en.wikipedia.org/wiki/Mazzaroth

Mazzaroth

Article   Talk

文A 3 languages ∨

Read   Edit   View history   Tools ∨

From Wikipedia, the free encyclopedia

Mazzaroth (Hebrew Transliteration: מַזָּרֹת *Mazzārōt*, LXX Μαζουρωθ, *Mazourōth*) is a Biblical Hebrew Word found in the Book of Job (38:32) and literally meaning "constellations," according to 10th-century biblical exegete Saadia Gaon,[1] while others interpret the word as *Garland of Crowns*,[2] but its context is that of Astronomical Constellations, and it is often interpreted as a term for the Zodiac or the Constellations thereof.[3] (Job 38:31–32 ⬀). The similar word *mazalot* (מַזָּלוֹת) in 2 Kings 23:3–5 ⬀ may be related.

The word itself is a hapax legomenon (i.e., a word appearing only once in a text) of the Hebrew Bible. In Yiddish, the term *mazalot* came to be used in the sense of "astrology" in general, surviving in the expression "mazel tov," meaning "good fortune."[4]

Biblical context [edit]

The stars were created as a witness:

Genesis 1:14
AND GOD SAID, "LET THERE BE LIGHTS IN THE VAULT OF THE SKY TO
SEPARATE THE DAY FROM THE NIGHT, AND LET THEM SERVE AS SIGNS
TO MARK SACRED TIMES, AND DAYS AND YEARS.

The Hebrew word translated above as "signs" means pledge
(promise) and witness:

> **g226. oth ▶ Strong's Concordance**
> **Definition**: *a sign, banners (1), omens (1), **pledge** (1), sign
> (43), signs (30), standards (1), **witness** (1), wondrous (1).*

The constellations are given to all mankind as a "witness" of the
Will of Yahuah:

Deuteronomy 4:19
AND WHEN YOU LOOK UP TO THE HEAVENS AND SEE THE SUN, THE
MOON, AND THE STARS—ALL THE HEAVENLY SCROLL—DO NOT BE
ENTICED INTO BOWING DOWN TO WORSHIP THE CONSTELLATIONS
(*they are signs not 'gods'*) FOR YAHUAH YOUR GOD HAS
APPORTIONED SUN, MOON, CONSTELLATION, AND STARS AS
SIGNS (*a witness*) TO ALL THE NATIONS UNDER THE HEAVENLY
SCROLL.

Psalm 19:1-6
1 THE HEAVENS (*Shamayim... the place in the sky where the
stars are located i.e. Zodiac*) ARE TELLING OF THE GLORY OF
YAHUAH (*the Glory of Yahuah is Yahusha! - 2 Corinthians 4:6*);
AND THEIR EXPANSE IS DECLARING (*witnessing*) THE WORK OF
HIS HANDS.

**So the stars/constellations are telling of the "Glory of Yahuah"
which is Yahusha! That is what Abraham was shown.**

Next, we will continue to seek out and clearly define the "faith of
our Forefathers" to build a foundation of Truth.

160

Jeremiah 6:16

THIS IS WHAT YAHUAH SAYS: "STAND AT THE CROSSROADS AND LOOK; ASK FOR THE ANCIENT PATHS, ASK WHERE THE GOOD WAY IS, AND WALK IN IT, AND YOU WILL FIND REST FOR YOUR SOULS. BUT YOU SAID, 'WE WILL NOT WALK IN IT!'"

The Faith of Our Forefathers
Introduction

Now that we have held the Tanakh to the same standard we hold the New Testament writings of the Nazarenes, we find the same issues with both:

- No original autographed copies.

- No known authors assembled over time, sometimes thousands of years removed.

- Additions and alterations by the scribes.

- Miracles seem to be parallels of other pagan gods.

- Contradictions.

- New doctrines and truths – "Anything true in the NT isn't new and anything new isn't true" does not hold up in the Tanakh as every covenant introduced new instructions and promises.

In short, the Tanakh fails the same tests when held to the same standard. If we are to reject the New Testament, then we must also reject the Tanakh! But should we reject either the Tanakh or the New Testament? Or have we fallen for the Lying Pen of the Scribes?

If we cannot trust the Scriptures that have been handed down to us which have been altered and oral tradition "of the elders" have been incorporated, then how do we know what "Truth and Righteousness" is?

What did the offshoot of the Samaritans who became known as

Essenes believe? This is paramount as the Nazarenes were an offshoot of the Essenes. Where did they put their faith? What faith influenced the Nazarene followers of John the Baptist and later Yahusha the Messiah? Were John, Yahusha, and many of the deciples Samaritans? Why did the Jews recognized Yahusha and his teachings to be of the faith of the Samaritans which they considered doctrines of demons.

John 8

48 THE JEWS ANSWERED HIM, "ARE WE NOT RIGHT TO SAY THAT YOU ARE A SAMARITAN AND YOU HAVE A DEMON?" 49 "I DO NOT HAVE A DEMON," YAHUSHA REPLIED, "BUT I HONOR MY FATHER, AND YOU DISHONOR ME.

So, what was Yahusha's message that so inflamed the Jews and especially the High Priests?

Before the Foundation of the World... The Ancient Path

To find The Way, the Ancient Path we must go back to creation:

1 Peter 1:20

HE WAS CHOSEN BEFORE THE CREATION OF THE WORLD (*as foretold in The Heavenly Scroll*), BUT WAS REVEALED IN THESE LAST TIMES FOR YOUR SAKE (*to fulfill The Plan of Salvation and show us The Way*).

Revelation 13:8

ALL INHABITANTS OF THE EARTH WILL WORSHIP THE BEAST—ALL WHOSE NAMES HAVE NOT BEEN WRITTEN IN THE LAMB'S BOOK OF LIFE, THE LAMB WHO WAS SLAIN FROM THE CREATION OF THE WORLD.

Where do we turn at this crossroads? If the lying pen of the scribes has totally falsified the written "word" passed down to us today and all we have are "nothing but lies"... then what is the Truth and where do we find it?"

Like ancient Israel, modern-day Christianity, and Judaism; will we too refuse to walk in the Ancient Path where the Truth is established? Will we too refuse to admit it?

Isaiah 48:3-6

3 I FORETOLD THE FORMER THINGS LONG AGO, MY MOUTH ANNOUNCED THEM AND I MADE THEM KNOWN; THEN SUDDENLY I ACTED, AND THEY CAME TO PASS. 4 FOR I KNEW HOW STUBBORN YOU WERE; YOUR NECK MUSCLES WERE IRON; YOUR FOREHEAD WAS BRONZE. 5 THEREFORE I TOLD YOU THESE THINGS LONG AGO; BEFORE THEY WERE FULFILLED, I ANNOUNCED THEM SO THAT YOU COULD NOT SAY, 'MY IMAGES BROUGHT THEM ABOUT; MY WOODEN IMAGE AND METAL GOD ORDAINED THEM.' 6 YOU HAVE HEARD THESE THINGS; LOOK AT ALL THEN ALL. WILL YOU NOT ADMIT THEM?-

What is "the ancient path", also called The Way, that we may seek it and travel down that path?

This path was revealed first to Enoch then passed down to Abraham through Moses and then the Zadok Priesthood at Samaria to John the Baptist then Yahusha the Messiah. Both anointed Zadokite High Priest of Israel.

At the time Yahuah declared through Jeremiah His Word had been completely corrupted by the scribes under the direction of a priesthood that had fallen into ruin (multiple times), we see Yahuah instruct us to seek "the ancient path" that long predated the giving of the Law to Moses. Ancient to Jeremiah was not Moses, but rather before Abraham.

Jeremiah 6:16

THIS IS WHAT YAHUAH SAYS: "STAND AT THE CROSSROADS AND LOOK; ASK FOR THE ANCIENT PATHS, ASK WHERE THE GOOD WAY IS,

AND WALK IN IT, AND YOU WILL FIND REST FOR YOUR SOULS. BUT YOU SAID, 'WE WILL NOT WALK IN IT!'"

Next, I am going to establish:

- The Faith of Enoch

- The Faith of Noah

- The Faith of Abraham

- The Faith of Moses

- The Faith of the High Priests

- The Faith of David

- The Faith of Jeremiah

- The Faith of Ezekiel

- The Faith of Isaiah

- The Faith of Zechariah

- The Faith of the Essenes/Nazarene

- The Faith of John the Baptist

- The Faith of Yahuhsa the Messiah

- The Faith of Sha'ul the Apostle

- The Faith of John of Patmos

- The Faith of the First Century Israelites

Then I will break down "the Ancient Path" so that we may choose to walk it and admit it or refuse to do either.

The Original Pre-Diluvian Zodiac

The Zodiac Signs (The Heavenly Scroll) were originally revealed to Adam and passed down to Seth and Enoch before the Flood. Their meaning was transmitted to Noah who preserved it, according to the Enoch and Hermetic literature, on an Emerald Prism, left hidden in Egypt.

From: *THE ORIGINAL PRE-DILUVIAN ZODIAC - Christian Hospitality*

The Great Pyramids of Egypt

The Egyptians called Adam's son, Seth "Agathodaimon", i.e. "The Good, or Beneficent, Spirit", and Seth's descendant Enoch "The First Thoth (Hermes)". The builder of the Great Pyramid, the Pharaoh Khufu or Cheops, is said in native Egyptian literature to have used the secret writings of "Thoth" (i.e. of Enoch) to build the Great Pyramid of Gizeh.

Pharaoh Khufu found the knowledge of the whereabouts of these writings of Thoth in the possession of a humble seer of very advanced age. Thus, the secrets of the star-signs were preserved after the Flood in Egypt and used to construct the Great Pyramid.

Testimony of Josephus

This Egyptian tradition, combined with the witness of the Enoch and Hermetic literature, confirms the testimony of Josephus that the antediluvian patriarchs discovered the secrets of the Zodiac and that their discoveries were inscribed on a monument of stone which remained standing to Josephus' own time in Northern Egypt (the Siriadic land as he calls it).

167

Ancient Myths and Astrology

*As early as 1811, modern researchers were examining evidence for knowledge of the precession of the equinoxes and astrological ages before Hipparchus. Sir William Drummond published Oedipus Judaicus: Allegory in the Old Testament in 1811. **Drummond expounds on his hypothesis that a greater part of the Hebrew Scriptures are merely allegorical writings that hide the true content.** Furthermore, the Orientalists were mainly concerned with astronomy and most of their ancient myths are really disguised astronomical records. Drummond believed that the 49th chapter of Genesis contains prophecies allied to astronomy and that the twelve tribes of Israel represented the 12 zodiac signs.*

Drummond makes his case that at the time of Abraham, the Amorites first recorded the shift from the Age of Taurus to the Age of Aries as represented by the year commencing with the Ram (Aries) rather than the bull (Taurus).

*The Book of Joshua indicates that by the time of Moses the equinoxes had already shifted from Taurus to Aries, as Moses had ordained that the civil year should commence with the month of Nisan (Aries) rather than the month of Taurus. **The feast of the Passover is probably a celebration of the Age of Aries with the Paschal Lamb representative of Aries, traditionally associated with the symbol of the ram or sheep.***

Drummond also hypothesizes that most number references in ancient texts were coded to hide their real value by multiples of 1,000. For example, in the Old Testament Joshua commanded 30,000 men, and he slew 12,000 inhabitants of the city of Ai. The historian Berosus stated the Babylonians commenced astronomical observations 49,000 years (7 × 7 x 1000) before Alexander the Great. Most early references were related to 7 (Sun, Moon, and five visible planets), 12 (number of zodiacal signs and months per year), 30 (degrees per sign of the zodiac), and higher combinations of these numbers and other numbers associated with astronomical observations and astrology.

Understanding Ancient Astrology

The problem of understanding the exact nature of ancient astrology is that it was only partly documented, leaving the question of the extent of their undocumented astrological knowledge. Michael Baigent in From the Omens of Babylon: Astrology and Ancient Mesopotamia suggests that there is evidence that there was probably an older or parallel oral tradition of astrology at the time of publication of Enuma Anu Enlil believed published over the period (1595–1157 BC).

Santillana and von Dechend believed that <u>the old mythological stories handed down from antiquity were not random fictitious tales but were accurate depictions of celestial cosmology clothed in tales to aid their oral transmission</u>. The chaos, monsters, and violence in ancient myths are representative of the forces that shape each age. They believed that ancient myths are the remains of preliterate astronomy that became lost with the rise of the Greco-Roman civilization.

*Santillana and von Dechend state that ancient myths have no historical basis but a cosmological one based on a primitive form of astrology. They recognized the importance of the heliacally rising constellation as markers for the astrological ages and wrote that knowledge of this phenomenon had been known for thousands of years previously. **They state that to understand ancient thinking it is necessary to understand astrology, not the modern sun-sign or horoscopic astrology, but the astrology of ancient times which was the lingua franca of ancient times.***

The Faith of Our Forefathers From Adam to Jacob

The Faith of Enoch

For more, read my book *Enoch the Scribe of The Heavenly Tablets*:

4 *Enoch* 3:10

10 AND HE SAID UNTO ME: "OBSERVE, ENOCH, THE HEAVENLY SCROLL AND READ WHAT IS WRITTEN THEREON, AND MARK EVERY INDIVIDUAL FACT."

3 *Enoch* 1:19

19 AND AFTER THAT THERE SHALL BE STILL MORE UNRIGHTEOUSNESS THAN THAT WHICH WAS FIRST CONSUMMATED ON THE EARTH; FOR I KNOW THE MYSTERIES OF THE HOLY ONES; FOR HE, YAHUAH, HAS SHOWED ME AND INFORMED ME, AND I HAVE READ THE HEAVENLY SCROLL.

1 *Enoch* 35:3

I BLESSED YAHUAH AUTHOR OF GLORY (*The Heavenly Scroll - Psalm* 19:1), WHO HAD MADE THOSE GREAT AND SPLENDID SIGNS (*of the Zodiac — Genesis* 1:14), THAT THEY MIGHT DISPLAY (*to all mankind - Deut.* 4:19) THE MAGNIFICENCE OF THE WORKS OF HIS HANDS (*The Plan of Salvation - Psalm* 19) TO ANGELS AND TO THE SOULS OF MEN; AND THAT THESE (*splendid signs in The Heavenly Scroll*) MIGHT GLORIFY ALL HIS WORKS AND OPERATIONS (*His Will - Daniel* 4:35); THAT WE MIGHT SEE THE EFFECT OF HIS POWER; AND THE HEAVENLY SCROLL MIGHT GLORIFY THE GREAT LABOR OF HIS HANDS; AND BLESS HIM FOREVER.

170

The Zodiac Signs were originally revealed by Adam and passed down to Seth and Enoch before the Flood. Their meaning was transmitted to Noah who preserved it.

From: Abraham - chabad.org

The Faith of Shem

Abraham was a great philosopher and astrologer. The Talmud teaches that, "Abraham held great astrology in his heart, and all the kings of the east and west arose early at his door." ... It is in the Holy Land where he met Malki Tzedek, King of Shalem, who was a priest to G d, the Most High (Genesis 14:18). Our Sages identify Malki Tzedek as Shem the son of Noah. There is evidence that the mystical tradition was taught to Abraham by Shem. According to some authorities, Abraham authored Sefer Yetzirah (the Book of Formation), one of the fundamental works of Kabbalah. The Talmud states that Abraham, Isaac, and Jacob all studied in the academies of Shem and Eber.

The Faith of Noah

In the Book of Jubilees, there are few terms whose sense is as rich and varied as that of the "heavenly tablets." The passages that mention The Heavenly Scroll are grouped into five categories: the tablets of the law; the heavenly register of good and evil; the Book of Destiny; the calendar and feasts.

An extended passage in Jubilees following the flood narrative explicitly expresses the conception of Shavuot as the festival of covenant.

Jubilees 6:17

FESTIVAL OF WEEKS DURING THIS MONTH—ONCE A YEAR—TO RENEW THE COVENANT EACH AND EVERY YEAR.

171

The purpose of the annual celebration of Shavuot is to renew the covenant between God and Israel. Shavuot as a Covenant Going Back to the Time of Creation.

According to Jubilees, the national covenant between God and Israel was not first established at Sinai, but existed from the dawn of time, when Israel was already chosen as God's nation in the first week of creation (written in The Heavenly Scroll):

Jubilees 6:19

19 HE SAID TO US: "I WILL NOW SEPARATE FOR MYSELF A PEOPLE AMONG MY NATIONS. AND THEY WILL KEEP SABBATH. I WILL SANCTIFY THEM AS MY PEOPLE, AND I WILL BLESS THEM. THEY WILL BE MY PEOPLE AND I WILL BE THEIR GOD." 20 AND HE CHOSE THE DESCENDANTS OF JACOB AMONG ALL OF THOSE WHOM I HAVE SEEN. I HAVE RECORDED THEM AS MY FIRST-BORN SON AND HAVE SANCTIFIED THEM FOR MYSELF FOR ALL THE AGES OF ETERNITY. THE SEVENTH DAY I WILL TELL THEM SO THAT THEY MAY KEEP SABBATH ON IT FROM EVERYTHING, 21 AS HE BLESSED THEM AND SANCTIFIED THEM FOR HIMSELF AS A SPECIAL PEOPLE OUT OF ALL THE NATIONS AND TO BE KEEPING SABBATH TOGETHER WITH US.

This accords with a deterministic, dualistic worldview expressed in a number of passages throughout Jubilees, according to which the status of Israel and the nations (and their heavenly angelic counterparts) was established by God as an integral part of the cosmos (in The Heavenly Scroll). Although Israel did not exist until over twenty generations later, its special position was determined in advance in The Heavenly Scroll.

The Foundation of the Written Scrolls

The existence of the covenant from the time of creation necessitated the existence of commandments, which are the stipulations of this covenant, and thus Jubilees posits that many commandments were already given (and passed down orally) prior to Mount Sinai.

172

Similarly, the covenant festival was relevant from the dawn of time as well: first observed by angelic beings in heaven from creation, until the time of Noah when it was first observed by human beings. It was then celebrated off and on until it was commanded at Mount Sinai:

Jubilees 6:18-19

THIS ENTIRE FESTIVAL OF SHAVUOT HAD BEEN CELEBRATED IN HEAVEN FROM THE TIME OF CREATION UNTIL THE LIFETIME OF NOAH— FOR 26 JUBILEES AND FIVE WEEKS OF YEARS [= 1309]. THEN NOAH AND HIS SONS KEPT IT FOR SEVEN JUBILEES AND ONE WEEK OF YEARS UNTIL NOAH'S DEATH [=350 YEARS]. FROM THE DAY OF NOAH'S DEATH HIS SONS CORRUPTED (IT) UNTIL ABRAHAM'S LIFETIME AND WERE EATING BLOOD. 19 ABRAHAM ALONE KEPT (IT), AND HIS SONS ISAAC AND JACOB KEPT IT UNTIL YOUR LIFETIME. DURING YOUR LIFETIME THE ISRAELITES HAD FORGOTTEN (IT) UNTIL I RENEWED (IT) FOR THEM AT THIS MOUNTAIN.

Jubilees thus commemorate this eternal covenant, which began in the first week of history and was renewed over time. The Sinaitic revelation is the culmination of a process, but is not the sole covenantal event at the heart of this festival of Shavuot.

The book of Jubilees, preserved in about 15 fragmentary copies in the Dead Sea scrolls, presents a rewriting of Genesis and Exodus, enriching them with additional material, often reflecting both halachic and/or chronological concerns.

The Faith of Abraham

We see as far back as 200 years BC, it was understood that Abraham was a Chaldean Astrologer. He was most probably the founder of the Chaldean School of Astrology. Daniel too was of the Chaldean school of Astrologers as I will show later.

173

THE ASTROLOGER IN JEWISH LITERARY TRADITION - –
scielo.org

From early in the Jewish exegetical tradition, there has been a tendency to interpret Genesis 15:5 and its stargazing as some sort of reference to astral divination, specifically to astrology. In contrast to how some exponents of critical biblical study, for example, von Rad, view the beginning of chapter 15 as derived from a cultic setting (divine revelation, followed by a salvation oracle and an acknowledgment of sedäqä), ***early Jewish exegesis clearly seems to have seen Abram here as a "wise man of Chaldea," so to speak, well-versed in astral divination. A tradition about Abraham as an astrologer can be found already in Josephus*** *(Ant. Iud. I 7.1.2, attributing the idea to Berossus), and another early reference (attributed to the possibly Samaritan writer Pseudo-Eupolemus) can be found in Eusebius of Caesarea (Praep. Evang. IX 17).6 Philo mentions Abraham as a knower of the stars (De Abrahamo 69-71), and Pseudo-Philo makes such a connection in his work Biblical Antiquities (18:5).*

Qumran Scrolls
Interestingly, the Qumran text Pseudo-Jubilees appears to allude to a similar astrological connection to the promise of descendants to Abraham (4Q225 2 I 3-8).7 It is notable that this tradition seems to have extended to non-Jewish sources as well. ***The second century CE astrological writer Vettius Valens mentions Abraham as an astrologer of repute (Anthologiae** 28-29)**, as does the fourth century Firmicus Maternus, who lists him along other semi-mythical icons of astrology*** *such as Nechepso-Petosiris (Mathesis 4. Proem. 5; 4.17.2, 5; 4.18.1).8*

174

The Talmud
Moving on to Rabbinic sources, *the Talmudic passage*
Bava Batra states
Abra(ha)m was a highly skilled astrologer whom the
kings of the east and the west would come to consult,
and it is quite likely that this idea emanates to a great deal
from an early exegesis of Genesis 15:5. Such an analysis
occurs already in the Genesis Rabbah (44:10, dealing with
the somewhat earlier Gen 15:3):10

From: Abraham - Chabad.org
Abraham was a great philosopher and astrologer. The
Talmud teaches that, "Abraham held great astrology in
his heart, and all the kings of the east and west arose
early at his door." ... It is in the Holy Land where he met
Malki Tzedek, King of Shalem, who was a priest to G d, the
Most High (Genesis 14:18). Our Sages identify Malki Tzedek
as Shem the son of Noah. There is evidence that the
mystical tradition was taught to Abraham by Shem.
The Talmud states that Abraham, Isaac, and Jacob all
studied in the academies of Shem and Eber.

From the Dead Sea Scroll – brill.com
The Astrologer at Qumran? The description of this promise
in 4Q225 2 i 3-8 is built on the three biblical formulations of
the promise in Genesis (13:16; 15:2-6; 22:17), but the
particularities of their reworking imply the view that
Abraham was versed in astrology.

From: Abraham: Father of Nations—and a Scientist,
Mathematician and Astronomer | ArmstrongInstitute.org
Consider the record of third-century B.C.E. Babylonian
historian Berossus: "In the 10th generation after the Flood,
there was among the Chaldeans a man righteous and great,
and skillful in the celestial science". While Berossus doesn't
give this great scientist a name, first-century Jewish

historian Josephus tells us that Berossus was writing about Abraham.... **What many historians are unwilling to admit is that Abraham possessed advanced astronomical knowledge that would not be rediscovered for thousands of years.** *Josephus further records that Abraham wasn't the first astronomer in his family.* **The study of astronomy originated with Seth, the third son of Adam.** *He wrote that "God gave [those who lived before the Flood] such long life that they might perfect those things which they had invented in astronomy" (Antiquities, 1.3.9).*

From: **Lives of Abraham: Seeing Abraham through the Eyes of Second-Temple Jews | The Interpreter Foundation**
Artapanus

One of the earliest "biographies" of Abraham is found in the fragmentary writings of a Jewish author named Artapanus, as preserved in the writings of Christian fathers Eusebius and Clement. Dates for the writing have proposed between 250 BC and 50 BC, though some scholars suggest a tenable date of 200 BC. Artapanus claims that Abraham "came to Egypt with all his household to the Egyptian king Pharethothes, and taught him astrology, that he remained there twenty years and then departed again for the regions of Syria." In this short fragment, key additional details beyond the original biblical story give us an interval for Abraham's Egyptian sojourn as well as testimony **that Abraham brought culture in the form of astrology to Egypt.**

The Faith of Jacob

Jubilees 32:21–26 tells the story of Jacob's third divine encounter at Bethel, in which heavenly writing is revealed to him.

Jubilees 32

AND JACOB GAVE HIS VOW: THUS HE TITHED AGAIN THE TITHE TO THE LORD AND SANCTIFIED IT, AND IT BECAME HOLY UNTO HIM. AND FOR THIS REASON IT IS ORDAINED ON THE HEAVENLY TABLES AS A LAW FOR THE TITHING AGAIN THE TITHE TO EAT BEFORE THE LORD FROM YEAR TO YEAR, IN THE PLACE WHERE IT IS CHOSEN THAT HIS NAME SHOULD DWELL, AND TO THIS LAW THERE IS NO LIMIT OF DAYS FOR EVER. THIS ORDINANCE IS WRITTEN (*in The Heavenly Scroll*) THAT IT MAY BE FULFILLED FROM YEAR TO YEAR IN EATING THE SECOND TITHE BEFORE THE LORD IN THE PLACE WHERE IT HATH BEEN CHOSEN,

The Faith of Our Forefathers From Joseph thru the Prophets

By Hellenizing the scriptures, the reality of the Mazzaroth 'the Heavenly Scroll' is hidden from our view. "Heaven" in Hebrew is shamayim and means "visible sky where the stars are located". It is speaking of the Mazzaroth. Today we call it the Zodiac where Yahuah authored the Plan of Salvation.

Understanding this simple truth brings new meaning to the scriptures. When we remove the effects of Hellenism the reality of these scriptures comes to life in light of The Heavenly Scroll.

For instance, when Yahusha prays to Yahuah:

Matthew 6:10
"YOUR KINGDOM COME, YOUR WILL BE DONE, ON EARTH AS IT IS IN HEAVEN."

Below is the Hebrew word for Heaven which is shamayim:

-----Brown-Driver-Briggs entry H8064-----
1. *a. visible heavens, sky, where stars, etc., are located*

We see that the primary definition 1.A is "visible sky where the stars are located" i.e. the Mazzaroth! What Yahusha REALLY said and meant is this:

Matthew 6:10
"YOUR KINGDOM COME, YOUR WILL BE DONE, ON EARTH AS IT IS (*written*) WHERE THE STARS ARE VISIBLE IN THE SKY (*Shamayim/Mazzaroth*)"

You see, Yahusha understood that the Plan of Salvation, His Kingdom, and Yahuah's Will were originally written in the stars! He was proclaiming his desire to see that Original Revelation come true on Earth exactly as it is written in the Mazzaroth. Let us look at other occurrences of the word 'shamayim' in scripture and reveal the meaning of those passages.

One was found among the Dead Sea Scrolls. Astrology was often practiced by rabbis. In the Middle ages, rabbis were often employed as astrologers.

The scholar Anthony J. Tomasino states in: *"Among the great medieval rabbis astrology was considered a science quite compatible with the Jewish faith."*
> *"For Origen, the important early Christian scholar, the stars are "heavenly writings, which the angels and the divine powers are able to read well . . ."*

> <u>*But around the 4th century after the Council of Nicaea a new religion emerged called Christianity. Christians began to denounce astrology.*</u>

No one can point to any verse in the Bible that supports such a condemnation when understood in context. Sure, there are mistranslated sound bites used to "imply" Yahuah condemns astrology. We can see the degree to which we "refuse to admit" the stars and constellation show us The Way and we refuse to walk in it.

I have had to wonder if Christianity banned astrological knowledge so that the Bible would become more obscure... "Lying Pen of the Scribes" comes to mind.

The Faith of Joseph

In Genesis 37:9, Joseph dreams "the sun and moon and eleven stars were bowing down to me." For Philo, the 1st century Jewish sage, this meant that Joseph was "thus classing himself as the twelfth, to complete the circle of the zodiac."

Genesis 37:9
9 THEN JOSEPH HAD ANOTHER DREAM AND TOLD IT TO HIS BROTHERS. "LOOK," HE SAID, "I HAD ANOTHER DREAM, AND THIS TIME THE SUN AND MOON AND ELEVEN STARS WERE BOWING DOWN TO ME."

The Faith of Moses, Aaron, and the Priesthood

Deuteronomy 4:19
AND WHEN YOU LOOK UP TO THE HEAVENS AND SEE THE SUN, THE MOON, AND THE STARS—ALL THE HEAVENLY SCROLL—DO NOT BE ENTICED INTO BOWING DOWN TO WORSHIP THE CONSTELLATIONS (*they are pictographs not gods*) FOR YAHUAH YOUR GOD HAS APPORTIONED SUN, MOON, CONSTELLATION, AND STARS AS SIGNS TO ALL THE NATIONS UNDER THE HEAVENLY SCROLL.

Deuteronomy 33:26
"THERE IS NONE LIKE THE ELOHIM OF YAHSHURUN, WHO (*ORION*) RIDES THE CLOUDS OF HEAVEN (*Milky Way Galaxy*) TO YOUR HELP, AND THE CLOUEDS IN HIS GLORY (*the works of His Hands are proclaimed through The Heavenly Scroll in His Majesty/Glory - Psalm 19, Enoch 35:3*).

The Law was transmitted from Adam to Moses orally. With Moses, the Law was transposed from oral to written in stone. In The Yahushaic Covenant, the Law is transposed from written in stone to written on our hearts. What Moses was given on Mt. Sinai was what is written in The Heavenly Scroll where true Righteousness is found.

Moses constructed the Tabernacle in the wilderness as a reflection of The Heavenly Scroll. There were images of the 4 constellations on the flags/standards carried by the four divisions of the host of Israelites in the wilderness. Each of the 4 division consisted of three tribes and were known by the name of the principal tribe which formed it.

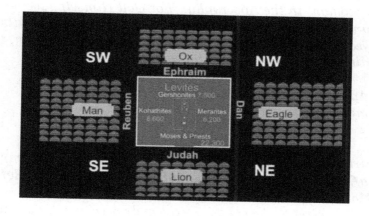

The images on the standards were a lion for Judah, a man for Reuben, a bull for Ephraim, and an eagle (or river) for Dan. In two cases multiple symbols are required to tell their story. For instance, Rueben. A man and a river, represents Aquarius the water-bearer pouring out a river of living water from on high.

From: *ASTROLOGY AND THE BIBLE – Worldspiritualality.org*

> *Solomon was credited with a knowledge of astrology. This is based on the passage in the "Book of the Wisdom of Solomon" in the Apocrypha: "For God Himself gave me unerring knowledge of the things that are – the circuits of years and the positions of stars – the thoughts of men, the diversities of plants and the virtues of roots."*
>
> *Apparently, in Solomon's time astrology and magic/pharmacy had merged into one.*

Breastplate of the High Priest

From: *Birthstones & Aaron's Breastplate* (vulcans-forge.com): *"The Secret of the Torah"*, A translation of Abraham ibn Ezra's *Sefer Yesod Mora Ve-Sod Ha-Torah*, by H. Norman Strickman.

> *"The secret of the ephod is extremely precious, for six names were inscribed on each one of the two sapphire stones that were on the ephod. One stone was on its right, and one was on its left.*

Name of Zodiac	Name in English	Name in Hebrew	Son of Jacob	Tribe Of Israel	Old Testament Prophet
Aries	Ram	Tleh	Zebulon	Judah	Malachi
Taurus	Bull	Shor	Issachar	Joseph	Haggai
Gemini	Twins	Teumi	Benjamin	Zebulon	Zachary
Cancer	Crab	Sartan	Issachar	Reuben	Amos
Leo	Lion	Ari	Judah	Simeon	Hosea
Virgo	Virgin	Betula	Naphtali	Gad	Micah
Libra	Scales	Moznaim	Asher	Ephraim	Jonah
Scorpio	Scorpion	Akrav	Dan	Menasseh	Obadiah
Sagittarius	Archer	Kashet	Gad	Benjamin	Zephaniah
Capricorn	Goat	Gedi	Simeon	Dan	Nahum
Aquarius	Water-Bearer	Dli	Reuben	Asher	Habakuk
Pisces	Fish	Dagim	Levi	Naphtali	Joel

Observe: There was no image on the stones [of the ephod]. This alludes to the twelve sections of the sky. These sections can be perceived only by the mind. They correspond to the number of the tribes of Israel.

The breastplate was like the work of the ephod (Shemot (Exodus) 28:15). It was square, corresponding to the four compass points. Each one of its stones was therefore unlike the other. The boxes and the rings that were permanently set in the breastplate allude to the celestial equator.

The urim are to be taken at face value. So is the tummim. The tummim corresponds to the cubed number. Moses first placed them on the breastplate, <u>in accordance with the position of the heavenly bodies</u>, on the day that he erected the tabernacle. The wise will understand."

More info: https://doormann.tripod.com/mazzarot.htm

According to Josephus, each of the twelve precious stones that formed the High Priest's breastplate bore the name of a tribe, connecting them with the signs of the zodiac. "And for the twelve stones," he states, "whether we understand by them the months, or whether we understand the like number of the signs of that circle which the Greeks call the Zodiac, we shall not be mistaken in their meaning." ...

The Faith of David

Psalm 19

2 THE HEAVENS (THE HEAVENLY SCROLL) ARE TELLING OF THE GLORY OF YAHUAH (*the Glory of Yahuah is Yahusha! - 2 Corinthians 4:6*); AND THEIR EXPANSE IS DECLARING THE WORK OF HIS HANDS. 2 DAY TO DAY THE HEAVENLY SCROLL POURS FORTH SPEECH, AND NIGHT TO NIGHT REVEALS KNOWLEDGE. 3 THERE IS NO SPEECH, NOR ARE THERE WORDS; THEIR (*signs of the Zodiac/Constellations*) VOICE IS NOT HEARD. 4 THEIR LINE (*signs of the Zodiac/Constellations*) HAS GONE OUT THROUGH (*and seen by*) ALL THE EARTH, AND THEIR (*constellations*) UTTERANCES TO THE END OF THE WORLD. IN THEM (*the constellations*) HE HAS PLACED A TENT FOR THE SUN (*the Zodiac*), 5 WHICH IS AS A BRIDEGROOM (*Yahusha*) COMING OUT OF HIS CHAMBER; IT REJOICES AS A STRONG MAN TO RUN HIS COURSE (*of a wedding - The Feast Cycle*). 6 ITS RISING IS FROM ONE END OF THE HEAVENS, AND ITS CIRCUIT (*Zodiac means circuit or path or The Way*) TO THE OTHER END OF THEM; AND THERE IS NOTHING HIDDEN FROM ITS HEAT.

Psalm 89:2

I WILL DECLARE THAT YOUR LOVE STANDS FIRM FOREVER, THAT YOU HAVE ESTABLISHED YOUR FAITHFUL PROMISE (*LOGOS / DEBAR*) OF SALVATION IN THE HEAVENLY SCROLL ITSELF.

Psalm 119:89

YOUR WORD (*LOGOS / DEBAR*), YAHUAH, IS ETERNAL; IT STANDS FIRM WRITTEN IN THE HEAVENLY SCROLL.

Psalm 97:6

THE HEAVENLY SCROLL PROCLAIMS HIS RIGHTEOUSNESS, AND ALL THE PEOPLES SEE HIS GLORY (*the stars/constellations declare the Glory of Yahuah and proclaim it day after day, night after night — Psalm 19*).

Psalm 50:3-6

YAHUAH SUMMONS THE HEAVENS ABOVE, AND THE EARTH, THAT HE MAY JUDGE HIS PEOPLE: "GATHER TO ME MY CONSECRATED ONES, WHO MADE A COVENANT WITH ME BY SACRIFICE." AND THE HEAVENS PROCLAIM HIS RIGHTEOUSNESS, FOR GOD HIMSELF IS JUDGE.

Psalm 147

4 HE DETERMINES THE NUMBER OF THE STARS (*in each constellation*) AND CALLS THEM (*the stars and constellations*) EACH BY NAME.

The Faith of Jeremiah

Jeremiah 6:16

THIS IS WHAT YAHUAH SAYS: "STAND AT THE CROSSROADS AND LOOK; ASK FOR THE ANCIENT (*Enochian*) PATHS (*The Heavenly Scroll*), ASK WHERE THE GOOD WAY IS, AND WALK IN IT (*AQUARIUS, Jeremiah 31, Ezekiel 36*), AND YOU WILL FIND REST FOR YOUR SOULS (*in the Kingdom Age of AQUARIUS*). BUT YOU SAID, 'WE WILL NOT WALK IN IT''.

Jeremiah 15:16

YOUR WORDS (*in The Heavenly Scroll - Ezekiel 3:1-3, Zechariah 5:2-3*) WERE FOUND, AND I ATE THEM, AND YOUR WORDS BECAME TO ME A JOY AND THE DELIGHT OF MY HEART, FOR I AM CALLED BY YOUR NAME, O YAHUAH, GOD OF HOSTS (*constellations are the "hosts of heaven" or "starry hosts"*).

Jeremiah 2:13

"FOR MY PEOPLE HAVE COMMITTED TWO EVILS: THEY HAVE FORSAKEN MY COVENANT OF PEACE (*brought by The Son of Man the Prince of Peace, ORION*) AND REJECTED THE FOUNTAIN OF LIVING WATERS (*poured out by AQUARIUS the Bearer of Living Water and Manna from The Heavenly Scroll*), THEY HEW

185

FOR THEMSELVES CISTERNS, BROKEN CISTERNS THAT CAN HOLD NO WATER (*cannot be filled with His Spirit*).

The Faith of Ezekial

Ezekiel 2:9-10
THEN I LOOKED (*into the heavens*), AND BEHOLD, A HAND WAS EXTENDED TO ME; AND LO, A SCROLL WAS IN IT.

Ezekiel 3
1 AND HE SAID TO ME, "SON OF MAN, EAT WHAT IS BEFORE YOU, EAT THIS SCROLL; THEN GO AND SPEAK TO THE PEOPLE OF ISRAEL." 2 SO I OPENED MY MOUTH, AND HE GAVE ME THE SCROLL TO EAT. 3 THEN HE SAID TO ME, "SON OF MAN, EAT THIS SCROLL I AM GIVING YOU AND FILL YOUR STOMACH WITH IT." SO I ATE IT, AND IT TASTED AS SWEET AS HONEY IN MY MOUTH.

I produced a video showing Ezekiel's Vision of The Heavenly Scroll (4 wheels within a wheel) below:

https://www.ravshaul.com/Creation_Cries_Out!/CCO_Chapter_10.htm#Ezekiel%E2%80%99s_vision_of_the_Enoch_Zodiac

The Faith of Isaiah

Isaiah 45:12
IT IS I WHO MADE THE EARTH, AND CREATED MAN UPON IT. IT WAS MY HANDS THAT STRETCHED OUT THE HEAVENS (*like a scroll*), AND I ORDAINED ALL THEIR (*the star's*) HOSTS (*constellations "host stars" and tell of His Glory - Psalm* 19).

Isaiah 34:4
AND ALL THE HOST OF HEAVEN (ZODIAC SIGNS/CONSTELLATIONS

186

"HOST STARS") SHALL BE DISSOLVED, AND THE HEAVENS SHALL BE ROLLED TOGETHER AS A SCROLL (I.E. THE HEAVENLY SCROLL).

Isaiah 9:6-7

"FOR TO US A CHILD IS BORN (*VIRGO*), TO US A SON (*of man*) IS GIVEN (*ORION*), AND THE GOVERNMENT SHALL BE ON HIS SHOULDERS (*TAURUS*) AND HE WILL BE CALLED WONDERFUL COUNSELOR (*AQUARIUS*), (*the perfect image of*) MIGHTY GOD (*CAPRICORNUSv*), (*fore*) FATHER OF EVERLASTING (*life*) (*CAPRICORNUS*), AND PRINCE OF PEACE (*CANCER*)." THERE WILL BE NO END TO THE INCREASE OF HIS GOVERNMENT OR OF PEACE, ON THE THRONE OF DAVID AND OVER HIS KINGDOM, TO ESTABLISH IT (*SAGITTARIUS*) AND TO UPHOLD IT WITH JUSTICE AND RIGHTEOUSNESS FROM THEN ON AND FOREVERMORE (*LEO*).

Isaiah 40:26

LIFT UP YOUR EYES AND LOOK TO THE HEAVENS (*stars and constellations*): WHO CREATED ALL THESE? HE WHO BRINGS OUT THE STARRY HOST (*constellations*) ONE BY ONE AND CALLS FORTH EACH OF THEM (*the constellations*) BY NAME. BECAUSE OF HIS GREAT POWER AND MIGHTY STRENGTH, NOT ONE OF THEM IS MISSING (*there are exactly* 12 *constellations in every culture dating back to the origin of man!*).

Isaiah 13:6-10

THE STARS OF HEAVEN AND THEIR CONSTELLATIONS WILL NOT SHOW THEIR LIGHT. THE RISING SUN WILL BE DARKENED AND THE MOON WILL NOT GIVE ITS LIGHT.

Isaiah 48:3-6

3 I FORETOLD THE FORMER THINGS LONG AGO (*WRITTEN IN THE STARS ON DAY 4 OF CREATION*). MY MOUTH ANNOUNCED THEM (*TO MY PROPHETS WHO ALL READ THE HEAVENLY SCROLL*) AND I MADE THEM KNOWN (*TO ALL MANKIND BY THE WORD OF MY TESTIMONY WRITTEN IN THE STARS PSALM 19, ENOCH 35:3, GIVEN TO ALL MANKIND DEUTERONOMY 4:19*); THEN SUDDENLY I ACTED, AND THE MESSAGE PROCLAIMED BY THE STARS/CONSTELLATIONS CAME TO PASS. 4 FOR I KNEW HOW

STUBBORN YOU WERE; YOUR NECK MUSCLES WERE IRON; YOUR FOREHEAD WAS BRONZE. 5 THEREFORE I TOLD YOU THESE THINGS (*IN THE HEAVENLY SCROLL*) LONG AGO (*AT CREATION SO THAT YOU ARE WITHOUT EXCUSE BECAUSE YAHUAH IS KNOWN THROUGH HIS HANDIWORK ROMANS 1:20*); BEFORE THEY WERE FULFILLED I ANNOUNCED THE PLAN OF SALVATION TO YOU (*IN THE HEAVENLY SCROLL - PSALM 19*) SO THAT YOU COULD NOT SAY, 'MY IMAGES BROUGHT THEM ABOUT (*BECAUSE THEY ARE WRITTEN INTO CREATION IN THE STARS AS SIGNS CALLED CONSTELLATIONS*); MY WOODEN IMAGE AND METAL GOD ORDAINED THEM.' 6 YOU HAVE HEARD THESE THINGS (*THAT THE STARS PROCLAIM DAY AFTER DAY, NIGHT AFTER NIGHT TO ALL MANKIND AS A WITNESS PSALM 19*); LOOK AT ALL THE STARS/CONSTELLATION (*IN THE HEAVENLY SCROLL*). **WILL YOU NOT ADMIT THEM**? ...

The Faith of Zechariah

Zechariah 5:2-3

AND HE SAID TO ME, "WHAT DO YOU SEE (*as you look into the heavens*)?" AND I ANSWERED, "I SEE A FLYING SCROLL!"

The Faith of Amos

Amos 5:8

YAHUAH WHO MADE THE PLEIADES (7 *stars/Orion's Belt*) AND ORION (*Orion represents the Son of Man coming of the clouds of heaven*)

Amos 9:6

YAHUAH BUILDS HIS LOFTY PALACE IN THE HEAVENS (*Mazzaroth/Heavenly Scroll*) AND SETS ITS FOUNDATION ON THE EARTH (*the heavens and Earth are intimately connected, what is portrayed in the heavens, plays out on Earth*).

The Faith of Job

Job 38:31-33

31 CAN YOU BIND THE CHAINS OF THE PLEIADES OR LOOSEN THE BELT OF ORION? 32 CAN YOU BRING FORTH THE CONSTELLATIONS IN THEIR SEASONS OR LEAD OUT THE BEAR AND HER CUBS? 33 DO YOU KNOW THE LAWS OF THE HEAVENS? CAN YOU SET THEIR (*constellations and the Law's*) DOMINION OVER THE EARTH?

Above, Yahuah provides a direct link to the constellations and The Law recorded in The Heavenly Scroll. Both having "dominion over the Earth".

The Faith of Daniel

Daniel is a very good example that using the Zodiac, interpreting dreams, and deciphering omens with the proper 'spirit' and seeking those answers from the Creator is acceptable. The Prophet Daniel was the "Chief Astrologer" in the Babylonian Court (actually under several empires/kings) ... so good was Daniel at his craft of divination (means seeking **DIVIN**e revel**ATION**), he was made King of the Chaldeans who were renowned Astrologers

189

dating back to Babylon and before to Abraham the founder!

The Bible calls those who use divination techniques to seek counsel from Yahuah... Prophets. Those who use divination and seek counsel from other gods... false prophets, soothsayers, etc.

Daniel was a Eunuch; he had no children/heirs. Daniel amassed a fortune serving at the highest levels of multiple empires and Kings as their 'advisor' i.e. chief astrologer... Daniel became the right hand of the Kings who deemed Daniel their King "by proxy". Daniel was one of the most powerful and wealthy men across several dynasties and Kings. Daniel trained the Chaldean Astrologers how to properly understand The Zodiac and how it foretold of the coming King/Messiah. He left specific instruction to those in his 'school of astrology' called Chaldean Astrologer how to find the newborn King using astrology and the signs in the sky/Zodiac.

We see Daniel below declare Yahuah's Will is written in the constellations:

Daniel 4:35
35 "ALL THE INHABITANTS OF THE EARTH ARE ACCOUNTED AS NOTHING, BUT HE DOES ACCORDING TO HIS WILL WRITTEN IN THE HOSTS OF HEAVEN. (*constellations 'host' stars*)

Daniel describes The Enoch Zodiac (The Heavenly Scroll) in great detail, see my video:

https://www.youtube.com/watch?v=FeoexwU0If4

See my book *Creation Cries Out! The Mazzaroth* for more information.

Next, I will continue to reveal the faith of our forefathers...

• The Faith of the Essenes/Nazarene
• The Faith of John the Baptist
• The Faith of Yahuhsa the Messiah
• The Faith of Sha'ul the Apostle
• The Faith of John of Patmos
• The Faith of the First Century Israelites

Then I will breakdown "the Ancient Path" so that we may choose to walk it and admit it or refuse to do either.

191

Chapter 6
The Faith of the First-Century Nazarenes

Chapter 6: Introduction

The Scriptures are vivid with references to The Heavenly Scroll.

1 *Corinthians* 15:23-24

23 BUT EACH IN TURN: THE MESSIAH, THE FIRSTFRUITS; THEN, WHEN HE (*ORION*) COMES (*riding on the clouds of heaven*), THOSE (*the Bride*) WHO BELONG TO HIM (*AQUARIUS*). 24 THEN THE END OF THE AGE OF PISCES (*The Messianic Age*) WILL COME (*and the Age of AQUARIUS / The Kingdom Age will begin*), WHEN HE (*ORION the Conquering King*) HANDS OVER THE KINGDOM (*TAURUS*) TO YAHUAH, THE FATHER, AFTER HE HAS DESTROYED ALL DOMINION, AUTHORITY, AND POWER (*LEO*).

Isaiah 9:6-7

"FOR TO US A CHILD IS BORN (*VIRGO*), TO US A SON (*OF MAN*) IS GIVEN (*ORION*), AND THE GOVERNMENT SHALL BE ON HIS SHOULDERS (*TAURUS*) AND HE WILL BE CALLED WONDERFUL COUNSELOR (*AQUARIUS*), (*THE PERFECT IMAGE OF*) MIGHTY GOD (*CAPRICORNUS*), (*FORE*) FATHER OF EVERLASTING (*LIFE*) (*CAPRICORNUS*), AND PRINCE OF PEACE (*CANCER*)." THERE WILL BE NO END TO THE INCREASE OF HIS GOVERNMENT OR OF PEACE, ON THE THRONE OF DAVID AND OVER HIS KINGDOM, TO ESTABLISH IT (*SAGITTARIUS*) AND TO UPHOLD IT WITH JUSTICE AND RIGHTEOUSNESS FROM THEN ON AND FOREVERMORE (*LEO*).

Isaiah 45:7

7 MY OWN HANDS STRETCHED OUT THE HEAVENS (*THE HEAVENLY SCROLL*); I MARSHALED THEIR STARRY HOSTS (*CONSTELLATIONS / SIGNS WHICH HOST STARS*)

Biblical Astrology

The proper use of astrology (discerning the Will of Yahuah in 'heaven' as to make it so on Earth) is still practiced today.

> **Rabbis. Rabbi Joel C. Dobin** explains:
> *"That all-in-existence is subject to God's will is an essential beginning for the astrologer: 'One Creator, One Creation' should be the mantra for every astrologer! For, combining this latest statement with its forerunner—then man, God, and universe are an essential unity—allows the astrologer to seek in the Heavens for the evidence of God's will for mankind, which will help the individual person as well as the community realize and act on the basic religious statement: 'Make Thy will, my will.' Astrology revealed to me His order and His beauty, and His place for me in the Divine balance that links God, man, and universe into One Balanced Process which never ends in this or on other planes of awareness of life."*

This was the same desire of Yahusha the Messiah. That there is one Creator, one creation, and that he, and all the sons are to be one with the Father, and not his will but "thine be done".
Yahusha's hope was that Yahuah's Will, as laid out and defined by Yahuah at creation and written in the stars, be done on this Earth.

Matthew 6:10
"YOUR KINGDOM COME, YOUR WILL BE DONE, ON EARTH AS IT IS IN 'HEAVEN/SHAMAYIM (*The Heavenly Scroll*)"

We see in Psalms 11, King David proclaim that Yahuah's throne is in "heaven". What is David referring to? We already know in Psalms 19, David proclaimed the meaning of the Zodiac in great detail.

Psalms 11

4 YAHUAH IS IN HIS HOLY TEMPLE; YAHUAH'S THRONE IS IN THE HEAVENLY SCROLL. HIS EYES WATCH; HIS EYES EXAMINE ALL PEOPLE.

We also see Isaiah proclaim:

Isaiah 66:1

THIS IS WHAT YAHUAH SAYS: "HEAVEN (*shamarym/Zodiac*) IS MY THRONE, AND THE EARTH IS MY FOOTSTOOL. WHERE IS THE HOUSE YOU WILL BUILD FOR ME? WHERE WILL MY RESTING PLACE BE?

We see Isaiah declare the exact same reality below. Remember "heavens" is actually specifically referring to the place in the sky where the stars are... i.e. the Zodiac. "Starry hosts" are the constellations that hosts the stars ...

Isaiah 40:26

LIFT UP YOUR EYES AND LOOK TO THE HEAVENS (*the Zodiac*): WHO CREATED ALL THESE (*stars/constellations*)? HE WHO BRINGS OUT THE STARRY HOST (*constellations*) ONE BY ONE AND CALLS FORTH EACH OF THEM (*stars/constellations*) BY NAME. BECAUSE OF HIS GREAT POWER AND MIGHTY STRENGTH, NOT ONE OF THEM IS MISSING (*to tell the Plan of Salvation i.e. His Will - Ephesians* 1:9-10).

Ephesians 1:9-10

9 HE MADE KNOWN TO US THE MYSTERY OF HIS WILL ACCORDING TO HIS GOOD PLEASURE, WRITTEN IN THE HEAVENLY SCROLL WHICH HE PURPOSED TO FULFILL IN THE YAHUSHAIC COVENANT (*Daniel 4:35*), 10 TO BE PUT INTO EFFECT WHEN THE AGES REACH THEIR FULFILLMENT (*Age of Aquarius*)

Again, we see David in Psalms 119 declare that Yahuah's "instructions" endure, they stand secure in heaven i.e. shamarym/Zodiac. The Mazzaroth/Zodiac is Yahuah's Original

Revelation to all mankind, laying out His Plan for Man (the timeframe through 2000 year reverse Ages) and His Plan of Salvation through Yahusha the Messiah (as told by the 12 signs from Virgo-Leo). Let's shed the light of "context" on this passage with Psalm 19:

Psalm 19

1 THE HEAVENS (*stars and constellations*) DECLARE THE GLORY OF YAHUAH; THE SKIES PROCLAIM THE WORK OF HIS HANDS. 2 DAY AFTER DAY THEY POUR FORTH SPEECH; NIGHT AFTER NIGHT THEY REVEAL KNOWLEDGE. 3 THEY HAVE NO SPEECH, THEY USE NO WORDS; NO SOUND IS HEARD FROM THEM. 4 YET THEIR VOICE GOES OUT INTO ALL THE EARTH, THEIR WORDS TO THE ENDS OF THE AGE. IN THE HEAVENS (*stars and constellations*) YAHUAH HAS PITCHED A TENT FOR THE SUN (*the Zodiac*). 5 IT IS LIKE A BRIDEGROOM COMING OUT OF HIS CHAMBER, LIKE A CHAMPION (*King*) REJOICING TO RUN HIS COURSE (*through the ecliptic*). 6 IT RISES AT ONE END OF THE HEAVENS AND MAKES ITS CIRCUIT (*Zodiac means circuit of circle or path*) TO THE OTHER; NOTHING IS DEPRIVED OF ITS WARMTH.

Rabbi Joel C. Dobin summarizes...

"Astrology helps man to understand God's will and to put himself in balance with Divine and universal forces, thus enriching his life and experience."

196

The question is how much of the references to The Heavenly Scroll did the first-century Jews understand? What anchored their faith? The problem of understanding the exact nature of ancient astrology is that it was only partly documented, leaving the question of the extent of their undocumented astrological knowledge.

Michael Baigent in From the Omens of Babylon: Astrology and Ancient Mesopotamia:

"that there is evidence that there was probably an older or parallel oral tradition of astrology at the time of publication of Enuma Anu Enlil believed published over the period between 1595–1157 BC.

Giorgio de Santillana (1902 – 1974) became professor of the History of Science in the School of Humanities at the Massachusetts Institute of Technology in 1954, and along with Hertha von Dechend, published Hamlet's Mill, An Essay on Myth and the Frame of Time in 1969.

"science and mythology of our ancestors had become separated by the ancient Greeks and the old mythological stories handed down from antiquity were not random fictitious tales but were accurate depictions of celestial cosmology clothed in tales to aid their oral transmission. The chaos, monsters, and violence in ancient myths are representative of the forces that shape each age. They believed that ancient myths are the remains of preliterate astronomy that became lost with the rise of the Greco-Roman civilization.

Ancient myths have no historical basis but a cosmological one based on a primitive form of astrology. They recognized the importance of the heliacally rising constellation as markers for the astrological ages and wrote that knowledge of this phenomenon had been known for thousands of years previously. They state that to understand ancient thinking it is necessary to understand

197

astrology, not the modern sun-sign or horoscopic astrology, but the astrology of ancient times which was the way of communicating between cultures of ancient times who spoke different languages.

Avraham Ibn Ezra, one of the most distinguished Jewish biblical commentators and philosophers of the Middle Ages stresses the proper use of Biblical astrology (not horoscopes, fortune telling, palm reading, etc.): *"Especially influential is Avraham Ibn Ezra's astrological treatise called Sefer HaOlam (The Book of the World). Its main message is to warn users against the wrong applications of astrology. Of course, like most scholars until modern times, he was an ardent believer in astrology, but only when it is practiced correctly."*

Notice above that most scholars, until modern times, were ardent believers in astrology! Over time, we slipped further and further into a physical science dictatorship and rejected the supernatural nature of Yahuah's creation. The truth in astrology was replaced by the abuse of His creation and the texts were corrupted.

According to Ramban (Moses ben Nachman) a leading medieval Jewish scholar states:
"There is some truth in Divination, sooth-saying, and astrology but we Jews are only to believe in God alone and inquire through prophecy and the Urim VeTummim of the Supreme being who is in control over the whole system and not through His celestial deputies who he appointed under Him. Ramban utilized the idea that the Jews are directly under G-d's Providence and are therefore not subject to the celestial constellations as are other nations to explain a large variety of biblical verses and laws. Yet, he maintained that this idea also assumed a universe determined by the stars."

The Faith of First Century Israel

Remains of many Jewish synagogues dating back to the 1st century CE through the 6th century CE have been uncovered by archeologist to reveal the Zodiac as a major function of their religion.

Many of them with elaborate mosaics of the Zodiac well preserved, alongside mosaics of Biblical stories. The 12 lunar Hebrew months of the year were closely associated with the 12 Zodiac signs. This association with the Zodiac and the Calendar was preserved in Hebrew writing on each corresponding Zodiac sign in these ancient synagogues. This demonstrates that if we look back in history at the last Divine Correction, we see the Zodiac and the Divine Clock were well understood and had a significant role in the places of worship.

Today, however, we are so arrogant as to believe "these early Jews had succumbed to Greek mythology!" No, they had come BACK to the truth of Yahuah following the last Divine Correction. The Zodiac was adopted by the Greeks FROM the Hebrews. It is we who, 2000 years later, have fallen from the truth of the Creator; not the other way around! The prevalence of the Zodiac and the prominence of these Zodiac mosaics in the Synagogues over the first 7 centuries dating all the way back to just before Yahusha came... speaks to the reality and importance of the message contained in the Zodiac.

Even the Talmud identified the 12 constellations of the Zodiac with the 12 months of the Hebrew calendar. The correspondence of the constellations with their names in Hebrew and the months is as follows:

1. Aries - Ṭaleh – Nisan

2. Taurus - Shor – Iyar

3. Gemini - Teomim – Sivan

4. Cancer - Sarṭon – Tammuz

5. Leo - Ari – Av

6. Virgo - Betulah – Elul

7. Libra - Moznayim – Tishrei

8. Scorpio - 'Aḵrab – Cheshvan

9. Sagittarius - Ḵasshat – Kislev

10. Capricorn - Gedi – Tevet

11. Aquarius - D'li – Shevat

12. Pisces - Dagim – Adar

The implication of the Zodiac being so prominently displayed in synagogues going back to the 1st Century is astounding. Remember, John, Yahusha, Sha'ul, and all the men in the Renewed Covenant taught in the synagogues. It is possible some of these Zodiac floor murals had the honor of the footprints of the Messiah; as he walked over them to speak to the people! Never once are they condemned in the New Testament writings or by the Messiah. These Zodiac mosaics were accepted right alongside mosaics of the Ark of the Covenant, Abraham sacrificing Isaac, Adam and Eve, and so on. They all were seen as "the story of salvation" proudly displayed in elaborate floor and ceiling mosaics that survive today.

Below is from Harper Collins Bible Dictionary on the role of the Jewish Synagogue:

http://www.bibleodyssey.org/places/related-articles/first-century-synagogues.aspx
First Century Synagogues by Chad Spigel
According to the New Testament Gospels, Jesus often taught in synagogues, one of which was in Capernaum (Mark 1:21-28), in northern Israel. The book of Acts suggests that the apostle Sha'ul also taught in synagogues (Acts 17:1-2). But what exactly were synagogues in the first century C.E.? Were they different from modern synagogues? The answers to these questions not only illuminate stories in the New Testament, they also shed light on the early years of an important Jewish institution.

"Synagogue" is a Greek word that literally means a gathering of people but also refers to the place of assembly. Although the origin of the synagogue as a Jewish institution is unclear, by the first century C.E. they were found in both Palestine and the

Diaspora, where they were used for a variety of communal needs:

- *as schools (Josephus, Antiquities 16.43),*

- *or communal meals (Josephus, Antiquities 14.214-216),*

- *as hostels,*

- *as courts of Law (Acts 22:19),*

- *as a place to collect and distribute charity (Matt 6:2),*

- *and for political meetings (Josephus, Life 276-289).*

In short, the Synagogue was the focus and expression of Jewish faith. Without a doubt, the most prominent feature of these ancient Jewish synagogues was... The Heavenly Scroll of Enoch's Zodiac! Given the Synagogue served the function of schools, legal courts, and politics; the prominent display of the Enoch Zodiac on the floors of these Jewish institutions speaks to reality that they understood the Zodiac to have been created by Yahuah, given to all mankind, and containing the Plan of Salvation from which their entire religion was revealed

Astrology, the Zodiac and its associated meaning, had played a role in Hebrew history for 6,000 years (the Ages of Taurus, Aries, and Pisces. It is the foundation of Yahuah proclaiming the Gospel to Abraham. As we have seen so far in this book, Yahuah took Abraham outside, under the canopy of stars, and instructed Abraham to look up and discern the meaning behind the Zodiac. The Zodiac came to mankind through Enoch. Then corrupted by the watchers.

As I have pointed out in this book, the Zodiac was literally the foundation from which the prophets of Yahuah made their predictions. They described the Zodiac perfectly, there is no doubt.

202

The role of the Zodiac continued to play a major role during the current Age of Pisces at least for 6 maybe 7 Centuries if not all the way up to the 16th Century before the false prophet (Pope) abolished it.

When you research into "what happened to Astrology" over the past several Centuries, Jewish and Christian authorities have a very difficult time explaining "why" the Enoch Zodiac (with all its meaning and implication) was removed from their religious traditions. Yet, the fact that Astrology/Enoch Zodiac played a key and integral role in both religions is simply indisputable.

To deny the importance of the Heavenly Scroll (Zodiac), we would have to turn a blind eye to countless references to the Zodiac in both testaments, declarations made by Yahuah and Yahusha, all the prophets, and ignore the archeological evidence that all loudly proclaim... Yahuah is the author!

> *Rabbi Joel C. Dobin*, *To Rule Both Day And Night*:
> *Astrology in the Bible*, *Midrash*, & *Talmud* explains:
> *"The basic philosophy of the astrologer is religious,
> regardless of the religious direction from which he seeks
> the truth. The basic philosophical thrust of astrology derives
> from the conviction that the human being, God, and the
> universe are in some way a unity; that man and universe, if
> you will, both swim in the sea of space-time whose substance
> is God."*

One of the most anointed and famous of all prophets of Yahuah, Daniel, was an astrologer! Daniel was "Chief Astrologer" under several kings and empires.

Daniel 5:11
"THERE IS A MAN IN YOUR KINGDOM WHO IS ENDOWED WITH A SPIRIT OF THE HOLY GODS. IN THE DAYS OF YOUR FATHER HE WAS FOUND TO HAVE ENLIGHTENMENT,

UNDERSTANDING, AND WISDOM LIKE THE WISDOM OF THE GODS. YOUR FATHER, KING NEBUCHADNEZZAR, MADE HIM CHIEF OF THE MAGICIANS, ENCHANTERS, CHALDEANS, AND DIVINERS."

Gone Astray

Where did we go astray from the ancient path?

Daniel 7:25

HE (*The False Prophet*) SHALL SPEAK WORDS AGAINST THE MOST HIGH, AND SHALL WEAR OUT THE SAINTS OF THE MOST HIGH, AND SHALL THINK TO CHANGE THE TIMES AND THE LAW; AND THEY SHALL BE GIVEN INTO HIS HAND FOR A TIME, TIMES, AND HALF A TIME.

It was by Papal Decree that the Sabbath was done away with, and Sunday worship was established. It was by Papal Decree that Yahuah became a Trinity. It was by Papal Decree that the Passover was changed to Easter. It was by Papal Decree that the Law was deemed to be "done away with". It was by Papal Decree that everything holy to Yahuah, all knowledge of the Creator was deemed "Old" and irrelevant to be replaced by a Babylonian counterfeit. And yes, that same system, the Beastly system prophesied to do all these things, is the source once again of yet another abomination... outlawing the Zodiac, the Heavenly Scroll.

In 1586, Pope Sixtus V issued papal bull Coeli et terras condemning judicial (mundane) astrology. This condemnation has deprived humanity (Catholics, Protestants, and all mankind) from the esoteric wisdom found in astrology to this day. Literally abolishing The Heavenly Scroll in the same way the Earthly Scroll (The Torah/Prophets) were abolished by the false prophet! In the article titled "Reconstructing Thomist Astrology: Robert Bellarmine and the Papal Bull coeli et terrae (2020)"...

Historians have portrayed the papal bull Coeli et terrae (1586) as a significant turning point in the history of the Catholic Church's censorship of astrology. They argue that this bull was intended to prohibit the idea that the stars could naturally incline humans towards future actions, but also had the effect of preventing the discussion of other forms of natural astrology including those useful to medicine, agriculture, and navigation. The bull, therefore, threatened to overturn principles established by Thomas Aquinas, which not only justified long-standing astrological practices, but also informed the Roman Inquisition's attitude towards this art.

From this point forward humanity, *being brainwashed by the corrupted use of astrology to believe there could be no righteous use of it*, rushed headlong into a scientific dictatorship that denied the power and authority of The Creator and the supernatural aspect of nature. It is the age old battle that began with the "watchers" giving humanity advanced knowledge outside of the context of The Creator.

Daniel Taylor in his article **The Scientific Dictatorship Explained** published in the Old Thinker News journal July, 26, 2011 made a very valid observation:

> *"The ideological roots of the Scientific Dictatorship can be traced to the works of Plato some 2,000 years ago. In truth, humanity has been battling the formation of this tyranny for much of known history."*

The proper use of astrology (*discerning the Will of Yahuah in 'heaven' as to make it so on Earth*) is still practiced today by many Rabbis. Rabbi Joel C. Dobin explains:

> *"That all-in-existence is subject to God's will is an essential beginning for the astrologer: 'One Creator, One Creation' should be the mantra for every astrologer! For, combining this latest statement with its forerunner—then man, God, and universe are an essential unity—allows the astrologer to seek in the Heavens for the evidence of God's will for mankind, which will help the individual person as well as*

206

the community realize and act on the basic religious statement: 'Make Thy will, my will.'

Astrology revealed to me His order and His beauty, and His place for me in the Divine balance that links God, man, and universe into One Balanced Process which never ends in this or on other planes of awareness of life."

This was the same desire of Yahusha the Messiah. That there is one Creator, one creation, and that he, and all the sons are to be one with the Father, and not his will but "thine be done". Yahusha's hope was that Yahuah's Will, as laid out and defined by Yahuah at creation and written in the stars, be done on this Earth.

MATTHEW 6:10
"YOUR KINGDOM COME, YOUR WILL BE DONE, ON EARTH AS IT IS IN 'HEAVEN/SHAMAYIM (WHERE THE STARS ARE VISIBLE IN THE SKY)"

As humanity further distanced itself from the ancient path, we gradually moved toward a world defined by science outside of the knowledge of Yahuah. Yahuah was denied His Glory as Creator and theories such as the "Big Bang" and "Evolution" replace His creative acts. Humanity has fallen so far from Yahuah as the Creator, even Yahuah's Original Revelation to all humanity, written in the stars as illustrated by the Zodiac has been outlawed by the very institutions that claim to represent Him!

Now that I have covered the faith of everyone from Adam through ancient Israel to the middle ages, I will explain why Yahusha is the Messiah.

Chapter 7
The Faith of the Essenes through First Century Nazarenes

Chapter 7: Introduction

I have been providing a response to those who have been led astray by Judaism to reject The Yahushaic Covenant on the grounds the NT is nothing but fairytales of other pagan gods.

We are now going to search for **"Truth and Righteousness"** to re-establish the validity of both the Tanakh and NT writings of the Nazarenes. Next, I will continue to reveal the faith of our forefathers...

- The Faith of the Essenes/Nazarene

- The Faith of John the Baptist

- The Faith of Yahusha the Messiah

- The Faith of Sha'ul the Apostle

- The Faith of John of Patmos

- The Faith of the First Century Israelites

Then I will break down "the Ancient Path" so that we may choose to walk it and admit it or refuse to do either.

Jeremiah 6:16
THIS IS WHAT YAHUAH SAYS: "STAND AT THE CROSSROADS AND LOOK; ASK FOR THE ANCIENT PATHS, ASK WHERE THE GOOD WAY IS, AND WALK IN IT, AND YOU WILL FIND REST FOR YOUR SOULS. BUT YOU SAID, 'WE WILL NOT WALK IN IT!'"

As I have shown in this series so far, the written word had been corrupted by rival factions within Judaism. Sadducees, Pharisees, Royal, and Priestly scribes transliterating the Scriptures to strengthen each of their position and authority over the people. All while downplaying the role of the other factions. Incorporating vague oral traditions that were shaped in the interpretation to their favor.

From Wikipedia: Documentary hypothesis

According to Simon, parts of the Old Testament were not written by individuals at all, but *by scribes recording their community's oral tradition, shrouded in mystery not having texts to back them up*.

Several portions of the Tanakh were passed down orally by a society in the process of becoming a nation, who at times were nomads, and at times were living among strangers in exile. Sacred texts were eventually recorded on separate scrolls over many centuries by different authors with varying agendas and styles to make their messages clear in their own contemporary societies.

By Jeremiah's time when Yahuah declared we should seek out, admit, and follow the "ancient path"... the written word had been so corrupted it contained "nothing but lies".

Again, in Jeremiah, we are told that our faith would be based on "nothing but lies". Not a "few lies", not "a little lie here or there", not "mostly lies", but TOTAL LIES... "Nothing but lies" there would be no truth in the twisted Scriptures we have had handed down to us.

Jeremiah 16:19

19 O Yahuah, my strength and my stronghold, And my refuge in the day of distress, To You the (*lost sheep among the*) nations will come From the ends of the earth and say, "Our fathers have inherited nothing but LIES, Idols and

210

WORTHLESS THINGS OF NO PROFIT." 20 CAN MAN MAKE GODS FOR HIMSELF (*Idols and demi-gods*)? YET THEY (*idols of the constellations*) ARE NOT GODS!

We see Yahuah speak through Isaiah that, again, we should seek out the Ancient Path (former things foretold long ago) and ask the simple question: "will we not admit them" speaking of the Plan of Salvation written in the stars/constellations:

Isaiah 48:3-6

3 I FORETOLD THE FORMER THINGS LONG AGO (written in the stars on Day 4 of Creation), MY MOUTH ANNOUNCED THEM (to My Prophets who all read The Heavenly Scroll) AND I MADE THEM KNOWN (to all mankind Deuteronomy 4:19); THEN SUDDENLY I ACTED, AND THE MESSAGE PROCLAIMED BY THE STARS/CONSTELLATIONS CAME TO PASS. 4 FOR I KNEW HOW STUBBORN YOU WERE; YOUR NECK MUSCLES WERE IRON; YOUR FOREHEAD WAS BRONZE. 5 THEREFORE I TOLD YOU THESE THINGS (in The Heavenly Scroll) LONG AGO (at Creation so that you are without excuse because Yahuah is known through His Handiwork Romans 1:20); BEFORE THEY WERE FULFILLED I ANNOUNCED THE PLAN OF SALVATION TO YOU (in The Heavenly Scroll Psalm 19) SO THAT YOU COULD NOT SAY, 'MY IMAGES BROUGHT THEM ABOUT; MY WOODEN IMAGE AND METAL GOD ORDAINED THEM.' 6 YOU HAVE HEARD THESE THINGS (that the stars Proclaim day after day, night after night to all mankind as a witness Psalm 19); LOOK AT ALL THE STARS/CONSTELLATION (in The Heavenly Scroll). WILL YOU NOT ADMIT THEM)?

So far, I have covered the faith of Adam through the Prophets. Now let us introduce the faith of the first century followers of the Messiah. The Faith or The Way that proves that Yahusha is the Messiah.

The Faith of the Essenes and Nazarenes

The Qumran and The Heavenly Scroll

Source: Horoscopes – Wikipedia
> *The Qumran Horoscopes are manuscripts found among the Dead Sea Scrolls; they are alternatively called "Astrological Physiognomies" (4Q186). Unlike most horoscopes, however, in 4Q186 no mention of the positions of astral bodies is found.*
>
> *Instead, the text uses the physiognomic features of a person to tell prophecy in the dabar (spoken promise in the stars). This blending of features- of horoscopes and of astrological physiognomies- makes it difficult to accurately title the fragments.*

We read in **The Complete Dead Sea Scrolls in English**. **Penguin Classics**. **pp**. 370–732.:
> *"The presence of 4Q186 Zodiac among the Qumran community should not, however, come as a surprise, "for if many Jews frowned on astrology, others... **credited the invention of astrology to Abraham**!""*

The Enochian Essenes

Their understanding of astrology stemmed from the Essenes devotion to the Book of Enoch. The Dead Sea Scrolls reveal the Essenes under John the Baptist, the Teacher of Righteousness, used the Book of Enoch extensively and followed the 364 day solar calendar given to Enoch.

The Enochians were visionaries and held mystical views for their day. Especially that a Messiah was necessary to fulfill The

Heavenly Scroll not just "arriving". The Enochian believed a Messiah would be needed to administer the final teachings of the Law and the Prophets.

They were followers of the "ancient path" dating back to Enoch whose faith was founded in The Heavenly Scroll:

4 *Enoch* 3:10
10 AND HE SAID UNTO ME: "OBSERVE, ENOCH, THE HEAVENLY SCROLL AND READ WHAT IS WRITTEN THEREON, AND MARK EVERY INDIVIDUAL FACT."

3 *Enoch* 1:19
19 AND AFTER THAT THERE SHALL BE STILL MORE UNRIGHTEOUSNESS THAN THAT WHICH WAS FIRST CONSUMMATED ON THE EARTH; FOR I KNOW THE MYSTERIES OF THE HOLY ONES; FOR HE, YAHUAH, HAS SHOWED ME AND INFORMED ME, AND I HAVE READ THE HEAVENLY SCROLL.

1 *Enoch* 35:3
I BLESSED YAHUAH AUTHOR OF GLORY (*The Heavenly Scroll - Psalm* 19:1), WHO HAD MADE THOSE GREAT AND SPLENDID SIGNS (*of the Zodiac — Genesis* 1:14), THAT THEY MIGHT DISPLAY (*to all mankind - Deut.* 4:19) THE MAGNIFICENCE OF THE WORKS OF HIS HANDS (*The Plan of Salvation - Psalm* 19) TO ANGELS AND TO THE SOULS OF MEN; AND THAT THESE (*splendid signs in The Heavenly Scroll*) MIGHT GLORIFY ALL HIS WORKS AND OPERATIONS (*His Will - Daniel* 4:35); THAT WE MIGHT SEE THE EFFECT OF HIS POWER; AND THE HEAVENLY SCROLL MIGHT GLORIFY THE GREAT LABOR OF HIS HANDS; AND BLESS HIM FOREVER.

The Essene Enochians believed there would be an end time and everyone must be prepared. They believed in a remnant, a "designated group" at the end. This theme is found throughout the Book of Enoch.
The Enochian spiritual emphasis would be the Book of Enoch. The text of Enoch became a continued influence within the Hebrew

Bible. Also, the Book of Enoch is represented in the New Testament. This would infer the Enochic vision as ongoing, a root of Judaism almost from the beginning, perhaps as early as the times of Enoch himself.

For more, read my book **Enoch the Scribe of The Heavenly Tablets**:

The Faith of John the Baptist

In the Dead Sea Scrolls, there is a figure called "The Great Notsri (Nazarene)" and "Teacher of Righteousness". He was said to have the proper understanding of the Torah, qualified in its accurate instruction, and be the one through whom Yahuah would reveal to the community *the hidden things in which Israel had gone astray*. He would rightfully be of the House of Zadok (a true High Priest) which had separated itself in Samaria at Mount Gerizim. This was Yahusha's mentor and teacher, John the Great Notsri, who was of The House of Zadok, and the "anointed High Priest" in succession to Yahusha III.

This description of "The Great Notsri" is found in the Damascus Document of the Dead Sea Scroll, which carbon dating has placed about +/- 44 BC, that would be around the time John was acting as High Priest in the wilderness. John was prophesied to fulfill this very role by his father Zechariah. In Luke 1:76 we see that John was to be a prophet of the Most High. His message was to give knowledge of salvation through Mikveh and restore the ancient path found in The Heavenly Scroll in verse 78 below:

Luke 1:76-80 - ZECHARIAH'S SONG

76 AND YOU, MY CHILD, WILL BE CALLED A PROPHET OF THE MOST HIGH; FOR YOU WILL GO ON BEFORE YAHUAH TO PREPARE THE WAY FOR HIM (*Yahusha*), 77 TO GIVE HIS PEOPLE THE KNOWLEDGE OF SALVATION THROUGH THE FORGIVENESS OF THEIR SINS, 78 *because of the tender mercy of our God, by which the rising sun will come to us from* (what is written in) *heaven* 79 TO SHINE ON THOSE LIVING IN DARKNESS AND IN THE SHADOW OF DEATH, TO GUIDE OUR FEET INTO THE PATH OF PEACE." 80 AND THE CHILD GREW AND BECAME STRONG IN SPIRIT; AND HE LIVED IN THE WILDERNESS UNTIL HE (*was trained as High Priest and*) APPEARED PUBLICLY TO ISRAEL.

215

The Great Notsri, founder of the Nazarenes, at that time, was undoubtedly John the Baptist; who was the rightful High Priest from the House of Zadok.

Matthew 11:11
"I TELL YOU THE TRUTH, AMONG THOSE BORN OF WOMEN, NO ONE HAS ARISEN GREATER THAN JOHN THE BAPTIST.

John's ministry was to proclaim and establish the "Gospel" message. Which was that Yahusha came to fulfill The Heavenly Scroll thereby revealing to the community *the hidden things in which Israel had gone astray*". Those things hidden in The Heavenly Scroll concerning the coming King and Kingdom:

Matthew 3:1-2
1 IN THOSE DAYS, JOHN THE BAPTIZER CAME, PREACHING IN THE WILDERNESS OF JUDEA, SAYING, 2 "REPENT, FOR THE KINGDOM OF (*proclaimed in - Psalm* 19) HEAVEN (*The Heavenly Scroll*) IS AT HAND!"

John was to correct where Israel had gone astray committing two evils in the sigh of Yahuah by refusing to admit and follow the Ancient Path:

Jeremiah 2:13
"FOR MY PEOPLE HAVE COMMITTED TWO EVILS: THEY HAVE FORSAKEN ME, THE FOUNTAIN OF LIVING WATERS (*Aquarius*), TO HEW FOR THEMSELVES CISTERNS, BROKEN CISTERNS THAT CAN HOLD NO WATER.

Mark 1:4
AND SO JOHN THE BAPTIST APPEARED IN THE WILDERNESS, PREACHING A MIKVEH OF REPENTANCE FOR THE FORGIVENESS OF SINS (*Ezekiel* 36:24-31).

Ezekiel 36

216

24 "'FOR I WILL TAKE YOU OUT OF THE NATIONS; I WILL GATHER YOU FROM ALL THE COUNTRIES AND BRING YOU BACK INTO YOUR OWN LAND. 25 I WILL SPRINKLE CLEAN (*Living*) WATER ON YOU (*Mikveh, Yahusha set this example when Mikveh'd by John for repentance of sin*), AND YOU WILL BE CLEAN.

John understood that in The Heavenly Scroll, the Feast Cycle and in the prophets (who read it); there was debate as to the their meaning. There appeared to be either two coming Messiahs or one that came twice. The Suffering Servant (Spring Feasts) and The Conquering King (Fall Feasts).

Spring Feasts

Virgo	Libra	Scorpio	Sagittarius	Capricorn	Aquarius
Virgin gives birth to Glorious Branch	Scales of Justice demand a price from the seed a cross to endure	Seed battles the Serpent	Servant/King defeats Serpent casts down the Dragon	Seed must die eternal life springs from his death	Seed pours out Living Water Bride given earnest guarantee to live again

Pesach/Unleavened Bread
(Passover Week)

Shav'uot
(Weeks)

FAll Feasts

Pisces	Aries	Taurus	Gemini	Cancer	Leo
Seed re-unites both houses Remnant Bride is revealed	The Lamb of God is found worthy	Conquoring King comes to execute Judgment	Two Witnesses Prince comes in Great Glory Marriage of the Lamb	Remnant Bride united, brought safely into the Kingdom	Lion of the Tribe of Judah rules as King

Messianic
Age of Pisces

Days of Awe

Yom Kippur
(Atonement)

Yom Teruah
(Trumpets)

Sukkot
(Booths)

Kingdom
Reign
(Last Great Day)

218

John had already declared Yahusha the Passover Lamb. This is why John asked Yahusha if he was the one who came twice or was there another who would come as the Conquoring King (LEO):

Matthew 11:3
NOW WHEN JOHN HEARD IN PRISON ABOUT THE DEEDS OF THE MESSIAH, HE SENT WORD BY HIS DISCIPLES AND SAID TO HIM, "ARE YOU THE ONE WHO IS TO COME, OR SHALL WE LOOK FOR ANOTHER?"

The Faith of Yahusha the Nazarene

John 8:28
THEN YAHUSHA SAID TO THEM: "WHEN YOU HAVE (*admitted The Heavenly Scroll - Isaiah 48:3-6*) AND LIFTED UP YOUR EYES TO THE STARS (*shamayim/The Heavenly Scroll*) TO SEE (*Spiritually perceive see with the mind G3708. horao*) THE SON OF MAN RIDING ON THE CLOUDS OF HEAVEN, THEN YOU WILL KNOW THAT I AM THE SON OF MAN (*ORION — 'the coming of The Branch, the Bearer of the Light of Life*), AND THAT I DO NOT DO MY OWN WILL, BUT THE WILL OF THE FATHER WRITTEN IN THE HEAVENLY SCROLL (*Hebrews* 10:7, *Matthew* 6:10)."

Yahusha expressed on multiple occasions that what qualified him as The Messiah was the same "faith of Abraham" in the Plan of Salvation written in The Heavenly Scroll (stars/constellations - Shamayim):

Hebrews 10:7
7 THEN I SAID, 'HERE I AM—IT IS WRITTEN ABOUT ME IN THE HEAVENLY SCROLL– I HAVE COME TO DO YOUR WILL, MY ELOHIM! (*Matthew* 6:10)

Matthew 6:10
10 YOUR KINGDOM (*declared in heaven - Matthew* 4:17) COME,

219

YOUR WILL BE DONE, ON EARTH AS IT IS WRITTEN IN THE HEAVENLY SCROLL (*Psalm* 19, *Daniel* 4:35).

John 17
5 AND NOW, FATHER, GLORIFY ME IN YOUR PRESENCE WITH THE GLORY I HAD WITH YOU (*written in The Heavenly Scroll*) BEFORE THE WORLD BEGAN (*the Light of Gen. 1:1: written into the stars on Day 4, then fulfilled in Yahusha on the 4th prophetic day as the Debar/Plan was fulfilled in the flesh John 1*).

Matthew 11:25
AT THAT TIME YAHUSHA ANSWERED AND SAID, I THANK YOU, O FATHER, KING OF THE HEAVENLY SCROLL (*Strong's H8064 'shamayim' - the place where the stars are located, i.e. The Mazzaroth/Zodiac*) AND EARTH, BECAUSE YOU HAVE HID THESE THINGS (*secrets preserved in the stars/heaven - Enoch 9:6*) FROM THE WISE AND PRUDENT, AND HAVE REVEALED THEM UNTO BABES.

Matthew 13:11
HE REPLIED, "BECAUSE THE KNOWLEDGE OF THE SECRETS OF THE KINGDOM OF HEAVEN (*the "secrets preserved in the heavens" - Enoch 6:9*) HAS BEEN GIVEN TO YOU, BUT NOT TO THEM.

Being trained by John the Baptist in the ancient path called The Way, Yahusha instructed us all in the Great Commission to proclaim he was the fulfillment of The Heavenly Scroll. You see, Yahusha told us to go and make disciples of all nations, bringing them into The Yahushaic Covenant through Mikveh, Circumcision, and Offering. That is The Great Commission. Then he said, he will be with us in that endeavor until the "end of the age of Pisces"...

Matthew 28
19 THEREFORE GO AND MAKE DISCIPLES OF ALL NATIONS, MIKVEH'ING THEM IN (*the covenant that bears*) MY NAME, 20 AND TEACHING THEM TO OBEY ALL THAT I HAVE COMMANDED YOU. AND SURELY I AM WITH YOU ALWAYS (*as Eternal High Priest*), TO THE

VERY END OF THE AGE (*of Pisces when he returns as Conquoring King*)."

Yahusha was intimately familiar with The Heavenly Scroll, which foretells that the Age of Pisces, a 2,000-year period is "the Messianic Age" where the Bride is called out and exposed on Earth.

-----PISCES-----
The Redeemer's people multiplied, supported and led by the Lamb, The Bride is exposed on earth, the Bridegroom is exalted.

The Faith of Sha'ul the Apostle

Ephesians 1:9-10
9 HE MADE KNOWN TO US THE MYSTERY OF HIS WILL ACCORDING TO HIS GOOD PLEASURE, WRITTEN IN THE HEAVENLY SCROLL WHICH HE PURPOSED TO FULFILL IN THE YAHUSHAIC COVENANT (*Daniel 4:35*), 10 TO BE PUT INTO EFFECT WHEN THE AGES REACH THEIR FULFILLMENT (*Age of Aquarius*) —

2 Corinthians 4:6
6 SEEING IT IS YAHUAH, THAT SAID, LIGHT SHALL SHINE OUT OF DARKNESS (*referring to day 1 of Creation when the "light" or Plan of Salvation was revealed*), WHO SHINED IN OUR HEARTS, TO GIVE THE LIGHT OF THE KNOWLEDGE (*proclaimed by the stars Psalms 19*) OF THE GLORY OF YAHUAH IN THE FACE OF YAHUSHA THE MESSIAH.

Sha'ul speaking to former pagans who knew and abused the Zodiac:

1 Corinthians 2
1 AND SO IT WAS WITH ME, BROTHERS AND SISTERS. WHEN I CAME TO YOU, I DID NOT COME WITH ELOQUENCE OR HUMAN WISDOM AS I

221

PROCLAIMED TO YOU THE TESTIMONY OF YAHUAH (*about Yahusha written in the stars*). 2 FOR I RESOLVED TO KNOW NOTHING WHILE I WAS WITH YOU EXCEPT YAHUSHA THE MESSIAH AND HIM CRUCIFIED (*before the foundation of the world written in the stars before our very eyes - Galatians 3*). 3 I CAME TO YOU IN WEAKNESS WITH GREAT FEAR AND TREMBLING. 4 MY MESSAGE AND MY PREACHING WERE NOT WITH WISE AND PERSUASIVE WORDS (*of human literal wisdom*), BUT WITH A DEMONSTRATION OF THE SPIRIT'S POWER, 5 SO THAT YOUR FAITH MIGHT NOT REST ON (*literal*) HUMAN WISDOM, BUT ON YAHUAH'S POWER (*in a Mystery Language*). 6 WE DO, HOWEVER, SPEAK A MESSAGE OF (SPIRITUAL) WISDOM AMONG THE (*spiritually*) MATURE, BUT NOT THE WISDOM OF THIS AGE OR OF THE RULERS OF THIS AGE (*who viewed the Zodiac literally and worshiped the signs and the Sun*), WHO ARE COMING TO NOTHING. 7 NO, WE DECLARE YAHUAH'S WISDOM, A MYSTERY THAT HAS BEEN HIDDEN (*in the Heavenly Scroll*) AND THAT YAHUAH DESTINED FOR OUR GLORY BEFORE TIME BEGAN (*writing it in the stars on day 4 of creation*). 8 NONE OF THE RULERS OF THIS AGE UNDERSTOOD IT (*because it was corrupted by the watchers - Enoch 9:6*)

Galatians 3
6 YOU FOOLISH GALATIANS! WHO HAS BEWITCHED YOU (*twisting the Zodiac into witchcraft*)? BEFORE YOUR VERY EYES (*in The Heavenly Scroll*) YAHUSHA THE MESSIAH WAS CLEARLY PORTRAYED AS CRUCIFIED ...7 UNDERSTAND THEN, THAT THOSE WHO HAVE FAITH (*in the message contained in the stars*) ARE CHILDREN OF ABRAHAM. 8 SCRIPTURE (*the word written in the heavens - Psalm 119:89*) FORESAW THAT YAHUAH WOULD JUSTIFY THE GENTILES BY FAITH, AND YAHUAH ANNOUNCED THE GOSPEL IN ADVANCE TO ABRAHAM (*via The Heavenly Scroll - Genesis 15:5; saying*): "ALL NATIONS WILL BE BLESSED THROUGH YOU."

Romans 10:17
CONSEQUENTLY, FAITH COMES FROM HEARING THE MESSAGE, AND THE MESSAGE IS HEARD THROUGH THE WORD ABOUT THE MESSIAH (*what "word" about Yahusha?*). 18 BUT I ASK: DID THEY NOT

HEAR (*what the stars proclaim night after night, day after day - Psalms* 19)? OF COURSE THEY DID: "THEIR (*constellations*) VOICE HAS GONE OUT INTO ALL THE EARTH, THEIR WORDS (*concerning Yahusha*) TO THE ENDS OF THE WORLD." (*Sha'ul quotes Psalms* 19)

Sha'ul had a vision as he was "taken to the third heaven"! Sha'ul deflects the attention away from himself with the age-old technique "I have a friend who" because he doesn't want to boast. He then goes on to say he was taken to the third heaven which is a metaphor for "shown advanced revelations of The Heavenly Scroll". The number 3 in The Mystery Language means:

> **Numbers in Scripture** by E.W, Bullinger
> "*Three stands for that which is solid, real, substantial, complete, and entire.*"

Sha'ul, below, is saying that Yahuah had given him visions of what is contained in The Heavenly Scroll that were "solid, real, substantial, complete, the ENTIRE revelation".

2 *Corinthians* 12

1 I MUST GO ON BOASTING. ALTHOUGH THERE IS NOTHING TO BE GAINED, I WILL GO ON TO VISIONS AND REVELATIONS FROM YAHUAH (*he did not literally go to a place called the third level of heaven, he saw VISIONS and REVELATIONS*). 2 I KNOW A MAN IN COVENANT WITH YAHUSHA (*he is speaking of himself in third person*) WHO FOURTEEN YEARS AGO (*when Sha'ul was nearly stoned to death, like Stephen he too saw the Heavenly Scroll open up*) WAS CAUGHT UP TO THE "*third*" HEAVEN (*was given 'solid, real, substantial, complete' understanding of The Heavenly Scroll*). WHETHER IT WAS IN THE BODY OR OUT OF THE BODY I DO NOT KNOW— YAHUAH KNOWS (*Sha'ul was unconscious from being stoned half to death*). 3 AND I KNOW THAT THIS MAN—WHETHER IN THE BODY OR APART FROM THE BODY I DO NOT KNOW, BUT YAHUAH KNOWS— 4 WAS CAUGHT UP TO PARADISE

(*shown The Heavenly Scroll like Daniel, Ezekiel, John, Enoch who were all 'taken to heaven' in the same way?*) AND HEARD INEXPRESSIBLE THINGS, THINGS THAT NO ONE IS PERMITTED TO TELL (*they are secrets preserved in The Heavenly Scroll - Enoch 9:6*). 5 I WILL BOAST ABOUT A MAN LIKE THAT, BUT I WILL NOT BOAST ABOUT MYSELF, EXCEPT ABOUT MY WEAKNESSES. 6 EVEN IF I SHOULD CHOOSE TO BOAST (*that this was speaking of himself*), I WOULD NOT BE A FOOL, BECAUSE I WOULD BE SPEAKING THE TRUTH. BUT I REFRAIN (*from saying it was me*), SO NO ONE WILL THINK MORE OF ME THAN IS WARRANTED BY WHAT I DO OR SAY, 7 OR BECAUSE OF THESE SURPASSINGLY GREAT *revelations* (*he was shown Yahusha coming as King of Heaven in The Heavenly Scroll*).

The Faith of John of Patmos

John was shown The Heavenly Scroll and described it in great detail as the "source of Revelation".

Revelation 4

1 THE THRONE IN HEAVEN AFTER THIS I LOOKED, AND BEHOLD, A DOOR WAS OPENED IN HEAVEN; AND THE FIRST VOICE WHICH I HEARD WAS (*Yahuah, the Aleph/Tav*), AS IT WERE, OF A LOUD SHOFAR BLAST TALKING WITH ME, WHICH SAID: COME UP HERE, AND I WILL SHOW YOU THINGS WHICH MUST BE AFTER THIS. 2 AND IMMEDIATELY I WAS IN THE SPIRIT (*seeing a vision of The Heavenly Scroll*); AND BEHOLD (*in the stars*), A THRONE WAS SET IN (*the middle of*) THE HEAVENLY SCROLL, AND ONE SAT ON THE THRONE. 3 AND HE WHO SAT THERE HAD THE APPEARANCE OF A JASPER AND A SARDIUS STONE, AND THERE WAS A RAINBOW SURROUNDING THE THRONE, LIKE THE APPEARANCE OF AN EMERALD. 4 AND SURROUNDING THE THRONE WERE TWENTY-FOUR SEATS, AND SITTING ON THE SEATS I SAW TWENTY-FOUR ELDERS (*represented by stars in the center of The Heavenly Scroll*), CLOTHED IN WHITE ROBES; AND THEY HAD CROWNS OF GOLD ON THEIR HEADS. 5 AND OUT OF THE THRONE PROCEEDED LIGHTNINGS, AND THUNDERINGS, AND VOICES; AND THERE WERE SEVEN LAMPS OF FIRE

(*Heavenly Menorah*) BURNING BEFORE THE THRONE, WHICH SIGNIFY AND REPRESENT THE COMPLETE PLAN OF YAHUAH (*7-spirits/7 stars of Pleiades*). 6 AND BEFORE THE THRONE THERE WAS A SEA OF GLASS, LIKE CRYSTAL (*blackness of space*). AND IN THE MIDST OF THE THRONE, AND SURROUNDING THE THRONE, WERE FOUR LIVING CREATURES FULL OF EYES BEFORE AND BEHIND. 7 AND THE FIRST CREATURE WAS LIKE A LION, AND THE SECOND CREATURE LIKE A CALF, AND THE THIRD CREATURE HAD A FACE AS A MAN, AND THE FOURTH CREATURE WAS LIKE A FLYING EAGLE. 8 AND EACH OF THE FOUR LIVING CREATURES HAD SIX WINGS (*Seraphim*), THEY WERE FULL OF EYES (*knowledge*) AROUND AND WITHIN (*foreknowlege*) ; AND THEY DID NOT CEASE DAY AND NIGHT, SAYING: HOLY, HOLY, HOLY, FATHER YAHUAH ALMIGHTY, WHO WAS, AND IS, AND IS TO COME. 9 AND WHEN THOSE CREATURES GIVE GLORY, AND HONOR, AND THANKS, TO HIM WHO SAT ON THE THRONE, TO HIM WHO LIVES FOREVER AND EVER, 10 THE TWENTY-FOUR ELDERS (*stars*) FALL DOWN BEFORE HIM WHO SAT ON THE THRONE (*in the Enoch Zodiac, there are exactly 24 stars and they are "falling" under the rainbow throne, the four beasts are seen singing "holy, holy, holy"*), AND WORSHIP HIM WHO LIVES FOREVER AND EVER, AND BOW WITH THEIR KIPPOT BEFORE THE THRONE, SAYING: 11 YOU ARE WORTHY, O YAHUAH, TO RECEIVE GLORY, AND HONOR, AND POWER; FOR YOU CREATED ALL THINGS, AND BY YOUR WILL THEY EXIST AND WERE CREATED!

I have produced a video on what John witnessed proving Yahuah was showing John The Heavenly Scroll:

https://www.youtube.com/watch?v=lWcV2tlHKX0

The Gospel of John is John's witness that Yahusha fulfilled The Heavenly Scroll. This Gospel has been twisted by the Lying Pen of the Scribe to promote the Spirit of the False Messiah which is incarnation.

I have retranslated the Gospel of John properly in the context of the rest of Scripture, the writing and beliefs of the Nazarenes, and in light of The Heavenly Scroll.

For more on the Gospel of John properly restored in context, see my book *The Testimony of Yahuchanon*.

The Faith of Peter

Peter directs us back to the first day of re-creation after the Earth had been destroyed by a flood. The first flood resulted from the fall of Lucifer and the Spirit of Yahuah hovering over the water that covered the Earth. The stars had already been created. We see Peter speak of Yahuah's Will existing in shamayim (translated 'heavens'). And that same plan written in The Heavenly Scroll is still the foundation until the day of judgment:

Peter 3:5-7
5 BUT THEY DELIBERATELY OVERLOOK THE FACT THAT LONG AGO BY GOD'S WORD EXISTED IN THE HEAVENS WHEN THE EARTH WAS FORMED OUT OF WATER AND BY WATER, 6 THROUGH WHICH THE WORLD OF THAT TIME PERISHED IN THE FLOOD (*of Lucifer*). 7 AND BY THAT SAME WORD (*written in heaven - Daniel 4:35, Psalm 89:2, Psalm 119:89, Psalms 97:6, Psalms 50:3-6 Enoch 35:3*), THE PRESENT HEAVENS AND EARTH ARE RESERVED FOR FIRE, BEING KEPT FOR THE DAY OF JUDGMENT AND DESTRUCTION OF UNGODLY MEN

The Faith of Steven

Stephen was given a vision of The Heavenly Scroll and Yahusha's role in it. We see Stephen while being stoned, was the first one to understand the witness of the Messiah as the "heavens opened up" and Steven saw Yahusha "coming in the clouds of heaven" in a vision:

Acts 7
55 BUT STEPHEN WAS FILLED WITH THE HOLY RUACH. HE LOOKED TOWARD THE HEAVENLY SCROLL, WHERE HE SAW OUR GLORIOUS ELOHIM AND YAHUSHA STANDING AT HIS RIGHT SIDE. 56 THEN STEPHEN SAID, "I SEE THE STARS/CONSTELLATIONS (*heaven/shamayim*) OPEN (*like a Scroll Revelation 6:14 and Hebrews 1:12*) AND THE SON OF MAN (*Orion*) STANDING AT THE RIGHT SIDE OF YAHUAH (*coming in the clouds of heaven the Milky Way*)!"

Chapter 8
Yahuah's Word Preserved in Heaven

Chapter 8: Introduction

What do all these verses in Scripture mean? The true meaning can only be understood when we properly translate the concept of "heaven" which in Hebrew is 'shamayim'. Shamayim means "place in the sky where the stars are located". In other words, 'heaven' is not some physical realm where Yahuah resides. Rather, it is a direct reference to The Heavenly Scroll in many cases. Only when we correct our Hellenized concept of 'heaven' can the true meaning come shining through.

We see below in the book of Enoch that Yahuah is the Author of Glory found in The Heavenly Scroll (stars and constellations):

ENOCH 35:3
I BLESSED YAHUAH AUTHOR OF GLORY (*The Heavenly Scroll - Psalm 19:1*), WHO HAD MADE THOSE GREAT AND SPLENDID SIGNS (*of the Zodiac – Genesis 1:14*), THAT THEY MIGHT DISPLAY (*to all mankind - Deuteronomy. 4:19*) THE MAGNIFICENCE OF THE WORKS OF HIS HANDS (*The Plan of Salvation - Psalm 19*) TO ANGELS AND TO THE SOULS OF MEN (*His Divine Counsel*); AND THAT THESE (*splendid signs in The Heavenly Scroll*) MIGHT GLORIFY ALL HIS WORKS AND OPERATIONS (*the Plan of Salvation*); THAT WE MIGHT SEE THE EFFECT OF HIS POWER (*as Creator to Write His Plan into the fabric of Creation on Day 4 and control the flow of history and fulfill His Promises*); AND THE HEAVENLY SCROLL MIGHT GLORIFY THE GREAT LABOR OF HIS HANDS (*and we might come to know Him - Romans 1, John 8:19 and His Son Psalm 19*); AND BLESS HIM FOREVER.

Like Enoch above, we see in Psalm 19 that The Heavenly Scroll tells of the Glory of Yahuah.

PSALM 19:1-6

[1]THE HEAVENLY SCROLL (*Shamayim - stars, Sun, and constellations*) ARE TELLING OF THE GLORY *(which is Yahusha - Hebrews 1:3)* OF ELOHIM *(John 1:14)*; AND THEIR EXPANSE (*The Divine Counsel*) IS DECLARING THE WORK OF HIS HANDS (*Enoch 35:3, John 1:3*). [2] DAY TO DAY THE HEAVENLY SCROLL POURS FORTH SPEECH, AND NIGHT TO NIGHT THE SUN/STARS/CONSTELLATIONS REVEAL KNOWLEDGE. [3] THERE IS NO SPEECH, NOR ARE THERE WORDS; THEIR VOICE IS NOT HEARD. [4] THEIR LINE (*Zodiac means 'line/path/way the Sun takes travels through the constellations'*) HAS GONE OUT THROUGH ALL THE EARTH (*the ecliptic plane*), AND THEIR UTTERANCES TO THE END OF THE WORLD *(John 1:9)*. IN THE STARS/CONSTELLATIONS YAHUAH HAS PLACED A TABERNACLE FOR THE SUN *(Luke 1:78-79, Matthew 4:16-17, the center of the Enoch Zodiac, the Throne in Heaven)*, [5] WHICH (*the Sun*) IS AS A BRIDEGROOM *(John 3:19)* COMING OUT OF HIS CHAMBER (*to marry the Bride - John 3:29*); IT REJOICES AS A STRONG MAN (*ORION*) TO RUN (*riding the clouds of heaven*) HIS COURSE (*of a wedding as the Groom... the feast Cycle/The Heavenly wedding*). [6] THE SUN'S RISING *(Luke 1:78, Matthew 4:16-17)* IS FROM ONE END OF THE HEAVENS (*Shamayim/stars*), AND ITS CIRCUIT (*Zodiac*) TO THE OTHER END OF THEM; AND THERE IS NOTHING HIDDEN FROM ITS LIGHT/REVELATION.

PSALM 89:2

I WILL DECLARE THAT YOUR LOVE STANDS FIRM FOREVER, THAT YOU HAVE ESTABLISHED YOUR FAITHFUL PROMISE (*LOGOS*) OF SALVATION IN THE HEAVENLY SCROLL ITSELF.

PSALM 119:89

YOUR WORD (*LOGOS / DEBAR*), YAHUAH, IS ETERNAL; IT STANDS FIRM WRITTEN IN THE HEAVENLY SCROLL.

PSALM 119:105

105 YOUR WORD (*LOGOS / DABAR eternally preserved in The Heavenly Scroll - Psalm 119:89*) IS A LAMP *(the Divine Counsel, we as His Bride are to keep our Lamps lit by keeping The Word of His Testimony - Isaiah 48)* UNTO MY FEET, AND A LIGHT (*revelation of the Sun/stars/constellations - Psalm 19, Enoch 35:3*) UNTO MY PATH (*The Heavenly Scroll is 'the Path of Righteousness' called The Way ... Isaiah 42:5-7*).

We see Sha'ul declare to the assemblies that they are without excuse for not accepting Yahusha as their Messiah. They (like Judaism today) were taught to expect only a conquering King. They did not understand Yahusha's role to fulfill the Spring Feasts first... then return as King to fulfill the Fall Feasts. Sha'ul points them back to The Heavenly Scroll which declares Yahuah's Will to have His Chosen King die for those he would later rule over:

GALATIANS 3:1

YOU FOOLISH GALATIANS! WHO HAS BEWITCHED YOU? BEFORE YOUR VERY EYES (*in the stars*) YAHUSHA THE MESSIAH WAS CLEARLY PORTRAYED AS CRUCIFIED *(in The Heavenly Scroll)*.

1 *CORINTHIANS* 2:7

NO, WE SPEAK OF THE MYSTERIOUS AND HIDDEN WISDOM OF GOD, WHICH HE DESTINED FOR OUR GLORY BEFORE TIME BEGAN.

TITUS 1:2

IN THE HOPE OF ETERNAL LIFE, WHICH GOD, WHO CANNOT LIE, PROMISED BEFORE TIME BEGAN.

We read in Deuteronomy that The Heavenly Scroll was given to all manking as a witness to the Will of Yahuah:

DEUTERONOMY 4:19
WHEN YOU LOOK UP TO THE SKY (sky is Hebrew 8064 'shamayim'/The Heavenly Scroll) AND SEE THE SUN, MOON, AND STARS (*speaking of the Zodiac/The Heavenly Scroll*) — THE WHOLE HEAVENLY CREATION (*Mazzaroth - Job 38:28*) — YOU MUST NOT BE SEDUCED TO WORSHIP AND SERVE THEM (*Signs/Divine Counsel/Starry Hosts/Hosts of Heaven... we call constellations which 'host stars'*) FOR YAHUAH YOUR ELOHIM HAS ASSIGNED THEM (*the stars/constellations*) TO ALL THE PEOPLE OF THE WORLD (*they were created by Yahuah to proclaim the coming Messiah Yahusha: see Psalm 19, they are not gods... they are Divine PICTOGRAPHS with meaning defined by their names which were given by Yahuah - Psalm 147:4, Isaiah 40:26*).

We read in Daniel His Will is written in The Heavenly Scroll:

DANIEL 4:35
35 "ALL THE INHABITANTS OF THE EARTH ARE ACCOUNTED AS NOTHING, BUT HE DOES ACCORDING TO HIS WILL WRITTEN IN *THE HOSTS OF HEAVEN*. (*sometimes translated as 'starry hosts' or 'heavenly hosts'. Constellations host stars, so this means 'constellations of The Heavenly Scroll'*)

Divine Love Story Written in the Stars

The Heavenly Wedding laid out in The Heavenly Scroll was fulfilled in the Feasts of Yahuah. The Spring Feasts are the Engagement, and the Fall Feasts are the Wedding festivities. Hebrew/Jewish weddings were pre-arranged marriages. They consisted of

- the father choosing a qualified Bride/Groom

- the Groom paying the dowry or "ransom" for the Bride.

- the Groom introduces himself to her father.

- the Bride presenting herself to the Bridegroom.

- the Bridegroom going away to prepare a place for her in his father's estate.

- the Bridegroom returning for his Bride.

- the wedding.

- the wedding banquet.

Remember, in Psalm 19, David described The Heavenly Scroll in great detail. He said the Sun was a shadow picture of the Messiah as the Bridegroom ran the course of a wedding. In Ephesians, Sha'ul goes into more detail the Divine Wedding that was pre-arranged before the foundation of the world written in The Heavenly Scroll:

Ephesians 1:3-11
3 BLESSED BE THE ONLY GOD AND FATHER OF OUR KING

YAHUSHA THE MESSIAH (*John* 17:3), WHO HAS BLESSED US IN MARRIAGE COVENANT WITH YAHUSHA AS HIS BRIDE WITH EVERY SPIRITUAL BLESSING PROCLAIMED IN THE HEAVENLY SCROLL. 4 JUST AS YAHUAH CHOSE US IN (*Marriage covenant with - Psalm* 19) YAHUSHA BEFORE THE FOUNDATION OF THE WORLD (*written into stars/constellations i.e. "heaven"*), THAT WE WOULD BE HOLY AND BLAMELESS BEFORE YAHUAH (*as Children through Mikveh - Ezekiel* 36:24-27). IN LOVE 5 YAHUAH PREDESTINED US TO ADOPTION AS SONS THROUGH (*Marriage*) COVENANT WITH THE MESSIAH YAHUSHA (*the Bridegroom - Matthew* 5:1-12, *John* 3:29, *Revelation* 8:23, *Mark* 2:18-20, *Psalm* 19) TO HIMSELF (*the Father of the Bridegroom*), ACCORDING TO THE KIND INTENTION OF HIS WILL (*proclaimed in The Heavenly Scroll - Ephesians* 1:9-10, *Daniel* 4:35, *Psalms* 97:6, *Psalm* 89:2, *Psalm* 119:89, *Psalms* 50:3-6), 6 TO THE PRAISE OF THE GLORY OF HIS GRACE, WHICH HE FREELY BESTOWED ON US IN THE BELOVED (*Family of Elohim*)....8 THAT HE LAVISHED ON US WITH ALL WISDOM AND UNDERSTANDING. 9 AND HE HAS MADE KNOWN TO US THE SECRET MYSTERY OF HIS WILL (*in The Heavenly Scroll*) ACCORDING TO HIS GOOD PLEASURE, WHICH HE PURPOSED (*in the beginning before the foundadtion of the world to be fulfilled*) IN COVENANT WITH YAHUSHA THE MESSIAH. 10 AS A PLAN (*LOGOS/DABAR*) TO BE FULFILLED AT THIS TIME (*4th Prophetic Day as laid out in The Heavenly Scroll the end of The Age of ARIES/Lamb dies*), **to bring all things written in The Heavenly Scroll to fulfillment on Earth perfectly fulfilled in Yahusha The Messiah** (*John* 17:4-5, *Hebrews* 10:7, *Matthew* 6:10) 11 IN COVENANT WITH YAHUSHA WE WERE ALSO THE CHOSEN BRIDE AND YAHUAH'S OWN CHILDREN (*John* 1:12), HAVING BEEN PREDESTINED ACCORDING TO THE PLAN OF SALVATION WRITTEN IN THE STARS BY YAHUAH WHO WORKS OUT EVERYTHING BY THE DIVINE COUNSEL (*the stars/constellations called The Heavenly Scroll or Divine Counsel*) WHICH DECLARE HIS WILL.

Sha'ul sums up why Yahusha is the Messiah and where our faith should be placed. The Plan of Salvation is a Divine Love Story foretold in The Heavenly Scroll before the foundation of the world.

This is the issue at hand. When dealing with Rabbinical Judaism you must prove Yahusha is the Messiah without using the New Testament's testimony of the Nazarenes. The true testimony that Yahusha is the Messiah is found in the "ancient path" also known as The Heavenly Scroll.

What was Yahusha's Claim to be the Messiah?

In this book, I have stressed the faith of our forefathers in the message contained in The Heavenly Scroll back to Adam. What is called "the Faith of Abraham" permeates and undergirds the written Tanakh and NT. The Heavenly Scroll is that which defines the role of the Messiah and is proof that Yahusha is the one promised in the stars/constellations.

EPHESIANS 1:9-10

9 HE MADE KNOWN TO US THE MYSTERY OF HIS WILL ACCORDING TO HIS GOOD PLEASURE, WRITTEN IN THE HEAVENLY SCROLL WHICH HE PURPOSED TO FULFILL IN THE YAHUSHAIC COVENANT (DANIEL 4:35), 10 TO BE PUT INTO EFFECT WHEN THE AGES REACH THEIR FULFILLMENT (AGE OF AQUARIUS) –

What is that "secret and mysterious" message the stars/constellations contain that is called Biblical Astrology?

Christianity would have us believe Yahusha was Yahuah in the flesh. They point to miracles to justify that their "Jesus" was God and for that reason, he is qualified to be the Messiah. Rabbinical Judaism would attempt to discredit Yahusha as the Messiah. They tell us the New Testament is a work of fiction.

The real question is what qualifies Yahusha to be the Messiah? Is it the miracles he performed? Is it because the NT says so? Because the Tanakh says so? How can we be sure if both have fallen prey to the "lying pen of the scribe"?

In this Chapter, we are going to firmly establish what qualifies Yahusha as the Messiah:

- *What claim did Yahusha make to being the Messiah?*

- *Contents of The Heavenly Scroll*

- *Fulfilled Yahuah's Spoken Promise - Word made flesh*

What qualifications did Yahusha claim to be the Messiah? Did he bear witness of himself? No. He laid claim to the Will of Yahuah as justification and witness of himself.

John 5:30-32

30 I CAN DO NOTHING BY MYSELF; I JUDGE ONLY AS I HEAR. AND MY JUDGMENT IS JUST, BECAUSE I DO NOT SEEK MY OWN WILL, BUT THE WILL OF HIM WHO SENT ME. 31 IF I TESTIFY ABOUT MYSELF, MY TESTIMONY IS NOT VALID. 32 THERE IS ANOTHER WHO TESTIFIES ABOUT ME, AND I KNOW THAT HIS TESTIMONY ABOUT ME IS VALID....

That "will of Yahuah" is that written in the stars/constellations called The Heavenly Scroll. The Heavenly Scroll is "the testimony of Yahuah" that Yahusha is the Messiah. The same testimony given to Abraham who "saw Yahusha's day" written in the stars and rejoiced.

John 8:56

YOUR FATHER ABRAHAM REJOICED TO SEE MY DAY (*written in The Heavenly Scroll - Genesis* 15:4-6), AND HE SAW IT (*written in the stars/constellations*) AND WAS GLAD."

Genesis 15:4-6

4 THEN THE WORD OF YAHUAH CAME TO ABRAM, SAYING, "THIS ONE WILL NOT BE YOUR HEIR, BUT ONE WHO COMES FROM YOUR OWN BODY WILL BE YOUR HEIR." 5 AND YAHUAH TOOK HIM OUTSIDE AND SAID, "NOW LOOK TO THE HEAVENS AND RECOUNT THE MEANING OF THE

STARS, IF YOU ARE ABLE." THEN HE TOLD HIM, "SO SHALL YOUR OFFSPRING BE." 6 ABRAM BELIEVED YAHUAH, AND IT (*his faith in the promise proclaimed in The Heavenly Scroll*) WAS CREDITED TO HIM AS RIGHTEOUSNESS.

Abraham was literally the "father of Astrology" and brought the knowledge of The Heavenly Scroll to Egypt. We are still being misled that it was Egypt that influenced Abraham.

From: **Abraham: Father of Nations—and a Scientist, Mathematician and Astronomer | ArmstrongInstitute.org**
> *Consider the record of third-century B.C.E. Babylonian historian Berossus: "In the 10th generation after the Flood, there was among the Chaldeans a man righteous and great, and skillful in the celestial science". While Berossus doesn't give this great scientist a name, first-century Jewish historian Josephus tells us that Berossus was writing about Abraham....* **What many historians are unwilling to admit is that Abraham possessed advanced astronomical knowledge that would not be rediscovered for thousands of years. Josephus further records that Abraham wasn't the first astronomer in his family. The study of astronomy originated with Seth, the third son of Adam.** *He wrote that "God gave [those who lived before the Flood] such long life that they might perfect those things which they had invented in astronomy" (Antiquities, 1.3.9).*

From: **Lives of Abraham: Seeing Abraham through the Eyes of Second-Temple Jews | The Interpreter Foundation**
> *Artapanus*
> *One of the earliest "biographies" of Abraham is found in the fragmentary writings of a Jewish author named Artapanus, as preserved in the writings of Christian fathers Eusebius and Clement. Dates for the writing have proposed between 250 BC and 50 BC, though some scholars*

suggest a tenable date of 200 BC. Artapanus claims that Abraham "came to Egypt with all his household to the Egyptian king Pharethothes, and taught him astrology, that he remained there twenty years and then departed again for the regions of Syria." In this short fragment, key additional details beyond the original biblical story give us an interval for Abraham's Egyptian sojourn as well as testimony **that Abraham brought culture in the form of astrology to Egypt.**

The Heavenly Scroll and the Ancient Path

The Talmud states that Abraham, Isaac, and Jacob all studied in the academies of Shem and Eber.

From: **Abraham: Father of Nations—and a Scientist, Mathematician and Astronomer | ArmstrongInstitute.org**

> *Consider the record of third-century B.C.E. Babylonian historian Berossus: "In the 10th generation after the Flood, there was among the Chaldeans a man righteous and great, and skillful in the celestial science". While Berossus doesn't give this great scientist a name, first-century Jewish historian Josephus tells us that Berossus was writing about Abraham....* **What many historians are unwilling to admit is that Abraham possessed advanced astronomical knowledge that would not be rediscovered for thousands of years. Josephus further records that Abraham wasn't the first astronomer in his family. The study of astronomy originated with Seth, the third son of Adam.** *He wrote that "God gave [those who lived before the Flood] such long life that they might perfect those things which they had invented in astronomy" (Antiquities, 1.3.9).*

We see this in the writings of the Nazarenes at Qumran.

From the Dead Sea Scroll: brill.com
The Astrologer at Qumran? The description of this promise in 4Q225 2 i 3-8 is built on the three biblical formulations of the promise in Genesis (13:16; 15:2-6; 22:17), but the particularities of their reworking imply the view that ***Abraham was versed in astrology.***

240

It is The Heavenly Scroll that defines and proves Yahsusha is the Messiah.

Hebrews 10:7

7 THEN I SAID, 'HERE I AM–IT IS WRITTEN ABOUT ME IN THE HEAVENLY SCROLL– I HAVE COME TO DO YOUR WILL, MY ELOHIM!

Matthew 6:10

10 YOUR KINGDOM (declared in heaven — Matthew 4:17) COME, YOUR WILL BE DONE, ON EARTH AS IT IS WRITTEN IN THE HEAVENLY SCROLL.

The promise Yahusha fulfilled was written in the stars/constellations as "signs" which means "witness" before the foundation of the world. Belief in The Heavenly Scroll is what defines "righteousness":

GENESIS 15:5-6

5 AND YAHUAH TOOK ABRAM OUTSIDE AND SAID, "NOW LOOK TO THE HEAVENS AND RECOUNT WHAT THE STARS PROCLAIM, IF YOU ARE ABLE." THEN HE TOLD HIM, "SO SHALL YOUR OFFSPRING BE." 6 ABRAM BELIEVED YAHUAH (WHEN HE READ THE STARS), AND IT WAS CREDITED TO HIM AS RIGHTEOUSNESS....

It defines "righteousness" and is the foundation of the faith of those in covenant with the Creator:

PSALMS 97:6

THE HEAVENLY SCROLL PROCLAIMS HIS RIGHTEOUSNESS, AND ALL THE PEOPLES SEE HIS GLORY (Psalm 19).

PSALMS 50:3-6

YAHUAH SUMMONS THE HEAVENS ABOVE, AND THE EARTH, THAT HE MAY JUDGE HIS PEOPLE: "GATHER TO ME MY CONSECRATED ONES, WHO MADE A COVENANT WITH ME

241

BY SACRIFICE." AND THE HEAVENS PROCLAIM HIS
RIGHTEOUSNESS, FOR GOD HIMSELF IS JUDGE.

To prove Yahusha is the promised seed of Abraham we must
understand what the faith of Abraham means and go back to
creation, called the "ancient path" or The Way.

> ### Rabbi Joel C. Dobin
> "_Astrology was so much part of Jewish life and experience_
> _and so well respected in our tradition and law that the_
> _abandonment of Astrology to follow the chimera of_
> _scientific linearality was one of the greatest religious_
> _tragedies that ever befell our people._ For in so doing, we
> abandoned as well the mystical realities of our faith, our
> abilities to balance our lives and attain Unity, and we have
> created of our synagogues and temples arenas of
> contention for power and concern for financial
> sufficiency.... I write as an astrologer, seeking to turn all
> those whose various faiths have seemed to abandon them
> back to their own faith."

Contents of The Heavenly Scroll

The Heavenly Scroll is literally the source of the Faith of our forefathers. Let us now clearly state exactly what the stars proclaim.

As the Sun is seen as "moving through its annual course" from west to east through the ecliptic, the moon completes 12 revolutions around the Earth. This "heavenly division" into 12 parts of 30 degrees each (12 x 30 = 360 degrees a complete circle) gives us 12 equal parts giving us what is called the Zodiac. Zodiac is derived from the primitive root 'zoad' which means The Way or walk. This is what the Bible calls the Ancient Path and the Nazarenes referred to as The Way.

Message Proclaimed in The Heavenly Scroll

VIRGO: A virgin will give birth to a beautiful Glorious and Righteous Branch. The seed of the woman will be a man of humiliation to rise to be the desire of nations and will become exalted first as Shepherd then as Harvester. **LIBRA**: The scales demand a price to be paid of this seed, a cross to endure; the victim will be slain and purchase a Crown. **SCORPIO**: There is a conflict between the seed and the serpent leading to a struggle with the enemy, the enemy is vanquished. **SAGITTARIUS**: The double-natured seed (Servant/King) triumphs as a warrior and pleases the heavens, builds fires of punishment, and casts down the dragon. **CAPRICORNUS**: Eternal life comes from his death, he's the Arrow of God, he is pierced, yet springs up again in abundant life. **AQUARIUS**: He pours out "Living Water" from on high, humanity

243

drinks of the heavenly river and the Faithful live again, he is the Deliverer of the good news (Gospel), Carrying the Cross over the Earth. *PISCES*: The Redeemer's people multiplied, supported, and led by the Lamb, The Bride is exposed on Earth, and the Bridegroom is exalted. *ARIES*: The Lamb is found worthy, the Bride is made ready, Satan is bound, and the strong man triumphs. *TAURUS*: The conquering Ruler comes, the sublime vanquisher, to execute the great judgment, he is the Ruling Shepherd King. *GEMINI*: The Marriage of the Lamb, the enemy is trodden down, the Prince comes in great Glory. *CANCER*: The great Bride, the two Houses of Judah and Israel are united, they are brought safely into the Kingdom. *LEO*: The Lion King is aroused for rending, the Serpent flees, the Bowl of Wrath is upon him, and his Carcass is devoured. The Lion of the Tribe of Judah Rules as King.

Psalms 147:1-5

HOW GOOD IT IS TO SING PRAISES TO OUR ELOHIM, HOW PLEASANT AND FITTING TO PRAISE HIM! YAHUAH BUILDS UP JERUSALEM; HE GATHERS THE EXILES OF ISRAEL. HE HEALS THE BROKENHEARTED AND BINDS UP THEIR WOUNDS. HE DETERMINES THE NUMBER OF THE STARS AND CALLS THEM EACH BY NAME. GREAT IS OUR ELOHIM AND MIGHTY IN POWER; HIS UNDERSTANDING HAS NO LIMIT.

Isaiah 40

26 LIFT UP YOUR EYES AND LOOK TO THE HEAVENS *(THE PLACE IN THE SKY WHERE THE STARS ARE LOCATED, THE ZODIAC)*: WHO CREATED ALL THESE? HE WHO BRINGS OUT THE STARRY HOST *(CONSTELLATIONS)* ONE BY ONE AND CALLS FORTH EACH OF THEM BY NAME *(SIGNS OF THE ZODIAC)*.

Isaiah 9:6-7

"FOR TO US A CHILD IS BORN *(VIRGO)*, TO US A SON *(of man)* IS GIVEN *(ORION)*, AND THE GOVERNMENT SHALL BE ON HIS SHOULDERS *(TAURUS)* AND HE WILL BE CALLED WONDERFUL COUNSELOR *(AQUARIUS)*, *(the perfect image of)* MIGHTY GOD *(CAPRICORNUS)*, *(fore)* FATHER OF EVERLASTING *(life)* *(CAPRICORNUS)*, AND PRINCE OF PEACE *(CANCER)*." THERE WILL BE NO END TO THE INCREASE OF HIS GOVERNMENT OR OF PEACE, ON THE THRONE OF DAVID AND OVER HIS KINGDOM, TO ESTABLISH IT *(SAGITTARIUS)* AND TO UPHOLD IT WITH JUSTICE AND RIGHTEOUSNESS FROM THEN ON AND FOREVERMORE *(LEO)*.

Each constellation is defined by the meaning behind the names Yahuah gave the 3 main stars and associated Decans.

The timeframe (The Sabbath Covenant) is read clockwise beginning with the "Living Creature" that is holding The Heavenly

Scroll. It is a 7,000-year plan covering 3 and ½ "Ages" which are 2,000 years each.

The Plan of Salvation which lays out the role and life of the Messiah is read counterclockwise beginning with Virgo and ending with Leo.

For much more on how to read The Heavenly Scroll, see my book Creation Cries Out! The Mazzaroth:

The Mazzaroth

Virgo

Book 1: Chapter 1

Short Story: <u>The Virgin / Young Maiden</u>
Virgin gives birth to a King, great shepherd and harvester

Tribe of Israel: <u>Naphtali</u>
Primary star

   Spica – means "ear of wheat/corn/grain". *Hebrew word for this star is Tsemech which means "the branch". Jer 23:5-6, Zech 3:8, 6:12, Isaiah 4:2. There are 20 different Hebrew words that mean "branch", yet only Tsemech is used of the Messiah; the same word for the name of the brightest star of Virgo. Virgo has a branch/ear of barely in one hand (John 12:21-24) and a "seed" in her other (Gen 3:15)*

Secondary star

Zavijaveh, meaning "gloriously beautiful." – *Isaiah* 4:2

Decans (secondary constellations)

Coma Decan – *meaning "the infant is the desired one" (Haggai 2:7). The image of this constellation is a woman holding an infant child.*

Centaurus decan – *meaning "the dart piercing a victim"*

Bootes decan – *meaning "the great shepherd and harvester"*

Overall story told by VIRGO

Seed of the Woman, Desire of Nations, Man of humiliation, becomes exalted Shepherd and Harvester. A virgin holding a branch and an ear of corn. Corn = seed (Latin Spica, the modern name of this bright star. Old name was Arabic Al Zimach meaning seed). Star Zavijaveh means "gloriously beautiful". So according to all cultures since the beginning of mankind, the constellation Virgo means "a virgin holding a branch and a seed that will be gloriously beautiful".

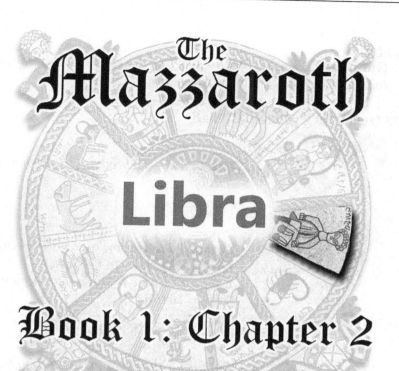

The Mazzaroth

Libra

Book 1: Chapter 2

Short Story: The Scales

> The scales demand a price to be paid, Cross to endure, the Victim slain, a Crown purchased.

Tribe of Israel: Asher

Primary star

Alpha: *Zuben al Genubi – means price deficient (Ps 49:7, 62:9*

Secondary star

Beta: *Zuben al Chemali – means price that covers (Rev 5:6). So "we fall short, another covers the gap)*

Third star

Gamma: *Zuben al Akrab – price of the conflict as it points toward Centaurus and victim slain*

Decans (secondary constellations)

The Cross *– Hebrew is Adom means "cut off"*

Lupus *– the victim, pierced to death, Hebrew Asedah "to be slain". Egyptian name is Sura which means "lamb" (Isa 53:7)*

Corona *– the crown (Heb 2:9). The Hebrew word Atarah means "royal crown" (Rev 5:9, Mt 27:29, Jas 1:12, Zech 9:16). To the south of Libra, we find the cosmic struggle of Serpens and Ophiuchus. A man wrestling with a serpent sticking his heel while his foot is on the scorpion's head (Genesis 3:15).*

Overall story told by Libra

The Balance, or Scales, symbolizes measurement and balance in general as well as justice and commerce. Speaking of the Messiah:

Job 31

6 LET YAHUAH WEIGH ME IN HONEST SCALES AND HE WILL KNOW THAT I AM BLAMELESS

REVELATION 6

5 WHEN THE LAMB OPENED THE THIRD SEAL, I HEARD THE THIRD LIVING CREATURE SAY, "COME!" I LOOKED, AND THERE BEFORE ME WAS A BLACK HORSE! ITS RIDER WAS HOLDING A PAIR OF SCALES IN HIS HAND.

An accurate balance with accurate weights was a symbol of Justice. Yahuah has perfect justice based upon His absolute Righteousness. The Scales of Divine Justice are accurately calibrated. Divine Judgment is without partiality. (Deut 10:17; Acts 10:34; Rom 2:11; Gal 2:6; Eph 6:9). Yahuah (His proxy King Yahusha) is the final Judge (2 Tim 4:1; Heb 4:12; 10:30; 12:23; Jas 4:12).

The Mazzaroth
Scorpio
Book 1: Chapter 3

Short Story

A Conflict, Serpent's coils, Struggle with the Enemy, the Evil Vanquisher. The "strong man" wrestles with the serpent who is reaching for the crown. The scorpion is stinging the heel of the strong man, who is treading on the scorpion.

Tribe of Israel: *Dan*

Primary star

Antares – wounding, cutting, tearing

Secondary star

Beta: Zuben al Chemali – *means price that covers (Rev 5:6). So "we fall short, another covers the gap)*

Third star

Gamma: Zuben al Akrab – *price of the conflict as it points toward Centaurus and victim slain*

Decans (secondary constellations)

Serpens and Ophiuchus decans – *the serpent and the **Serpent Bearer**, or **Healer**. A man wrestling with the serpent. He has one foot on the scorpions head and the other on the scorpion's tail.*

GENESIS 3:15

I WILL PUT ENMITY BETWEEN YOU (THE SERPENT) AND THE WOMAN, AND BETWEEN YOUR SEED AND HER SEED; HE SHALL CRUSH YOUR HEAD, AND YOU SHALL CRUSH HIS HEEL.

Hercules decan – *the mighty man. This Decan is the foundation of myths and idols of the Greeks.*

253

Overall story told by Scorpio

Scorpius, the Scorpion, symbolizes Satan, the enemy of Yahuah and His chosen family. Satan was the enemy of the Messiah in Hypostatic Union, who inspired the execution on the stake (Jn 13:2, 27), but was defeated at the stake through resurrection (Jn 3:14-15, 12:31-32, 16:11). The scorpion (Dt 8:15; Ezek 2:6; Lk 10:19; 11:12) is a desert creature, as is the snake, which also symbolizes Satan.

Snakes and scorpions, the symbols of Satan, were the enemies of Israel. "Fiery serpents" is the Hebrew nachash, serpent, and saraph, meaning burning, fiery, or serpent. The two words together mean literally burning snakes, which were so called for their inflammatory bite, filled with heat and poison.

The constellation, Scorpius, Is near other snake symbols. It Is near the constellation Serpens, the Serpent, and Ophiuchus, the Snake Holder. Since both snakes and scorpions are symbols of Satan, the sign of Scorpius applies to both. Therefore, scripture for snakes as well as scorpions apply in the study of Scorpius.

The scorpion is also a symbol of the Centaur demon assault army of Abaddon (Rev 9:3, 5, 10), which, of course, is from Satan. Scorpius symbolizes the enemy attack of Satan, but it also symbolizes the victory at the stake (Yahusha was nailed to a stake or tree not a cross). The Greek word for serpent is o[fi" (ophis), which is also used in the Septuagint for the serpent in the Garden (Gen 3:1), the fiery serpents (Deut. 8:15), and the brass serpent in the desert (Num 21:6-9).

255

The Mazzaroth

Sagittarius

Book 1: Chapter 4

Short Story: The Archer
> *The double-natured One triumphs as a Warrior, Pleases the Heavens, Builds fires of punishment, Casts down the Dragon. Same meaning in several languages (Rev. 6:2). Star Naim = The gracious one.*

Tribe of Israel: *Benjamin*

Primary star

> *El Asieh* – "the one to whom we bow" (Isaiah 45:23)

256

Secondary star

Beta: Zuben al Chemali – *means price that covers (Rev 5:6). So "we fall short, another covers the gap)*

Third star

Gamma: Zuben al Akrab – *price of the conflict as it points toward Centaurus and victim slain*

Decans (secondary constellations)

Lyra – The harp. *The name indicates the praise of Yahuah. Brightest star is **Vega** = He shall be exalted. (Ps. 2 1:13)*

Ara – *the Altar. The burning fire prepared for His enemies.*

Draco – The Dragon. *The name comes from the Greek = Trodden on (Ps. 91:13). Brightest star Thuban = The subtle. Names of other stars all refer to similar aspects of the dragon.*

Overall story told by Sagittarius

The heavenly sign shows the archer with his bow bent and an arrow fitted to the string. It is aimed directly at Antares, the star in the heart of Scorpio. In Sagittarius the emphasis shifts from the wounding by the adversary, to one of victory. The arrows of God are shot at the heart of the enemy. In the Zodiac of Dendera under the image of this constellation is the word Knem, meaning "He conquers." We find the same word under the last sign of the Dendera Zodiac, that of Leo the Lion who is standing upon a serpent. This affirms that the Lion of Leo, and the Centaur of Sagittarius, refer to the same person. Numerous Scriptures come to mind in relation to this sign.

PSALM 45:3-5

GIRD YOUR SWORD UPON YOUR THIGH, O MIGHTY ONE, WITH YOUR GLORY AND YOUR MAJESTY. AND IN YOUR MAJESTY RIDE PROSPEROUSLY BECAUSE OF TRUTH, HUMILITY, AND RIGHTEOUSNESS; AND YOUR RIGHT HAND SHALL TEACH YOU AWESOME THINGS. YOUR ARROWS ARE SHARP IN THE HEART OF THE KING'S ENEMIES; THE PEOPLES FALL UNDER YOU.

PSALM 64:7

GOD SHALL SHOOT AT THEM WITH AN ARROW; SUDDENLY THEY SHALL BE WOUNDED.

REVELATION 6:2

AND I LOOKED, AND BEHOLD, A WHITE HORSE, AND HE WHO SAT ON IT HAD A BOW; AND A CROWN WAS GIVEN TO HIM; AND HE WENT OUT CONQUERING, AND TO CONQUER.

The Mazzaroth
Capricorn
Book 2: Chapter 1

Short Story: Goat / Scapegoat

Life comes from death; He's the Arrow of God, Pierced, springs up again in abundant life.

Ancient pictures are half goat, half fish; i.e. the sacrifice and those who it is sacrificed for.

Tribe of Israel: *Zebulun*

Primary star

Gedi - Hebrew for "cut off"

Secondary star

Daneb Al Gedi - meaning "The Sacrifice Comes." (Isaiah 53:7-8)

Decans (secondary constellations)

Sagitta Decan – the Arrow

Aquila Decan – the Eagle

Delphinus Decan – the Dolphin

Overall story told by Capricorn

Capricorn is the top half of a goat, and the bottom half is the tail of a fish. It is called the **Sea Goat** *(Capricornus). It is wounded and on one knee, and some of the ancient star names indicate that it is a sacrifice. The goat was one of the sacrificial animals in the Law of Yahuah given to Moses. It was the animal used as the scapegoat that took upon itself the sins of Israel on the Day of Atonement (Lev. 16:10). After John the Immerser Mikveh'd Yahusha and laid his hands on our Messiah's*

261

head, Yahusha "fled into the wilderness" in fulfillment of the shadow picture of the scapegoat.

The Mazzaroth

Aquarius

Book 2: Chapter 2

Short Story: The Water Bearer

Life-waters from on High, Drinking the heavenly river, delivering the Good News, Carrying the wood of the sacrifice over all the earth.

Tribe of Israel: *Reuben*

Primary star

Sa'ad Al Melik - means "record of the outpouring"

Secondary star

Al Sund – means "the pourer out."

Decans (secondary constellations)

Picus Australis – the southern fish. Star Fom al Haut = the mouth of the fish.

Pegasus – the winged horse

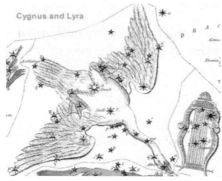

Cygnus – The Swan. Brightest star Deneb = The Judge or Adige = flying swiftly.

264

Overall story told by Aquarius

A man pouring out water on the Earth, living water (John 4:10, John 7:37-38, Isaiah 44:3-4). Aquarius is a Latin name meaning "the pourer forth of water." The brightest star is located in the right shoulder and is called Sa'ad Al Melik, meaning "record of the outpouring." The next star in brightness is Al Sund, "the pourer out." A star in the urn bears the Egyptian name Mon, or Meon, being interpreted "the urn." It is not difficult to find in the Scriptures references to Yahusha and the pouring forth of water.

When Yahusha encountered the woman of Samaria at the well, He said, "If you knew the gift of God, and who it is who says to you, 'Give Me a drink,' you would have asked Him, and He would have given you living water" (John 4:10). In John 7:37-38 Yahusha cried out at the water ceremony of Sukkot ""If any man is thirsty, let him come to Me and drink. He who believes in Me, as the Scripture said, 'From his innermost being shall flow rivers of living water.'"

The Mazzaroth
Pisces
Book 2: Chapter 3

Short Story: The Two Fish / Two Houses of Israel

> *The Redeemer's People multiplied, Supported and led by the Lamb, The Bride is exposed on earth, the Bridegroom is exalted. Star names indicate "the fish (multitudes) of those who will follow"- i.e. The chosen of Yahuah (Ps. 115:14).*

Tribe of Israel: *Simeon*

Primary star

> *Al Deramin* - means the Quickly-Returning.

Secondary star

Al Phirk – means the Redeemer **Decans (secondary constellations)**

The Band – (that unites the two fish) (Hos. 11:4, Ephesians 2:15)

Decans

Andromeda – The Chained Woman (who will be delivered).

Cepheus – The Crowned King.

267

Overall story told by Pisces

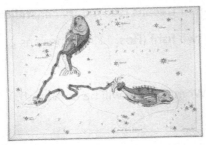

The unusual feature of this constellation is that the two fish are drawn as being held together by a band. This band is a shadow picture of the Messiah who makes out of the two houses of Israel (the two fish) one new "man" or Remnant Israel.

EPHESIANS 2:14-15

14 FOR YAHUSHA IS OUR PEACE, WHO HATH MADE BOTH (JEWS AND GENTILES) ONE, AND HATH BROKEN DOWN (THE DEATH DECREES IN THE LAW WHICH WERE) THE MIDDLE WALL OF PARTITION BETWEEN US; 15 HAVING ABOLISHED (NAILED THE DEATH DECREES TO THE CROSS) IN HIS FLESH WHICH WERE THE *CAUSE OF THE ENMITY* (OUR FEAR OF THE DEATH) *TOWARD* THE LAW, COMMANDMENTS AND ORDINANCES; FOR TO MAKE IN HIMSELF OF TWO, ONE NEW MAN, SO MAKING PEACE.

Pisces, of course, is symbolic of the redeemed of Yahuah, His called-out ones. Yahusha told His disciples, "I will make you fishers of men."

The shackles (on the Bride/Andromeda) of sin weigh down all mankind and have need of being broken. Isaiah, spoken by Yahusha as He began His ministry, was cited. "He has sent Me to proclaim release to the captives, and recovery of sight to the blind, to set free those who are downtrodden, to proclaim the favorable year of Yahuah." In Pisces, we see the conflict of man, a conflict that Yahusha triumphantly overcame.

The Mazzaroth

Aries

Book 2: Chapter 4

Short Story: The Ram / Lamb

The Lamb is found worthy, the Bride (after being released from chains of sin) is made ready, Satan is bound, the Breaker (of chains) triumphs. Brightest star El Nath = wounded, slain; (others similar).

Tribe of Israel: *Gad*

Primary star

El Nath – wounded, slain; (others similar).

269

Secondary star

Schedir – (Hebrew) = freed.

Third star

Caph – The Branch (of victory). (Is. 54:1-8, 62:3-5).

Decans (secondary constellations)

Cassiopeia, Perseus, and Andromeda grouped together tell the story of the woman (bride) held captive to be delivered and enthroned as Queen.

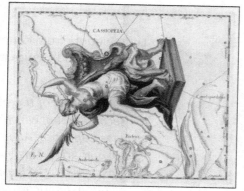

Cassiopeia – The Beautiful Enthroned Woman. The captive woman (Andromeda) now delivered.

Cetus – the sea monster (Revelation 13). The enemy bound.

Perseus – The Breaker. Hebrew = Peretz. Greek = Perses (Micah 2:13). Winged feet = coming swiftly. Head he carries wrongly called Medusa by Greeks; Hebrew Rosh Satan = Head of the Adversary.

271

Overall story told by Aries

Let me quote from Kenneth Fleming, in God's Voice in the Stars:

"Aries is the last of the signs in the second group, which includes Capricorn, Aquarius, Pisces, and Aries. This quartet of signs pictures the blessings of salvation. Capricorn signifies the blessings of salvation. Capricorn signifies the blessing of life from death. Aquarius pictures the blessing of salvation's fullness. Pisces signifies the delay of the promised blessing. Now in Aries we see the blessing fully realized...

Aries has a most interesting and instructive message for the student of the biblical prophecy and the history of salvation. Aries usually carries the symbol of the ram, but many of the oldest zodiacs portray a lamb (with no horns), and in some ancient zodiacs the lamb has a circular crown on its head... The Hebrew name for Aries was Taleh, which means Lamb, while the Arabic name, Hamal, means Sheep, Gentle, Merciful... In Syriac the name for Aries is Amroo, meaning Lamb. The New Testament in that language uses the same word for the Lord Jesus; John the Baptist cried, "Behold the Lamb of God!" (John 1:29)"

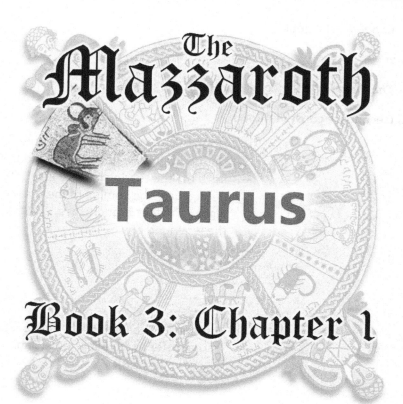

The Mazzaroth

Taurus

Book 3: Chapter 1

Short Story: The Bull

> *The conquering Ruler comes, the sublime Vanquisher, the great Judgment, the ruling Shepherd. The Pleiades = The congregation of the judge.*

Tribe of Israel: *Ephraim*

Primary star

> *Al Nitak* – the wounded one.

Secondary star

Capella – she goat

Third star

The Pleiades – The congregation of the judge.

Decans (secondary constellations)

Orion – The coming Prince. Hebrew Oarion = light. He holds a club and the head of "the roaring lion" (1 Pet. 5:8). Betelgeuz = The coming of the branch. Rigol = the foot that crushes. Al Nitak = the wounded one.

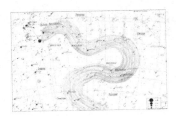

Eridanus – The River of the Judge. Star names refer to "flowing" etc. (Dan. 7:10; Nahum 1:8).

Auriga – The Shepherd (Isaiah 40:10-11). Hebrew root = shepherd. Star Capella (Latin) = she goat.

Overall story told by Taurus

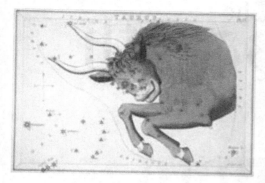

He is a great white bull of the variety of wild ox which has two long forward-pointing golden horns. His forelegs suggest that he is charging forward. On the other hand, he has seven doves on his back (the Seven Sisters), and some have suggested that the bent legs indicate that he is peacefully reclining. Here it is not the Greek myths, but the Book of Enoch (section 4, Chapter 85) which makes it clear what the white bull represents. It is the millennial Kingdom of Yahuah which will soon govern the earth for a thousand years, after the destruction of the wicked.

The Mazzaroth

Gemini

Book 3: Chapter 2

Short Story: The Twins

> *The Marriage of the Lamb, the Enemy is trodden down, the Prince comes in great Glory. There is some confusion of the pictures for this constellation in the different languages, but they generally refer to two people probably referring to the House of Israel and the House of Judah. The picture is also rendered as a man and a woman a picture of the Bride and Groom.*

Tribe of Israel: *Manasseh*

276

Primary star

> *Castor* – "the mortal Twin",

Secondary star

> *Pollux* - "the immortal Twin"

Decans (secondary constellations)

> **Lepus** – The Hare (the enemy); trodden under Orion's foot. Star names refer to "the deceiver" etc.

Canis Major (The Dog) or Sirius (The Prince). Sirius is the brightest of all stars. (Is. 9:6). **Canis Minor** – The Second Dog. Star Procyon Redeemer

Overall story told by Gemini

The tenth zodiac constellation is the **two joined together** (Gemini), who are the Bride and Groom and the Two Houses of Israel. This constellation has many "meanings" depending on the culture looking at it. If we consider the Plan of Salvation this constellation could be in reference to the dual nature of the Messiah. First coming as a man, the suffering servant; then returning divine as the conquering king. It can mean the reunification of the Two Houses of Israel. It can represent the Marriage between the Bride and Groom.

Yom Kippur is represented by Gemini. The story told by the major stars in the constellation Gemini are that of the Prince, having conquered his enemies and made them his footstool, comes in Great Glory to gather his Bride from all nations to attend The Wedding to unite the two houses of Israel.

When looking at this constellation in terms of "2000-year ages" it would be symbolic of Adam and Eve.

The Mazzaroth

Cancer

Book 3: Chapter 3

Short Story: The Crab

In Hebrew it is 'Ash' or Butterfly. To the Indians it was a Crab. Ancient Sumerians saw it as a Crayfish. In each case, the creature concerned rose to a new life out of its old shell. The brightest star is Acubene which is related to the Hebrew word for "hiding place." This picture is reinforced by the Praesepe cluster. The word comes from Latin, means "a crib, a manger, a hive, or a fold for animals." In Job 38:32, God asked if Job could "Guide the constellation Ash ('Butterfly') with his 'Multitude' ('Offspring' or 'Children' or 'Sons')". This refers to Cancer and the Praesepe cluster. It is all the more significant since Job had stated in his discussion in Job 19:25 "I know that my Redeemer Lives, and He will stand on the Earth in the Last Days. And though

279

after death worms consume my body, yet in my flesh will I see God, whom my own eyes will behold, and not another's."

The name "Cancer" may be related t" Ara'Ic. In old Arabic this sign was "Khan Ker" which means "priest-prince."

The meanings of the name of the constellation itself and the associated stars may have to do with the Priest-Prince coming out of his hiding place dwell among men.

Sukkot is represented by Cancer. The Messiah was on the first day of Sukkot and circumcised on the 8th day, the Last Great Day.

Tribe of Israel: *Issachar*

Primary star

> *Acubene – Hiding place*

Secondary star

> *Praesepe – a crib, a manger, a hive, or a fold for animals*

Decans (secondary constellations)

The first decan of Cancer is the strongest as it is a double dose of the same zodiac sign energies and characteristics. The second and third decans are modified by the qualities and traits of the other two signs belonging to the element of Water – Scorpio & Pisces.

Ursa Minor – The Little Bear. No bears found in any ancient Zodiacs. Confusion may be from Hebrew Dohver Sheepfold, Dovh Bear.

Ursa Major – The Great Bear. Possibly "Sheepfold" as Ursa Minor as Al Naish "assembled together"; Dubhe = "Herd of animals or a flock" etc. Many stars similarly named.

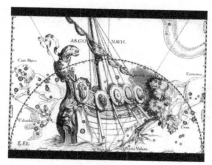

Argo – Meaning is the "Return of the travelers".

Overall story told by Cancer

The crab can pick up things in its powerful right hand and deliver them to the desired destination. The Great Deliverer descended into hell and the gates of hell could not prevent him from delivering his people to freedom from the bondage of death and hell. This deliverance has not only happened in the past, it will yet happen in the future just before the beginni"g of'the millennial reign of Yahusha. At that time, the righteous will again be delivered from the grasp of the seven-headed dragon kingdom (which has enslaved much of the entire world). This is where we are currently in the Heavenly Scroll.

281

The Mazzaroth

Leo

Book 3: Chapter 4

. **Short Story: The Lion of the Tribe of Juda**

The Lion King is aroused for rending, the Serpent flees, the Bowl of Wrath is upon him, and his Carcass is devoured. The Lion of the tribe of Judah (Rev. 5:5). Hebrew name means "Lion hunting down its prey". Name in other languages similar. Denebola Judge who cometh.

Tribe of Israel: *Judah*

Primary star

    Alpha Regulus – treading under foot

Secondary star

Denebola – the judge comes (Num 24:8-9, Rev 5:5)

Decans (secondary constellations)

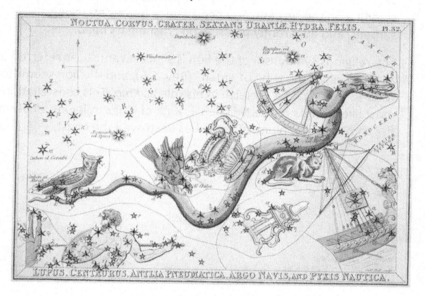

Hydra – The Serpent. Hydra means "He is abhorred". Star names similar.

Crater – The Cup. The pouring out of wrath on the wicked. (Ps 75:8, 11:6, Rev 14:10)

Corvus – The Raven. Birds of prey devouring the Serpent. (Prov 30:17, Rev 19:1)

Overall story told by Leo

The twelfth and last zodiac constellation is the **Lion** (Leo). He is a magnificent Lion which is pouncing on the head of the fleeing giant Water Serpent. In the Egypian planisphere, he is shown actually standing on the serpent. So once again, a hero is attacking a serpent; and apparently focusing on crushing its head.

The religious symbolism of the lion is similar. Yahusha is referred to as the "Lion of the tribe of Judah" (Rev. 5:5), and the lion seems to refer to Yahusha the Messiah in his role as *King*. This constellation most likely refers to the Messiah as King of Kings, reigning all during the coming Millennium, after he has destroyed the beast.

Conclusion

Mankind has always erred in giving what is Yahuah's Glory to graven images, pagan gods, mythological figures, etc. When it comes to Creation, Yahuah alone reserves the Glory and He will not give it to anyone or anything else... that is why any act such as divination, fortune telling, sorcery, magic, witchcraft, etc. are strictly forbidden in the context of "familiar spirits'; because those are the terms for using Creation improperly or seeking divine counsel outside of the Spirit of Yahuah!

Isaiah 45:5-12

5 I AM YAHUAH, AND THERE IS NO OTHER; APART FROM ME THERE IS NO GOD. 7 I FORM THE LIGHT AND CREATE DARKNESS, I BRING PROSPERITY AND CREATE DISASTER; I, YAHUAH, DO ALL THESE THINGS. 12 IT IS I WHO MADE THE EARTH AND CREATED MANKIND UPON IT. MY OWN HANDS STRETCHED OUT THE HEAVENS (STARS); I MARSHALED THEIR STARRY HOSTS (CONSTELLATIONS).

In every culture since the creation of man, "God" is seen as the author of The Zodiac.

Above, notice "God" is authoring the Zodiac with his son "on his mind"

Isaiah 44

24 "THIS IS WHAT YAHUAH SAYS— YOUR REDEEMER, WHO FORMED YOU IN THE WOMB: I AM YAHUAH, THE MAKER OF ALL THINGS, WHO STRETCHES OUT THE HEAVENS (*to tell a story*), WHO SPREADS OUT THE EARTH BY MYSELF.

Isaiah 46

5 "TO WHOM WILL YOU COMPARE ME OR COUNT ME EQUAL? TO WHOM WILL YOU LIKEN ME THAT WE MAY BE COMPARED? 8 "REMEMBER THIS, FIX IT IN MIND, TAKE IT TO HEART, YOU REBELS. 9 REMEMBER THE FORMER THINGS, THOSE OF LONG AGO; I AM GOD, AND THERE IS NO OTHER; I AM GOD, AND THERE IS NONE LIKE ME. 10 I MAKE KNOWN THE END FROM THE BEGINNING (*written in the Zodiac*), FROM ANCIENT TIMES, WHAT IS STILL TO COME. I SAY: MY PURPOSE WILL STAND, AND I WILL DO ALL THAT I PLEASE.

The bottom line is that Yahuah created the stars and the constellations, named them, gave them their meaning, proclaimed the Gospel in them, and will not give that Glory to another. So any use of the Zodiac outside of the Spirit of Yahuah is... sin.

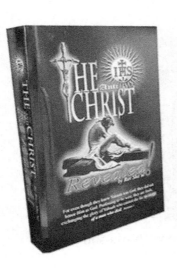

Therein lies the Battle of the Ages, the battleground is the Zodiac, the Heavenly Scroll! Who is the Messiah who fulfills it? Pagan demi-god 'Christs', or Yahusha the Messiah? All pagan 'Christs' were assimilated into one demi-god at the Council of Nicaea named Hesus Horus Krishna. We know this false image today as Jesus H. Christ. The reason Jesus represents the sun rituals of Christmas, Easter, the Trinity, and so forth is because that image is based on the corrupted version of the Zodiac. See my book *The*

286

Antichrist Revealed! For an in depth analysis of this false messianic image.

The Battle of the Ages has come down to Jesus vs. Yahusha; one is the fulfillment of the true message in the Zodiac, the other the twisted version of the Zodiac. Whom do you follow?

Could it be that the reason there are no real prophets left on Earth, like those of the likes of Moses, Jeremiah, Elijah, Daniel, Yahusha, and John the revelator; is because we have denied Yahuah the very basic foundation of all prophecy. The Zodiac? We have turned out back on any form of divination even when it is done seeking counsel from Yahuah like all the aforementioned prophets?

The three-level world of astrology: the twelve mundane houses surrounding the twelve Zodiac signs and the seven planets (seals over the Heavenly Scroll), with the earth at the centre. The entire system is shown to be under God's control... The British Library, C.4.c.9

Chapter 9
Yahusha Fufills Yahuah's Will on Earth as it is written in Heaven

Chapter 9: Yahusha Fufills Yahuah's Will on Earth as it is written in Heaven

HEBREWS 10:7
THEN I SAID, 'HERE I AM—IT IS WRITTEN ABOUT ME IN THE HEAVENLY SCROLL—I HAVE COME TO DO YOUR WILL, MY GOD! (MATTHEW 6:10)

MATTHEW 6:10
YOUR KINGDOM COME, YOUR WILL BE DONE, ON EARTH AS IT IS (WRITTEN) IN (THE) HEAVEN(LY SCROLL).

As I will show, Yahusha's claim to being the Messiah does not depend on the Tanakh or the NT. Rather, solely depends on Yahuah's Witness written into the stars "before the foundation of the world".

EPHESIANS 1:9-10
9 HE MADE KNOWN TO US THE MYSTERY OF HIS WILL ACCORDING TO HIS GOOD PLEASURE, WRITTEN IN THE HEAVENLY SCROLL WHICH HE PURPOSED TO FULFILL IN THE YAHUSHAIC COVENANT (*Daniel 4:35*), 10 TO BE PUT INTO EFFECT WHEN THE AGES REACH THEIR FULFILLMENT (*Age of Aquarius*) —

The stars/constellations are given to all mankind as "signs". The Hebrew word h226 "signs" in *Genesis* 1:14 also means "witness".

289

◀ 226. oth ▶

Strong's Concordance

oth: a sign

Original Word: אוֹת
Part of Speech: Noun Feminine
Transliteration: oth
Phonetic Spelling: (oth)
Definition: a sign

NAS Exhaustive Concordance

Word Origin

from avah

Definition

a sign

NASB Translation

banners (1), omens (1), pledge (1), sign (43), signs (30), standards (1), witness (1), wondrous (1).

We see that the stars/constellations were created by Yahuah and given to all mankind as a witness of His Will:

Deuteronomy 3:19

WHEN YOU LOOK UP TO THE SKY (*sky is Hebrew shamayim/Zodiac*) AND SEE THE SUN, MOON, AND STARS — THE WHOLE HEAVENLY CREATION (*The Heavenly Scroll*)— YOU MUST NOT BE SEDUCED TO WORSHIP AND SERVE THEM (STARS/CONSTELLATIONS), FOR YAHUAH YOUR ELOHIM HAS ASSIGNED THEM (*the signs of the Zodiac*) TO ALL THE PEOPLE OF THE WORLD (*as signs/witness - Genesis* 1:14).

Let's review what His Will is, that Yahusha came to fulfill. There are the 12 major constellations that lie in the path of the Sun. Then there are 36 minor constellations (3 associated with each of the 12 major constellations) that compliment and further define the main 12.

12 Major Constellations: The Plan of Salvation

VIRGO: A virgin will give birth to a beautiful Glorious and Righteous Branch. The seed of the woman will be a man of humiliation to rise to be the desire of nations and will become exalted first as Shepherd then as Harvester. **LIBRA**: The scales demand a price to be paid of this seed, a cross to endure; the victim will be slain and purchase a Crown. **SCORPIO**: There is a conflict between the seed and the serpent leading to a struggle with the enemy, the enemy is vanquished. **SAGITTARIUS**: The double-natured seed (Servant/King) triumphs as a warrior and pleases the heavens, builds fires of punishment, casts down the dragon. **CAPRICORNUS**: Eternal life comes from his death, he's the Arrow of God, he is pierced, yet springs up again in abundant life. **AQUARIUS**: He pours out "Living Water" from on high, humanity drinks of the heavenly river and the Faithful live again, he is the Deliverer of the good news (Gospel), Carrying the Cross over the Earth. **PISCES**: The Redeemer's people multiplied, supported and led by the Lamb, The Bride is exposed on Earth, the Bridegroom is exalted. **ARIES**: The Lamb is found worthy, the Bride is made ready, Satan is bound, the strong man triumphs. **TAURUS**: The conquering Ruler comes, the sublime vanquisher, to execute the great judgment, he is the Ruling Shepherd King. **GEMINI**: The Marriage of the Lamb, the enemy is trodden down, the Prince comes in great Glory. **CANCER**: The great Bride, the two Houses of Judah and Israel are united, they are brought safely into the Kingdom. **LEO**: The Lion King is aroused for rending, the Serpent flees, the Bowl of Wrath is upon him, his Carcass is devoured. The Lion of the Tribe of Judah Rules as King.

36 Minor Constellations (Decans)

A young Maiden mother of an Infant Prince who is both servant and king (**CENTAUR**) and who will grow up to be the Good Shepherd (**BOOTES**). He will pay the price of sin (**LIBRA**/scales) through his suffering (**CRUX**) as a sacrifice in order to win the Crown (**CORONA BOREALIS**). A great Healer who will crush sickness and death (**SCORPION**). He is the Savior (**SAGGITARIUS**, **HERCULES**) who slays the Dragon (**DRACO**), resulting in great rejoicing (**LYRA**). He is also the Goat (**CAPRICORNUS**) sacrificed on the Altar (**ARA**), but then resurrecting (**DELPHINUS**). He is the messenger (**ORION**) of his Father (**AQUILA and SAGITTA**). He is the Master Teacher (**AQUARIUIS**), who pours out knowledge and blessings on his church (**PISCIS AUSTRINUS**), carrying it upward (**PEGASUS**) to someday be glorified (**CYGNUS**). He is the Ram (**ARIES**) who breaks the Bands of Death, and the Hero who looses the chains of hell which bind and shackle both the House of Israel and House of Judah (**PISCES**) to the awful Sea Monster (**CETUS**). The Hero is also the Bridegroom who then marries his Bride (**ANDROMEDA**). He is enthroned as the King (**CEPEUS**) and the glorified Bride becomes his Queen (**CASSIOPEIA**). At the beginning of the Millennium, Yahusha reigns as King (**CEPHEUS**) and King of the Kingdom of Yahuah (**LEO**). As the royal Hunter (**ORION**) he destroys the harlot (**LEPUS**) who has perverted religions and governments worldwide, and he executes judgment on the wicked (**ERIDANUS**). He is the "double-natured seed" (**SAGITTARIUS**) being both the High Priest and King (**GEMINI**). He who comes in power (**ORION**) to destroy the great harlot (**LEPUS**) at the Second Coming (**CANIS MAJOR**) is also he who came in meekness and allowed himself to be slain (**LIBRA**) by her at the First Coming (**CANIS MINOR**). He is the Deliverer (**CANCER**) who leads the dead up out of hell (**ARGO NAVIS**) and delivers his flocks (**URSA MAJOR AND MINOR**). As the millennial King (**LEO**), he permanently overcomes the fleeing Water Serpent (**SERPENDS, OPHICIUS**), who suffers the Cup of the wrath of God (**CRATER**), and whose corpse (**HYDRA**) is eaten by birds of prey (**CORVUS, NOCTUA**).

This is the Will of Yahuah written into the stars, His "Word" or Dabar/Logos which means "Spoken Promise" that Yahusha came to fulfill.

Daniel 4:35
35 "ALL THE INHABITANTS OF THE EARTH ARE ACCOUNTED AS NOTHING, BUT HE DOES ACCORDING TO HIS WILL WRITTEN IN THE HOSTS OF HEAVEN. (*sometimes translated as 'starry hosts' or 'heavenly hosts'. Constellations host stars, so this means 'constellations of The Heavenly Scroll'*)

Psalm 89:2
2 I WILL DECLARE THAT YOUR LOVE STANDS FIRM FOREVER, THAT YOU HAVE ESTABLISHED YOUR FAITHFUL PROMISE (*Dabar/Logos*) OF SALVATION IN THE HEAVENLY SCROLL ITSELF.

Psalm 119:89
89 YOUR WORD (*Dabar/Logos*), YAHUAH, IS ETERNAL; IT STANDS FIRM WRITTEN IN THE HEAVENLY SCROLL.

Psalm 97:6
THE HEAVENLY SCROLL PROCLAIMS HIS RIGHTEOUSNESS, AND ALL THE PEOPLES SEE HIS GLORY (*The stars/constellations declare the Glory of Yahuah and proclaim it day after day, night after night — Psalm 19*).

Psalm 50:3-6
YAHUAH SUMMONS THE HEAVENS ABOVE, AND THE EARTH, THAT HE MAY JUDGE HIS PEOPLE: "GATHER TO ME MY CONSECRATED ONES, WHO MADE A COVENANT WITH ME BY SACRIFICE." AND THE HEAVENS PROCLAIM HIS RIGHTEOUSNESS, FOR GOD HIMSELF IS JUDGE.

Hebrews 10:7
7 THEN I SAID, 'HERE I AM—IT IS WRITTEN ABOUT ME IN THE HEAVENLY SCROLL– I HAVE COME TO DO YOUR WILL, MY ELOHIM! (*Matthew 6:10*)

293

Matthew 6:10
10 YOUR KINGDOM (*DECLARED IN HEAVEN - MATTHEW 4:17*) COME, YOUR WILL BE DONE, ON EARTH AS IT IS WRITTEN IN THE HEAVENLY SCROLL (*Psalm* 19, *Daniel* 4:35).

This is Yahuah's Testimony called "the Word of His Testimony" that Yahusha is the Messiah written into Creation. Fulfilled in The Yahushaic Covenant when His Word was fulfilled in the flesh (the promise was fulfilled when Yahusha was born/created).

Ephesians 1:9-10
9 HE MADE KNOWN TO US THE MYSTERY OF HIS WILL ACCORDING TO HIS GOOD PLEASURE, WRITTEN IN THE HEAVENLY SCROLL WHICH HE PURPOSED TO FULFILL IN THE YAHUSHAIC COVENANT, 10 TO BE PUT INTO EFFECT WHEN THE AGES REACH THEIR FULFILLMENT (*AGE OF AQUARIUS*)

With this knowledge, I will demonstrate why Yahusha is unique in human history to be qualified as The Messiah. Not because of the Tanakh or the NT... but by the Will of the Father alone and the fact Yahusha's life uniquely fulfilled it.

Fulfilled Yahuah's Spoken Promise

The "Word Made Flesh"

The Spirit of the False Messiah makes use of the following out-of-context sound bite to "prove" Yahusha was Yahuah.

John 1:1-2

1 IN THE BEGINNING WAS THE WORD, AND THE WORD WAS WITH GOD, AND THE WORD WAS GOD. 2 HE WAS WITH GOD IN THE BEGINNING.

"The Word was God" ... or "the Spoken Promise exists Divinely Preserved in the Heavens"?

John Chapter 1 has been mistranslated by pagan scribes to incorporate pagan doctrines and philosophies into what John actually wrote. We have been misled to literally blaspheme Yahuah by our English Bibles! We must correct this grave error in translation and restore The Truth. Yahusha was not a pre-existing member of a triune deity, he was not a god, and the Word is not a "person" it is an "it"!

So, let us correct the "Lying Pen of the Scribes" and restore the Truth and "come out of Babylon". Let's begin with John 1:1... Below is the twisted version we find in every modern translation:

John 1:1-2

1 IN THE BEGINNING WAS THE WORD, AND THE WORD WAS WITH GOD, AND THE WORD WAS GOD. 2 HE WAS WITH GOD IN THE BEGINNING.

I am going to prove that is a gross mistranslation of the text, a violation of the rules of the languages, and built on Greek Philosophy not the Hebraic Mindset. Remember, John was written in HEBREW by a Nazarene as I will show. Joun used the word "dabar" not "logos" which means "God's Predestined Plan or Spoken Promise" referring to The Heavenly Scroll, not a pre-existing demi-god! It should read:

John 1:1

IN THE BEGINNING WAS THE SPOKEN PROMISE, AND THE SPOKEN PROMISE WAS WITH YAHUAH (*in The Beginning Gen.* 1:2 *and Yahuah SAID "let there be light"*), AND THE SPOKEN PROMISE EXISTS DIVINELY WRITTEN IN HEAVEN (*in the stars at Creation called The Heavenly Scroll - Psalm* 19, *Psalms* 97:6 , *Psalms* 50:3-6, *and many more*).

I am going to address each word in the phrase "*Word was God*". I will prove it is a mistranslation and twisting of the text under The Spirit of the False Messiah. Used to elevate The Messiah into a Greek demigod in idolatry (see Romans 1). In the following image, I have "*Logos en Theos*" as written in Latin from what John wrote *in Hebrew* (most probably to win the Samaritans as I have shown in this book). I have included screenshots of the meaning of the words "Word was God" in English.

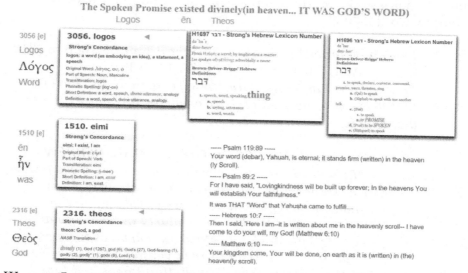

We see *'Logos'* can mean "*divine utterance*". 'Word' in English, Latin, and Hebrew all implies an "it", the spoken word... not a God.

The word *'eimi'* translated "*was*" in the past tense means *'exists'* present tense.

And finally, 'theos' can mean "divinely".

So, which is the proper translation if context of the Scriptures and The Heavenly Scroll is kept in focus? "***Word was God***" or "***Spoken promise exists divinely*** (written in The Heavenly Scroll)"? Is Yahusha literally the "word made flesh" or "the predestined plan written in the stars fulfilled in the flesh"?

The Encyclopedia Judaica admits that the style of most of the writings in The New Testament is, in fact, Hebraic. The Greek versions we have today of The New Testament are later Hellenized versions translated from earlier Hebrew original versions that were most likely burned after the council of Nicea. So "logos" is a mistranslation; the original version of John Chapter 1 used the Hebrew word debar

> *The Encyclopedia Judaica, Volume* 12, *page* 1060 in THE LANGUAGE OF THE NEW TESTAMENT.
> *Although the language of the New Testament, in the form that it exists today, is Greek, two earlier influences are still discernible.*
>
> > (1) *THE INFLUENCE OF THE ARAMAIC-HEBREW ORIGINALS. Because most of the authors were Jewish Nazarenes, they spoke, for the most part, Aramaic, and some also mishnaic Hebrew. This influence, which was detectable particularly in the original versions of Mark and Matthew, survives to some degree in their extant Greek versions and in several of the Epistles as well, including James and Jude.*
> > (2) *THE SEPTUAGINT.*
> >
> > *Since this translation was used by many authors, the New Testament contains not only Aramaic words and phrases, which the disciples heard from Jesus and took care to remember out of reverence for their master (e.g. Talitha Kumi (Mark 5:41), Kum, Rabboni, Eli, Eli (Elohi, Elohi) lama sabachthani (Matt. 27:46; Mark 15:24)), but also expressions and phrases which retain their Hebrew flavor although they were transmitted through the Greek translation of the Hebrew Bible.*

John wrote under the inspiration of Yahuah, not of a pre-existent God-savior, but of the wonderful Plan of Yahuah which is what the Hebrew word debar implies. The Anchor Bible shows us from the Talmud that seven things were in Yahuah's mind showing us what the Hebraic mindset was. His Plan was from the beginning and this plan included the Savior. This is the mindset of John Chapter 1 not the pagan philosophy of "Logos":

> **The Anchor Bible**, **Ephesians** 1-3, **page** 111
> *IN THE TALMUD tractate Pesachim 54a; cf. Nedarim 39b, seven things, i.e. the law, repentance, paradise, Gehinnom, the throne of glory, the heavenly sanctuary, and the messiah are not called pre-created, but pre-conceived in (Yahuah's) thoughts.*

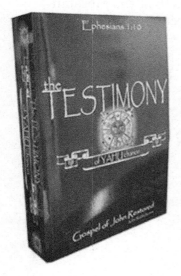

For a detailed breakdown of the Gospel of John and how it has been manipulated into a complete "lie" today, see my book **The Testimony of Yahuchanan**.

Fulfilled the Passover Lamb
End of the Age of Aries

The sacrifice of a lamb on Passover was an "annual reminder" of when the Messiah would come to pay the dowry for his bride. The Age of Aries is symbolized by the lamb. It is when the Age of Aries ends or "the lamb dies" laid out in The Heavenly Scroll that the Messiah is foretold to come. We see the birth of the Messiah foretold by the constellation Virgo intersect with the cusp of Aries and Pisces.

Birth of Messiah foretold in The Heavenly Scroll

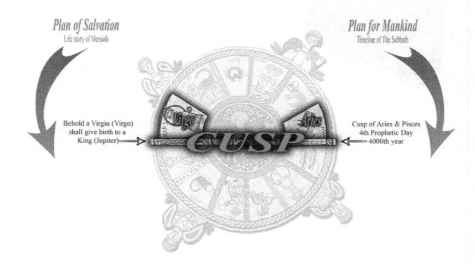

Plan of Salvation
Life story of Messiah

Plan for Mankind
Timeline of The Sabbath

Behold a Virgin (Virgo) shall give birth to a King (Jupiter)⟶

Cusp of Aries & Pisces
4th Prophetic Day
⟵ 4000th year

https://en.wikipedia.org/wiki/Astrological_age

> *"Drummond makes his case that at the time of Abraham, the Amorites first recorded the shift from the Age of Taurus to the Age of Aries as represented by the year commencing with the Ram (Aries) rather than the bull (Taurus).* **The feast of the Passover is probably a celebration of the Age of Aries with the Paschal Lamb representative of Aries, traditionally associated with the symbol of the ram or sheep.**"

In Hebrews we read:

HEBREWS 10

1 THE LAW IS ONLY A SHADOW (*physical example/rehearsal*) OF THE GOOD THINGS THAT ARE COMING (*The Spiritual Kingdom of Yahuah*)—NOT THE (*spiritual*) REALITIES THEMSELVES. FOR THIS REASON, IT (*the physical examples/rehearsals in The Law*) CAN NEVER, <u>BY THE SAME (*physical*) SACRIFICES (*of a lamb*) REPEATED ENDLESSLY YEAR AFTER YEAR</u>, MAKE PERFECT THOSE WHO DRAW NEAR TO WORSHIP. 2 OTHERWISE, WOULD THEY (*physical sacrifices*) NOT HAVE STOPPED BEING OFFERED? FOR THE WORSHIPERS WOULD HAVE BEEN CLEANSED ONCE FOR ALL, AND WOULD NO LONGER HAVE FELT GUILTY FOR THEIR SINS. 3 BUT THOSE SACRIFICES ARE **AN ANNUAL REMINDER OF SINS**. 4 IT IS IMPOSSIBLE FOR THE BLOOD OF BULLS AND GOATS TO TAKE AWAY SINS (*they were rehearsals*). 5 THEREFORE, WHEN THE MESSIAH CAME INTO THE WORLD (*to fulfill Passover*), YAHUSHA SAID: "SACRIFICE AND OFFERING YOU DID NOT DESIRE, BUT A (*sinful*) BODY YOU PREPARED FOR ME; 6 WITH (*physical*) BURNT OFFERINGS AND SIN OFFERINGS YOU WERE NOT PLEASED. 7 THEN I SAID, 'HERE I AM—IT IS WRITTEN ABOUT ME IN THE (*HEAVENLY*) SCROLL (*as a lamb that was slaughtered before the foundation of the world **Revelation 13:8**)* — I HAVE COME (*as the suffering servant*) TO DO YOUR WILL (*to die at the end of the age of aries to fulfill the meaning of the passover lamb*), <u>MY GOD</u>.'"

Lamb Slaughtered / Age of Aries Ends

before the world was... portrayed as crucified in The Heavenly Scroll

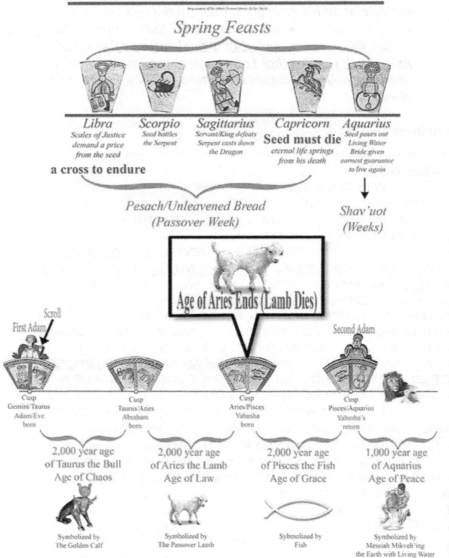

Spring Feasts

Libra	Scorpio	Sagittarius	Capricorn	Aquarius
Scales of Justice demand a price from the seed	Seed battles the Serpent	Servant/King defeats Serpent casts down the Dragon	**Seed must die** eternal life springs from his death	Seed pours out Living Water Bride given earnest guarantee to live again

a cross to endure

Pesach/Unleavened Bread (Passover Week)

Shav'uot (Weeks)

Age of Aries Ends (Lamb Dies)

Scroll
First Adam

Second Adam

Cusp Gemini/Taurus Adam/Eve born	Cusp Taurus/Aries Abraham born	Cusp Aries/Pisces Yahusha born	Cusp Pisces/Aquarius Yahusha's return
2,000 year age of Taurus the Bull Age of Chaos	2,000 year age of Aries the Lamb Age of Law	2,000 year age of Pisces the Fish Age of Grace	1,000 year age of Aquarius Age of Peace
Symbolized by The Golden Calf	Symbolized by The Passover Lamb	Symbolized by Fish	Symbolized by Messiah Mikveh'ing the Earth with Living Water

Fulfilled the Feast Cycle
The Divine Love Story

Each year, The Plan of Salvation is rehearsed through the Spring and Fall Feasts. That Plan of Salvation was originally written into the stars at creation called The Heavenly Scroll. It was in that Heavenly Scroll that Yahuah gave Glory to Yahusha before the world was.

In that scroll Yahuah promised that Yahusha would be a Bridegroom and would pay the dowry for his Bride with his life. He would be resurrected into eternal life and salvation would be through a marriage covenant. Yahusha would be crowned eternal King, and his Bride would be Queen and together they would rule Creation.

That glory (in The Heavenly Scroll) was then further elaborated in The Spring and Fall Feasts in greater detail, as The Heavenly Wedding (Plan of Salvation) would be rehearsed and fulfilled.

Isaiah 49:18
LIFT UP YOUR EYES AND BEHOLD (*The Heavenly Scroll*); ALL YOUR CHILDREN GATHER AND COME TO YOU. AS SURELY AS I LIVE," DECLARES YAHUAH, "YOU WILL WEAR THEM (*the constellations*) ALL AS ORNAMENTS; YOU WILL PUT THEM (*the stars*) ON, **LIKE A BRIDE**.

Psalm 19:1-6
1 THE HEAVENLY SCROLL (*Shamayim - stars, Sun, and constellations*) ARE TELLING OF THE GLORY (*which is Yahusha Hebrews* 1:3) OF ELOHIM; AND THEIR EXPANSE IS DECLARING THE WORK OF HIS HANDS. 2 DAY TO DAY THE HEAVENLY SCROLL POURS FORTH SPEECH, AND NIGHT TO NIGHT THE SUN/STARS/CONSTELLATIONS REVEAL KNOWLEDGE. 3 THERE IS NO SPEECH, NOR ARE THERE WORDS; THEIR VOICE IS NOT HEARD. 4

THEIR LINE HAS GONE OUT THROUGH ALL THE EARTH, AND THEIR UTTERANCES TO THE END OF THE WORLD. IN THE STARS/CONSTELLATIONS YAHUAH HAS PLACED A TABERNACLE FOR THE SUN, 5 WHICH (*THE SUN*) IS **AS A BRIDEGROOM** COMING OUT OF HIS CHAMBER (*to marry the Bride - John* 3:29); IT REJOICES AS A STRONG MAN TO RUN HIS COURSE (*of a wedding as the Groom... the feast Cycle/The Heavenly wedding*).

The Spring Feasts celebrate the courtship and engagement, while the Fall Feasts celebrate the Wedding and following banquet. For more on The Heavenly Wedding, see my book ***The Fall Feasts: An Invitation to the Wedding Banquet.***

Fulfilled the Suffering Servant and Conquering King

The Messiah is represented in The Heavenly Scroll to die first and suffer; to earn the right to reign as King. The prophets understood this and represented the Messiah in Scripture as a double-natured servant/king. These prophecies are known as The Messiah ben Joseph (The Suffering Servant) and The Messiah ben David (The Conquering King). The Spring Feast gives us the role of Messiah ben Joseph, as the Messiah must suffer and die for the forgiveness of sin. Then the Messiah is raised from the dead, granted eternal life, and returns as Conquering King (Messiah ben David) which is foretold in the Fall Feasts.

The Jews lost sight of The Heavenly Scroll which dictates the order the Messiah must fulfill in the Plan of Salvation. He MUST come first as "shepherd" and die, then as "harvester" to gather into one the two houses and rule as King (Leo). Being weary after spending over 500 years in captivity, Israel simply did not want to submit to The Plan of Salvation, therefore, denying Yahusha as the Messiah because he did not come as their "King" first. He came to fulfill The Heavenly Scroll... not their selfish desires.

We see Yahusha refer to The Heavenly Scroll and the role of The Son of Man (the constellation Orion which represents The Coming of The Branch in the stars):

Matthew 20:28
"28 JUST AS THE SON OF MAN DID NOT COME TO BE SERVED (*as King*), BUT TO SERVE (*as the Suffering Servant*), AND TO GIVE HIS LIFE AS A RANSOM FOR MANY (*pay the dowry for his Bride*)."

Yahusha was well aware that he was the Fulfillment of The Plan of Salvation written in The Heavenly Scroll and what that Scroll declares about his life and purpose. In The Heavenly Scroll, The Son of Man/Branch was foretold that he would battle the serpent and that his death would result in Eternal Life. He would come first as Shepherd, then Harvester. The last constellation that must be Fulfilled is that he would defeat the Dragon and Rule as The Lion of the Tribe of Judah.

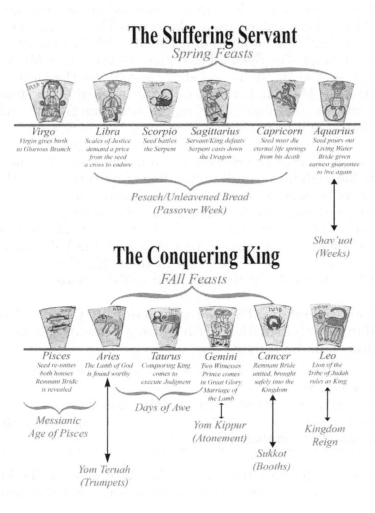

The Suffering Servant
Spring Feasts

Virgo	Libra	Scorpio	Sagittarius	Capricorn	Aquarius
Virgin gives birth to Glorious Branch	*Scales of Justice demand a price from the seed a cross to endure*	*Seed battles the Serpent*	*Servant/King defeats Serpent casts down the Dragon*	*Seed must die eternal life springs from his death*	*Seed pours out Living Water Bride given earnest guarantee to live again*

Pesach/Unleavened Bread
(Passover Week)

Shav'uot
(Weeks)

The Conquering King
FAll Feasts

Pisces	Aries	Taurus	Gemini	Cancer	Leo
Seed re-unites both houses Remnant Bride is revealed	*The Lamb of God is found worthy*	*Conquering King comes to execute Judgment*	*Two Witnesses Prince comes in Great Glory Marriage of the Lamb*	*Remnant Bride united, brought safely into the Kingdom*	*Lion of the Tribe of Judah rules as King*

Messianic Age of Pisces

Days of Awe

Yom Kippur
(Atonement)

Kingdom Reign

Yom Teruah
(Trumpets)

Sukkot
(Booths)

306

Chapter 10
Yahusha the Mechi Tsedek

Chapter 10: Introduction

In this last chapter, I will show how the Messiah must fulfill The Heavenly Scroll. Also, I will show that Yahusha stands alone in history to:

- *Restore the Fallen Priesthood - Line of Zadok.*
- *Restore the Fallen Throne of David.*
- *Fulfill the Light to the Nations - Showed us The Way.*
- *Worthy to Read the Secrets Contained in The Heavenly Scroll.*

The proof that Yahusha is the Messiah does not depend on what is written in what we call the New Testament. It is in his "blood" and written in the stars!

The Messiah Must Genetically Restore the Throne and Priesthood

The false doctrine that Jesus is the incarnate God born outside of the seed of Joseph alone disqualifies "Jesus Christ" from being the true Messiah. The true Messiah was foretold by the prophets of Yahuah as the one who would restore the Throne of David being a direct blood descendant of David through Solomon. That bloodline runs through Yahusha's father Joseph! But that is outside the scope of this book.

The throne is not passed to "stepchildren" it is passed to the firstborn son by blood. It is that bloodline that is the witness of Yahuah and the testimony that Yahusha is the Messiah... BLOOD.

Let's take a look at the prophecies Yahusha must fulfill by blood to be the Messiah concerning the Throne of David. Below we see that Yahuah prophesied a "righteous branch" that would restore both the Throne of David and the Priesthood of Aaron and the Levites within the context of The New Covenant:

Jeremiah 33

14 'BEHOLD, THE DAYS ARE COMING,' SAYS YAHUAH, 'THAT I WILL PERFORM THAT GOOD THING WHICH I HAVE PROMISED TO THE HOUSE OF ISRAEL AND TO THE HOUSE OF JUDAH (REFERRING TO THE YAHUSHAIC COVENANT SEE JEREMIAH 31 WHERE THE LAW WOULD BE WRITTEN ON OUR HEARTS): 15 'IN THOSE DAYS AND AT THAT TIME I WILL CAUSE TO GROW UP (in the bloodline) TO DAVID A BRANCH OF RIGHTEOUSNESS (VIRGO); HE SHALL EXECUTE JUDGMENT AND RIGHTEOUSNESS IN THE EARTH (Leo). 16 IN THOSE DAYS JUDAH WILL BE SAVED, AND JERUSALEM WILL DWELL SAFELY. AND THIS IS THE NAME BY WHICH HE WILL BE CALLED: YAHUAH OUR RIGHTEOUSNESS... 17 "FOR THUS SAYS YAHUAH: 'DAVID SHALL NEVER LACK A MAN TO SIT ON THE THRONE OF THE HOUSE OF

ISRAEL; 18 NOR SHALL THE PRIESTS, THE LEVITES, LACK A MAN TO OFFER BURNT OFFERINGS BEFORE ME, TO KINDLE GRAIN OFFERINGS, AND TO SACRIFICE CONTINUALLY.'"

Now consider a much-misunderstood passage of prophecy. If you begin reading the 18th verse of the 21st chapter of Ezekiel, you will see plainly that Yahuah is speaking of the captivity of Judah by the king of Babylon.

And, beginning in the 25th verse, He says:

Ezekiel 21:25-27

"AND THOU PROFANE WICKED PRINCE OF ISRAEL, WHOSE DAY IS COME, WHEN INIQUITY SHALL HAVE AN END, THUS SAITH YAHUAH YOUR GOD; REMOVE THE DIADEM, AND TAKE OFF THE CROWN (*as did happen, through the first half of Jeremiah's commission*): THIS [*the crown*] SHALL NOT BE THE SAME: EXALT HIM THAT IS LOW, AND ABASE HIM THAT IS HIGH. I WILL OVERTURN, OVERTURN, OVERTURN, IT: AND IT SHALL BE NO MORE, UNTIL HE COMES WHOSE RIGHT IT IS; AND I WILL GIVE IT TO HIM." (*this a reference to the Messiah who would RESTORE the Kingly Line*)

This prophecy, in fact, predicts the interruption of the Throne of David reflected in Amos 9: 11-12 and Acts 15: 16-18.

Ezekiel 21: 27

"TAKE OFF THE CROWN...A RUIN, RUIN, RUIN I WILL MAKE IT; THERE SHALL NOT BE A TRACE OF IT *until he comes whose right is; and to him will I give it*"

Amos prophesies what will happen when the Messiah returns:

Amos 9: 11-12

"ON THAT DAY (*at the return of the Messiah*) I WILL RAISE UP THE HOUSE OF DAVID (*the bloodline of David*), WHICH HAS FALLEN

310

DOWN, AND REPAIR ITS DAMAGES; I WILL RAISE UP ITS RUINS, AND REBUILD IT AS IN THE DAYS OF OLD; THAT THEY MAY POSSESS THE REMNANT OF EDOM, AND ALL THE GENTILES WHO ARE CALLED BY MY NAME," SAYS YAHUAH WHO DOES THIS THING.

Simon declared the prophecy in Amos to those in Jerusalem in Acts 15: 16-18. Jeremiah repeats this prophecy concerning Remnant Israel in Jeremiah 23:5-6.

If Yahusha is the true Messiah then he would by blood witness of Yahuah fulfill these prophecies and restore both the Throne of David and the priesthood by his bloodline. Yahusha was anointed King of Israel and High Priest of Israel directly by Yahuah when he fled into the wilderness after being Mikveh'd by John.

311

Restored the Fallen Priesthood

Below is an excerpt from my book *Melchizedek and the Passover Lamb*.

The Zadok Priesthood established itself in the time that King David fought against the revolt of his son Absalom. Zadok was a Levite High Priest, having descended down from Aaron, through Eleazar. Only descendants of Aaron through Eleazar could be High Priests. The entire tribe of Levi was chosen to be Temple Priests but not all could be High Priests.

As the Dead Sea Scrolls indicate, Zadokites were "to be as one in following the Law and (sharing) wealth and reconciling (based on) the mouth of the sons of Zadok the keepers of the covenant." You can learn more about the line of priests descending from Zadok here: http://en.wikipedia.org/wiki/Zadok

The Hebrew Bible records how, before his death, Aaron was accompanied by his brother Moses and his sons Eleazar and Ithamar. Upon entry to the cave where he was to die, Aaron saw his brother Moses dress his elder son, Eleazar, with the garments of the High Priest. Moses anointed Eleazar the successor to Aaron as High Priest of Israel. Jewish commentaries on the Bible say that this initiation ceremony served as the catalyst for the stipulation that all future candidates of High Priesthood be patrilineal descendants of Eleazar the elder son of Aaron and not Ithamar, the younger son.

This is the line that flows through Zadok the High Priest who served David and Solomon. This is the blood lineage that flowed

312

through the veins of both John the Baptist and Yahusha the Messiah.

Zadok was a patrilineal descendant of Eleazar, the son of Aaron, the High Priest (2 Samuel 8:17; 1 Chronicles 24:3). The lineage of Zadok is presented in the genealogy of Ezra (his descendant) as being of ninth generation and direct patrilineal descent from Phineas the son of Eleazar; Ezra 7:1:

Ezra 7:1-4
...ZADOK, THE SON OF AHITUB, SON OF AMARYAH, SON OF AZARYAH, SON OF MIRAYOTH, SON OF ZERACHYAH, SON OF UZZI, SON OF BUKKI, SON OF AVISHUA, SON OF PHINEAS..

Similarly, the Hebrew Bible relates how at the time Phineas son of Eleazar appeased Yahuah's anger, he merited the Divine blessing of Yahuah that his descendant would inherit the promises of the Eternal High Priesthood:

Numbers 25:13
PHINEAS THE SON OF ELEAZAR THE SON OF AARON THE PRIEST. BEHOLD I GIVE TO HIM MY COVENANT OF PEACE, AND WILL BE HIS, AND HIS PROGENY AFTER HIM, COVENANT OF EVERLASTING PRIESTHOOD IN TURN OF HIS ZEALOUSNESS FOR HIS ELOHIM, AND HE ATONED FOR THE SONS OF ISRAEL.

This is extremely important when tracing the right of Yahusha to be the Eternal High Priest. Yahusha must have come from the lineage of Zadok which is the bloodline of High Priest prepared for him and to which is entrusted the "Covenant of Peace, Covenant of Eternal High Priest, and the right to Atone for sin" as defined in Numbers 25:13 above. It is the convergence of the bloodline of David through Solomon and The House of Zadok that resulted in the "Ruling Zadok" or Melchizedek.

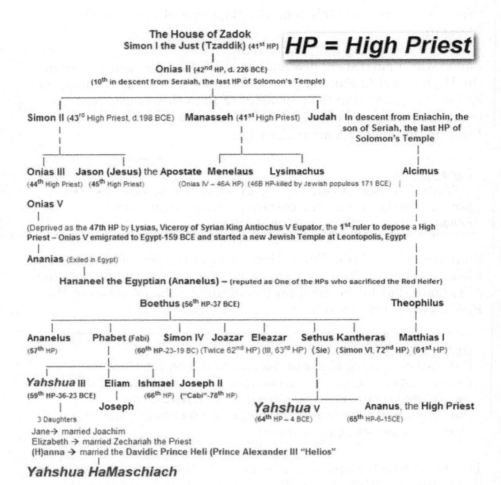

The House of Zadok
Simon I the Just (Tzaddik) (41st HP)

HP = High Priest

Onias II (42nd HP, d. 226 BCE)
(10th in descent from Seraiah, the last HP of Solomon's Temple)

Simon II (43rd High Priest, d. 198 BCE)   **Manasseh** (41st High Priest)   **Judah**   In descent from Eniachin, the son of Seriah, the last HP of Solomon's Temple

Onias III   **Jason (Jesus) the Apostate**   **Menelaus**   **Lysimachus**   **Alcimus**
(44th High Priest)   (45th High Priest)   (Onias IV – 46A HP)   (46B HP-killed by Jewish populous 171 BCE)

Onias V

(Deprived as the 47th HP by Lysias, Viceroy of Syrian King Antiochus V Eupator, the 1st ruler to depose a High Priest – Onias V emigrated to Egypt-159 BCE and started a new Jewish Temple at Leontopolis, Egypt

Ananias (Exiled in Egypt)

Hananeel the Egyptian (Ananelus) – (reputed as One of the HPs who sacrificed the Red Heifer)

Boethus (56th HP-37 BCE)   **Theophilus**

Ananelus   **Phabet** (Fabi)   **Simon IV**   **Joazar**   **Eleazar**   **Sethus**   **Kantheras**   **Matthias I**
(57th HP)   (60th HP-23-19 BC) (Twice 62nd HP) (III, 63rd HP) (Sie) (Simon VI, 72nd HP) (61st HP)

Yahshua III   **Eliam**   **Ishmael**   **Joseph II**
(59th HP-36-23 BCE)   (66th HP) ("Cabi"-78th HP)   **Yahshua V**   **Ananus, the High Priest**
Joseph   (64th HP – 4 BCE)   (65th HP-6-15CE)

3 Daughters
Jane→ married Joachim
Elizabeth → married Zechariah the Priest
(H)anna → married the Davidic Prince Heli (Prince Alexander III "Helios"

Yahshua HaMaschiach

Restored the Fallen Throne of David through Solomon

Yahusha was the descendant and heir to the Throne of David by blood through Joseph's bloodline. Yahusha was heir to the office of High Priest being the great-grandson (through Mary's maternal line) of the High Priest over the rebuilding of the Second Temple Yahusha III.

So by blood Yahusha fulfilled the requirements that the Messiah would restore the priesthood and the throne of David. Yahusha is the Messiah by the witness of Yahuah as he fulfilled the prophets who foretold of Yahusha.

The Throne of David had to be restored because it fell into judgment for kings who committed idolatry against Yahuah. This is the reason there is an extended period when no man has sat on the Throne of David as King. The prophets foretold of a human Messiah (Messiah means anointed King of Israel) that would come and restore the Throne of David from its fallen state as well as restore the priesthood of Aaron and Levi that had fallen into idolatry.

It is clear that Yahuah brought judgment on the Kingly Line of David and cast it to the ground. It is even clearer, through prophecy of the coming Messiah, that Yahuah would restore that Kingly Line of David/Solomon and re-establish the priesthood.

Yahuah's promise to David was eternal to be fulfilled by the Messiah. However, that promise was conditional to every other king who sat on that throne. Later King's rebelled and Yahuah, while keeping the eternal promise alive to David, disciplined the Kings and Israel for rebellion.

We see the big "IF" below as these promises were conditional to every king:

I *Kings* 8:25

NOW YAHUAH, GOD OF ISRAEL, KEEP FOR YOUR SERVANT DAVID MY FATHER THE PROMISES YOU MADE TO HIM WHEN YOU SAID, 'YOU SHALL NEVER FAIL TO HAVE A MAN TO SIT BEFORE ME ON THE THRONE OF ISRAEL, **IF** ONLY YOUR SONS ARE CAREFUL IN ALL THEY DO TO WALK BEFORE ME AS YOU HAVE DONE!'

In other words, Yahuah made it clear that there would be discipline and the throne would be suspended if all the Kingly Line were not obedient to His Law and governed righteously as David had done.

I *Kings* 9:4-7

4 "NOW, **IF** YOU WALK BEFORE ME AS YOUR FATHER DAVID WALKED, IN INTEGRITY OF HEART AND IN UPRIGHTNESS, TO DO ACCORDING TO ALL THAT I HAVE COMMANDED YOU, AND **IF** YOU KEEP MY STATUES AND MY JUDGMENTS, **THEN** I WILL ESTABLISH THE THRONE OF YOUR KINGDOM OVER ISRAEL FOREVER, AS I PROMISED DAVID YOUR FATHER, SAYING, 'YOU SHALL NOT FAIL TO HAVE A MAN ON THE THRONE OF ISRAEL.' **BUT** IF YOU OR YOUR SONS AT ALL TURN FROM FOLLOWING ME, AND DO **NOT** KEEP MY COMMANDMENTS AND MY STATUTES WHICH I HAVE SET BEFORE YOU, BUT GO AND SERVE OTHER GODS AND WORSHIP THEM, **THEN I WILL CUT OFF ISRAEL FROM THE LAND** WHICH I HAVE GIVEN THEM; AND THIS HOUSE [OF DAVID] WHICH I HAVE SANCTIFIED FOR MY NAME I WILL CAST OUT OF MY SIGHT. ISRAEL WILL BE A PROVERB AND A BYWORD AMONG ALL PEOPLES."

This is exactly what happened, the Kings rebelled and followed after other gods, and did not exercise righteous judgment. The Throne of David ceased when Yahuah cursed King Coniah and his sons, and the Throne of David was thrown to the ground because the King did not obey the Law of Yahuah. Coniah was dethroned by the King of Babylon, as prophesied by Jeremiah, and the House of Judah was sent into Babylonian Captivity:

Jeremiah 22:5; 24; 28-30

5 BUT IF YOU WILL NOT HEAR THESE WORDS, I SWEAR BY MYSELF," SAYS YAHUAH, "THAT THIS HOUSE SHALL BECOME A DESOLATION." ... 24 "AS I LIVE," SAYS YAHUAH, "THOUGH CONIAH THE SON OF JEHOIAKIM, KING OF JUDAH, WERE THE SIGNET ON MY RIGHT HAND, YET I WOULD PLUCK YOU OFF... 28 "IS THIS MAN CONIAH A DESPISED, BROKEN IDOL—A VESSEL IN WHICH IS NO PLEASURE? WHY ARE THEY CAST OUT, HE AND HIS DESCENDANTS, AND CAST INTO A LAND WHICH THEY DO NOT KNOW? 29 O EARTH, EARTH, EARTH, HEAR THE WORD OF YAHUAH! 30 THUS SAYS YAHUAH: 'WRITE THIS MAN *(Coniah specifically)* DOWN AS CHILDLESS, A MAN WHO SHALL NOT PROSPER IN HIS DAYS; FOR NONE OF HIS *(direct)* DESCENDANTS SHALL PROSPER, SITTING ON THE THRONE OF DAVID, AND RULING ANYMORE IN JUDAH.'"

King Coniah sat on the throne of David for 3 months before Yahuah fulfilled His Word through Jeremiah and dethroned him and sent him and the Southern Kingdom of Judah (the House of Judah) into Babylonian Captivity. No descendent of David has ever ascended the throne after that... until Yahusha that is.

Fulfilled the Light to the Nations

Matthew 4:16-17

THE PEOPLE LIVING IN DARKNESS (*following The Way of the Gentiles, the corrupted Zodiac - Romans* 1) HAVE SEEN A GREAT LIGHT (*as 'the Sun has come to us from The Heavenly Scroll' to show us The Way/Doctrine of Righteousness of Mikveh, Circumcision, and Offering Luke* 1:77-78, *Malachi* 4:2); ON THOSE LIVING IN THE LAND OF (*THE GENTILES WHO LIVE IIN*) THE SHADOW OF DEATH. 'I WILL MAKE YOU A COVENANT TO THE NATIONS, I WILL ALSO GIVE YOU FOR A LIGHT, (*fulfillment of The Light of the Sun, to the Gentiles' - Isaiah* 42:7-9), A LIGHT HAS DAWNED (*been fulfilled on Earth in the flesh John* 1:1-4, *Luke* 1:77-79).17 FROM THAT TIME ON YAHUSHA BEGAN TO TEACH THE WAY OF MIKVEH, CIRCUMCISION, AND OFFERING SAYING, REPENT (*Circumcision of Heart*) AND BE MIKVEH'D (*washed clean of your sin - Jeremiah* 31 *and Ezekiel* 36), FOR THE KINGDOM PROCLAIMED IN THE HEAVENLY SCROLL IS WITHIN YOUR REACH (*he has come to fulfill it*).

Below is an excerpt from **The Witness of the Stars... by E. W. Bullinger**:

The constellation ORION is mentioned by name, as being perfectly well known both by name and appearance, in the time of Job; and as being an object of familiar knowledge at that early period of the world's history. See Job 9:9; 38:31, and Amos 5:8 (Heb. Chesil, which means a strong one, a hero, or a giant).

Thus beautifully is set forth the brilliancy and glory of that Light which shall break forth when the moment comes for it to be said, "Arise, shine, for thy light is come." The picture presents us with "the Light of the world."

318

John 1-10
THE HEAVENLY SCROLL IS "THE TRUE LIGHT THAT ENLIGHTENS ALL MANKIND"

Yahuah's Plan/debar or "Purpose" is called "the Light" in Psalm 119:105. The Light in Genesis 1:1, is "The Plan of Salvation" (the Word of Yahuah that became flesh, the Debar written in the stars on day 4) by which Yahuah accomplished everything in the final 7th covenant (The Yahushaic Covenant - **Ephesians** 1:9-10).

After creating the Light "in the beginning" Yahuah grouped the sun/moon/stars on Day 4 and wrote the "Plan of Salvation" into the signs or constellations, called The Heavenly Scroll. The Heavenly Scroll then became the "Light of the World" literally, as a physical-to-spiritual parallel that foretells of the coming Messiah (Psalm 19).

Yahusha said "I am the Light of the World" because he was the Fulfillment of that Plan/debar and the sun was a metaphor for the coming Messiah as David Proclaims in Psalm 19. The Yahushaic Covenant is the shadow cast by The Heavenly Scroll.

Worthy to Read the Secrets Contained in The Heavenly Scroll

Excerpt from my book Creation Cries Out! The Mazzaroth:

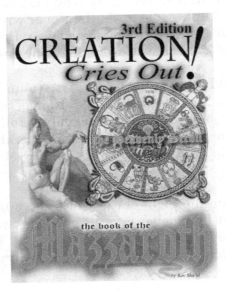

Note: See my video on this topic: https://youtu.be/3HQfqIuQ_rs

It is Yahuah who prophesied the end from the beginning, writing His Plan of Salvation in the stars in the Heavenly Scroll we call the Zodiac.

Isaiah 46

I AM ELOHIM, AND THERE IS NO OTHER; I AM ELOHIM, AND THERE IS NONE LIKE ME. 10 I MAKE KNOWN THE END FROM THE BEGINNING, FROM ANCIENT TIMES (*the foundation of the world*), WHAT IS STILL TO COME. I SAY: MY PURPOSE (*proclaimed in The Heavenly Scroll*) WILL STAND, AND I WILL DO ALL THAT I PLEASE.

Ephesians 1:9-10

9 HE MADE KNOWN TO US THE MYSTERY OF HIS WILL ACCORDING TO HIS GOOD PLEASURE, WRITTEN IN THE HEAVENLY SCROLL WHICH HE PURPOSED TO FULFILL IN THE YAHUSHAIC COVENANT (*Daniel 4:35*), 10 TO BE PUT INTO EFFECT WHEN THE AGES REACH THEIR FULFILLMENT (*Age of Aquarius - fulfillment of The Sabbath Covenant*)

His instructions for Earth, i.e. Plan of Salvation and Divine Clock are securely written in the Heavenly Scroll, safe from human hands.

Psalm 119:89

O YAHUAH, YOUR INSTRUCTIONS ENDURE; THEY STAND SECURE WRITTEN IN THE HEAVENLY SCROLL.

Yahusha prayed the will of Yahuah be done on Earth as it laid out in the Heavenly Scroll of the Mazzaroth/Zodiac.

Matthew 6:10

YOUR KINGDOM (*proclaimed in the heavenly scroll*) COME, YOUR WILL BE DONE, ON EARTH AS IT IS WRITTEN IN THE STARS.

We see that once the Heavenly Scroll is fulfilled, that the "heavens open up like a scroll" as the Book of the Mazzaroth is opened. The "starry hosts" or signs of the Zodiac "fall" at the feat of the one found worthy to open the Heavenly Scroll as they are fulfilled.

Revelation 6:14

THE HEAVENS (*stars/constellations*) RECEDED LIKE A SCROLL BEING ROLLED UP

Isaiah 34:4

ALL THE STARS IN THE SKY WILL BE DISSOLVED AND THE HEAVENS (*stars/constellations*) ROLLED UP LIKE A SCROLL; ALL THE STARRY

HOST (CONSTELLATIONS) WILL FALL *(before the one who fulfills them)*

It is only after Yahusha fulfills the final Zodiac Sign of Leo and conquers the dragon, that the Lion of the Tribe of Judah is revealed. Having fulfilled The Heavenly Scroll, he is found to be the only one worthy to open it, and read it publicly to proclaim that he was chosen by Yahuah from the foundation of the World.

The "heavenly scroll' is that witness to confirm that he alone is the Messiah. The proof of this is not found in the Tanakh or NT, but by fulfilling The Heavenly Scroll:

Revelation 5

5 THEN I SAW, IN THE RIGHT HAND OF THE ONE WHO WAS SEATED ON THE THRONE *(over the Kingdom that governs Creation, Yahusha)*, A SCROLL WRITTEN ON THE FRONT AND BACK *(3-D scroll of the Zodiac signs along the ecliptic plane)* AND SEALED WITH SEVEN SEALS *(the 7 visible planets from Earth, seen as seals over the scroll)*. 2 AND I SAW A POWERFUL ANGEL PROCLAIMING IN A LOUD VOICE: "WHO IS WORTHY TO OPEN THE SCROLL AND TO BREAK ITS SEALS?" 3 BUT NO ONE IN HEAVEN OR ON EARTH OR UNDER THE EARTH WAS ABLE TO OPEN THE SCROLL OR LOOK INTO IT. 4 So I BEGAN WEEPING BITTERLY BECAUSE NO ONE WAS FOUND WHO WAS WORTHY TO OPEN THE SCROLL OR TO LOOK INTO IT. 5 THEN ONE OF THE ELDERS SAID TO ME, "**Stop weeping**! **Look, the Lion of the tribe of Judah** *(Yahusha fulfills the sign of Leo; completing the Heavenly Scroll)*, **the root of David, has conquered** *(the dragon, the meaning of the sign of LEO)*; **thus** *(because only he has fulfilled the meaning of the scroll)* **he can open the scroll and its seven seals**."

The contents of the Heavenly Scroll or book of the Mazzaroth is held secret, revealed through the Ruach (Spirit) to His chosen prophets.

Matthew 13:11

HE REPLIED, "BECAUSE THE KNOWLEDGE OF THE SECRETS OF THE KINGDOM OF HEAVEN (*the Zodiac or Heavenly Scroll*) HAS BEEN GIVEN TO YOU, BUT NOT TO THEM

Conclusion

When seeking Yahuah's Word, do we seek Truth in the written texts or seek "DIVINe revelATION" from Creation? Both!

The Lying Pen of the Scribe, as laid out in this book, can only be overcome when the written Scriptures are translated in light of their source... The Heavenly Scroll. In like manner, The Heavenly Scroll is further defined by the prophets in the Tanakh and New Testament.

The Heavenly Scroll is the source and means by which Yahuah communicated with His Prophets. It is the source of the life of the Messiah and the standard by which the Messiah is identified and justified.

DANIEL 4:35
"ALL THE INHABITANTS OF THE EARTH ARE ACCOUNTED AS NOTHING, BUT HE DOES ACCORDING TO HIS WILL WRITTEN IN THE STARRY HOST (*Constellations "host stars"*).

EPHESIANS 1:9-10
9 HE MADE KNOWN TO US THE MYSTERY OF HIS WILL ACCORDING TO HIS GOOD PLEASURE, WRITTEN IN THE HEAVENLY SCROLL WHICH HE PURPOSED TO FULFILL IN THE YAHUSHAIC COVENANT (*Daniel 4:35*), 10 TO BE PUT INTO EFFECT WHEN THE AGES REACH THEIR FULFILLMENT (*Age of Aquarius*) —

PSALM 89:2
I WILL DECLARE THAT YOUR LOVE STANDS FIRM FOREVER, THAT YOU HAVE ESTABLISHED YOUR FAITHFUL PROMISE (*LOGOS*) OF SALVATION IN THE HEAVENLY SCROLL ITSELF.

PSALM 119:89
YOUR WORD (*LOGOS / DEBAR*), YAHUAH, IS ETERNAL; IT STANDS FIRM WRITTEN IN THE HEAVENLY SCROLL.

PSALM 89:2
FOR I HAVE SAID, "LOVINGKINDNESS WILL BE BUILT UP FOREVER; IN THE HEAVENLY SCROLL YOU WILL ESTABLISH YOUR FAITHFULNESS."

Judaism claims the New Testament is a "fairy tale" of pagan gods and the new revelations in The Yahushaic Covenant are not valid. They judge the writings of the Nazarenes based on their twisted translations promoted by the false religion of Christianity handed down by Hellenized scribes. The following standards are used to disqualify the writing of the Nazarenes (New Testament):

- No original autographed copies

- No known authors

- The New Testament was assembled long after Yahusha and the Apostles Lived

- Additions and alterations by the scribes

- Miracles were parallels of other pagan gods

- Contradictions

- New doctrines and truths – "Anything true in the NT isn't new and anything new isn't true"

When judged by that same standard, the Tanakh fails every test as well. Instead of being maticulously maintained error free, the Jewish Torah is the product of competing scribes twisting the Tanakh in their favor, mixed with vague unproven oral traditions, based on discarded scribal notes. It is the product of multiple authors written over thousands of years. There are pagan myths that mirror the "miracles" in the Tanahk. And new revelations came with each progressive covenant.

However, when translated in context and in light of The Heavenly Scroll, both the New Testament and the Tanakh can be fully understood. We must seek out, admit, then follow the ancient path revealed to Abraham. Understanding then applying the beliefs of the Nazarenes we can follow the "faith of Abraham" which is also called "the ancient path" or just "The Way".

What testifies to Yahusha as the Messiah is that he fulfilled The Heavenly Scroll. That is the ONLY testimony of Yahuah about His firstborn again son. And that is what Yahusha came to fulfill and what the prophets based their revelations upon.

EZEKIEL 2:9-10
THEN I LOOKED (*into the heavens*), AND BEHOLD, A HAND WAS EXTENDED TO ME; AND LO, A SCROLL WAS IN IT (*The Heavenly Scroll*).

HEBREWS 10:7
THEN I SAID, 'HERE I AM—IT IS WRITTEN ABOUT ME IN THE HEAVENLY SCROLL—I HAVE COME TO DO YOUR WILL, MY GOD! (*Matthew 6:10*)

MATTHEW 6:10
YOUR KINGDOM COME, YOUR WILL BE DONE, ON EARTH AS IT IS WRITTEN IN THE HEAVENLY SCROLL.

EPHESIANS 1:9-10

9 HE MADE KNOWN TO US THE MYSTERY OF HIS WILL ACCORDING TO HIS GOOD PLEASURE, WRITTEN IN THE HEAVENLY SCROLL WHICH HE PURPOSED TO FULFILL IN THE YAHUSHAIC COVENANT (*Daniel 4:35*), 10 TO BE PUT INTO EFFECT WHEN THE AGES REACH THEIR FULFILLMENT (*Age of Aquarius*)

REVELATION 6:14

THE HEAVENS (*Mazzaroth/Zodiac*) RECEDED LIKE A SCROLL BEING ROLLED UP.

ZECHARIAH 5:2-3

AND HE SAID TO ME, "WHAT DO YOU SEE (*as you look into the heavens*)?" AND I ANSWERED, "I SEE A FLYING SCROLL!"

ISAIAH 34:4

AND ALL THE HOST OF HEAVEN (*Zodiac Signs/Constellations "host stars"*) SHALL BE DISSOLVED, AND THE HEAVENS SHALL BE ROLLED TOGETHER AS A SCROLL (*i.e. The Heavenly Scroll*).

ISAIAH 48

13 MY HAND HAS LAID THE FOUNDATION OF THE EARTH (*all by Himself - Isaiah 44:24*), AND MY RIGHT HAND HAS SPANNED (*spread out like a tent*) THE HEAVEN(*ly Scroll - Psalm 19*); WHEN I SUMMON THEM (*stars/constellations*) TOGETHER, THEY WILL MINISTER TOGETHER (*to proclaim the Messiah/Plan of Salvation - Psalm 19*). 14 ALL OF YOU, GATHER YOURSELVES TOGETHER AND HEAR (*what the stars proclaim day after day, night after night - Psalm 19*)! WHO AMONG THEM HAS FORETOLD THESE THINGS (*written in the stars*)?

The Messiah Yahusha came at the cusp of Aries to Pisces and fulfilled the role of Messiah ben Joseph laid out in the first 6 constellations from Virgo through Aquarius.

327

Lamb Slaughtered / Age of Aries Ends

before the world was... portrayed as crucified in The Heavenly Scroll

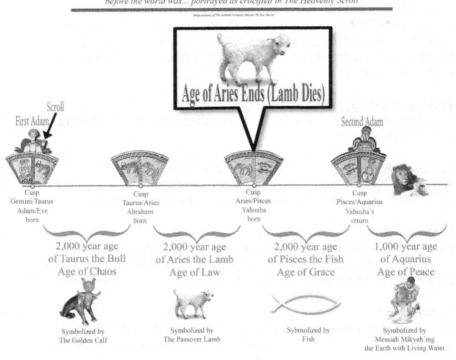

Judaism seeks to deny the Messiah has come, choosing instead to reject The Heavenly Scroll and the meaning of the Passover Lamb. It denies the Messiah must come first to serve as High Priest and make the final sacrifice to cover the Death Decrees as laid out in The Heavenly Scroll.

While Judaism denies the meaning of the Passover Lamb, thereby rejecting Yahusha as the Messiah. Christianity has adopted what the Bible calls "the Abomination of Desolation" which is the slaughter of the Ishtar Pig (Easter).

The first century Nazarenes rejected Christianity's "doctrines" and the Jewish Torah. They, instead, used the Samaritan Torah and were persecuted into hiding by both Judaism and Christianity. The Nazarenes faith can be established when we admit they were an offshoot of the Essenes who were an offshoot of the Samaritans.

Judaism, dating back to the first century, still denies the Messiah because he did not come as the "Conquering King" to unite the two houses of Israel, defeat her enemies, and setup his kingdom. Christianity seeks to replace the Messiah with a false Messiah based on pagan myths and traditions.

Both err in their understanding. He comes when the Age of Aries (the Lamb) ends (dies). He returns at the cusp of Pisces and Aquarius to fulfill Messiah ben David and "Mikveh the Earth with Living Water".

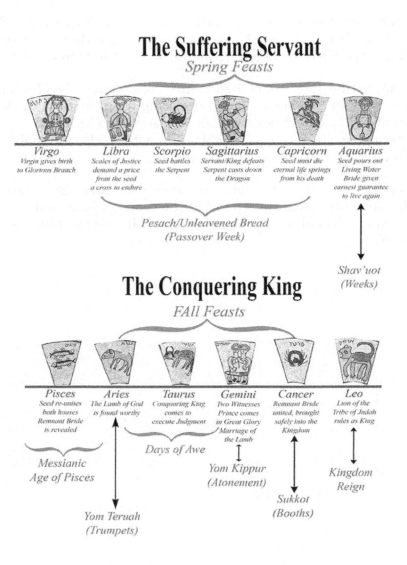

The Suffering Servant
Spring Feasts

Virgo	Libra	Scorpio	Sagittarius	Capricorn	Aquarius
Virgin gives birth to Glorious Branch	Scales of Justice demand a price from the seed a cross to endure	Seed battles the Serpent	Servant/King defeats Serpent casts down the Dragon	Seed must die eternal life springs from his death	Seed pours out Living Water Bride given earnest guarantee to live again

Pesach/Unleavened Bread
(Passover Week)

Shav'uot
(Weeks)

The Conquering King
FAll Feasts

Pisces	Aries	Taurus	Gemini	Cancer	Leo
Seed re-unites both houses Remnant Bride is revealed	The Lamb of God is found worthy	Conquering King comes to execute Judgment	Two Witnesses Prince comes in Great Glory Marriage of the Lamb	Remnant Bride united, brought safely into the Kingdom	Lion of the Tribe of Judah rules as King

Messianic
Age of Pisces

Days of Awe

Yom Kippur
(Atonement)

Kingdom
Reign

Yom Teruah
(Trumpets)

Sukkot
(Booths)

The problem we face is that Yahusha has yet to fulfill the Fall Feasts and return as Conquering King. At that time, the elect among the House of Judah will see Yahusha more clearly as their Messiah.

Appendix
Bookshelf
Available on Amazon Books. Please check often for new books I release. Search author Rav Sha'ul.

Book 1
Creation Cries Out!
The Mazzaroth

In this book I trace the great deception back to its origin and explain how the "Gospel message in the stars" was corrupted into another gospel. I reestablish the message contained in the Heavenly Scroll and give Yahuah the Glory He deserves as the Creator of all things. In this book, the original revelation found written in the stars is broken down, defined, and glorified.

I explain how the watchers corrupted the true message and taught mankind to worship the Creation over the Creator. Creation Cries Out! Reveals the secrets preserved in the Heavens and provides clear instruction so that the Great Seal over the Bible and the books of prophecy can be opened. Every prophet of Yahuah based their predictions on the Heavenly Scroll and described it in great detail.

Book 2
Mystery Babylon the
Religion of the Beast

In this book I explain how that corrupted message was formulated into a formal religion in Babylon and define that religion as it existed then. We will go back to the very beginning of "paganism" and examine the gods and rituals that define this false religion.

We will trace this religion, show how it evolved, who created it, and how it came to dominate all mankind. This information is vital as there is prophesied to be, at the end, a religion on Earth based on Mystery Babylon that deceives all humanity.

The only way to properly identify that religion today that has fulfilled this prophecy is to fully understand Mystery Babylon.

Book 3
Christianity and the
Great Deception

I compare Christianity to Mystery Babylon and prove that it is a carbon copy and is the prophesied false religion. Every description of "God" is taken directly from Babylon. From the Trinity to calling the Creator "The LORD" are all based on sun worship.

I explain where Jesus H. Christ came from, who created that false image, and how that false messiah is a carbon copy of the second member of the Babylonian Trinity named Tammuz.

From the false sacrifice of a pig on Easter, to Sunday worship, to Christmas... every aspect of the Christian Religion is a carbon copy of Mystery Babylon!

I document everything carefully from historical sources, the Catholic Church documents, and the Bible. No one who has read this book has remained a "Christian" after finishing it.

Book 4
The Antichrist
Revealed!

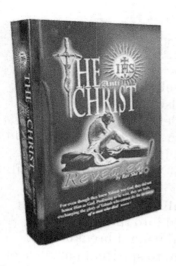

In this book I prove that Jesus H. Christ is the false image of the true messiah, and I demonstrate how he meets every prophecy of the "Antichrist".

I define in great detail such things as the Abomination of Desolation, the Spirit of the Antichrist, the Spirit of Error, the other Gospel, and much more. In this book, I demonstrate through Biblical prophecy that the false messiah is an "image" of the true Messiah not an actual person.

This book is 500 pages of solid proof that the "god" of this Earth, Jesus Christ is the "Abominable Beast" foretold by name, sacrifice, and rituals. I prove that "Jesus" is not the name of the Messiah in any language much less Hebrew. We dissect that name and prove how the name of the Messiah was intentionally altered to give glory to Zeus over Yahuah. The true name of the Messiah is Yahusha.

Book 5
The Kingdom

With the false religion, the false messiah, the false sacrifice, the false rituals clearly defined in the first 4 books, I begin to relay a firm foundation in what is true. In this book I define The Kingdom of Yahuah in great detail.

I explain how all previous 6 covenants were transposed into the final 7th Covenant of Yahusha. I breakdown every aspect of the Kingdom using physical to spiritual parallels of a kingdom on Earth. What is this Kingdom, what is its purpose, what is its domain, who is its King, what is its constitution, who are its citizens, and what responsibility to the citizens who gain citizenship? All answered in this book.

Book 6
The Yahushaic Covenant: The Mediator

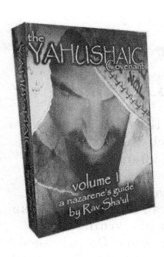

In this book I break down The New Covenant and explain who Yahusha is in relation to Yahuah, what our roles are in the covenant of Yahusha, and much more. The Yahushaic Covenant is the "Salvation of Yahuah Covenant".

I explain the role the Law plays in our lives under covenant with Yahusha. I explain the effects of Hellenism and blending the truth with paganism. I breakdown the Scripture in context, shedding light on the writings in the Renewed Covenant with the original Scriptures (Old Testament if you must).

I re-teach the Scriptures in light of the ancient language and cultural matrix of the 1st Century people of Yahuah living in the land of Israel.

Book 7
The Law and the
Pauline Doctrine

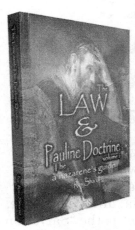

In this book, I explain the role the Law plays in our lives and re-teach Sha'ul's writings from the standpoint of intent.

I overcome the Christian lie that Sha'ul taught against the Torah. We go in and take a hard look at how Sha'ul's writing were translated and "twisted" by the Greeks into another Gospel called The Pauline Doctrine. In this book, I introduce us all to Rav Sha'ul the leader of the Nazarenes! What does that mean, and what does that one fact say about the way his writings have been translated today?

I explain the various aspects of The Law, how it was transposed over time from the Mind of Yahuah, to written in the stars at Creation, to given orally, to written in stone, to finally written on our hearts. I explain the various jurisdictional aspects of the Law, look at the Law from the standpoint of intent, and provide solid instruction to the Nazarene today in how to approach the Law of Yahuah.

Book 8
Melchizedek and the Passover Lamb

What does Melchizedek really mean? In this book I explain how Yahusha became the King of Kings and the Eternal High Priest by blood lineage to King David and the ordained Zadok Priesthood. We travel back 2,000 years to the time of the Messiah's birth to fully understand the mindset of that time. A time of great expectation toward the coming Messiah. We look back into historical documents surrounding that time period to identify the lineage of Yahusha. Lineage that was lost to antiquity when Rome burned the original manuscripts. Who were Yahusha's "other grandparents" that contributed equally to his bloodline, we have just never been introduce to? How is Yahusha "King of Israel". How is Yahusha the "High Priest of Israel".

The Bible declares Yahusha inherited those titles. If so, how and from whom? This book is a must read and introduction to the REAL Messiah in a way you have never known him.

Book 9
'The Narrow Gate'

In this book I explain how keeping the Feasts of Yahuah properly is a prerequisite of entering the Kingdom. The Feast Cycle is the "Narrow Gate" of a wedding, and we must rehearse these events from the standpoint of "a Bride". This is called The Plan of Salvation which is written in the stars "before the foundation of the world" on Day 4 of Creation.

What is the true meaning of the feasts, what are they rehearsing, how do we keep them? All these questions are answered and more in the final book in this series, The Narrow Gate.

Book 10
The Mistranslated
Book of Galatians

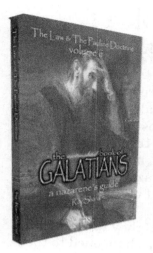

The letter to the Galatians is one of the most mistranslated (*purposely*) books in the Bible. The Greeks twisted the words of Sha'ul into a lie to abolish the Law.

In this book, I go verse by verse showing were and how the words were twisted, showing the proper translation, and then using all of Sha'ul's writing to shed light on what Sha'ul was talking about in this letter. The resulting translation is the first of its kind! The real letter to the Galatians says the exact opposite of what you read in your English Bibles. The basic foundation of the Christian Church is found to be a lie and the truth revealed in this book about what Sha'ul actually taught concerning The Law, Circumcision, and many other things.

341

Book 11
The Nazarene

In this book, we are going to find out how little we actually ever knew about The Nazarene. Most who use this title are nowhere near true Nazarenes by what they believe, much closer to Christians that Nazarenes. Accepting the Torah does not one a Nazarene!

I will show us who they were, what they believed, what happened to them. Who are they today? We are going much deeper into who the Messiah really was and exactly what those closest to him knew about him and believed.

We are going to wipe out 1,700 years of altered texts, pagan doctrines, twisted teachings, and get back to the basics of The Nazarene as he/they existed 2000 years ago.... before Constantine forced the Cult of Sol Invictus down humanities throat at the threat of death... and the Nazarenes went into hiding.

Book 12
The Fall Feasts: An invitation to the Wedding

In all our attempts to be obedient to the letter of the Law, we again fail our Father in Spiritual Intent. We remain addicted to milk, lacking teeth to digest the meatier matters of what The Feast Cycle was designed to teach us.

Hebrews 5:12

In fact, though by this time you ought to be teachers (of the Intent of the Law), you need someone to teach you the elementary truths of Yahuah's Word all over again. You need milk (the letter), not solid food (Spiritual Intent. The Law is Spiritually appraised *1 Corinthians 2:14*)!

Teachers who bring us under condemnation to the "letter of the Law" treat us as if we are Spiritual Children; telling us everything has to be done "just like this... or just like that"; yet never tell us "why" these things are done which is the more important MEAT. These teachers are a dime a dozen, not called to teach and lack the anointing required to mentor Spiritual Men and Women! These are infant teachers themselves... teaching infants, all feeding on milk! Nothing has changed in 2,000 years because we do not have mature teachers teaching the Spiritual Law, we have immature teachers trying to "look knowledgeable" with all their impressive carnal/literal knowledge of the letter.

Book 13
Unlocking the Book
of Revelation

The Book of Revelation is a documented account of what is written in the stars that must take place on Earth over what the Bible calls the "last days" which is the Age of PISCES. John is given visions as he looked up into the night sky and the angel Gabriel came to him on behalf of Yahuah and Yahusha to reveal the contents of The Heavenly Scroll. the Book of Revelation has been misunderstood, mistranslated, and mistaught for 2000 years as the ones doing the "teaching" have rejected the very source of its message... The Heavenly Scroll. These men and women who mislead the masses over the years are all filled with The Spirit of the False Messiah as they all worship the Beast Χξϛ ! They are blinded to the meaning of the words of this book as prophesied on its pages, do not understand the prophetic language, and have rejected The Word of His Testimony written in the stars.

This book reveals the meaning behind all the cryptic language, images, shadow pictures, and mysteries in the Book of Revelation. For the first time in history, teaching the Book of Revelation in context of the rest of the Prophets and The Heavenly Scroll.

344

Book 14
Blasphemy of the Holy Spirit

Blasphemy of the Holy Spirit is an opposing Spirit the Bible calls the **Spirit of the Antichrist**. It is at heart the denial of The Shema (*the greatest commandment*). It is declaring that "**Yahuah came to Earth as a man and died to save us**". We call this the Doctrine of Incarnation. The "carn" in "incarnation" refers to flesh or meat (of the human body). Thus, "incarnate" means "in the flesh". REINCARNATION is a word that means "to be born again (in the flesh)". Any concept of a Trinity or a Bi-Entity is blasphemy as Yahuah has declared He is ONE and He is Spirit and cannot and will not "come in the flesh". The phrase "in the flesh" means... "natural/physical origin (*not Spiritual*), born of natural origin ONLY, mere human/natural birth only... APART FROM DIVINE INFLUENCE, prone to sin and opposed to Yahuah".

g4561 'sarki' - Thayer:
2a) the body of a man 2b) used of natural or physical origin, generation or relationship 2b1) born of natural generation 4) the flesh, denotes mere human nature, the Earthly nature of man apart from Divine influence, and therefore prone to sin and opposed to God"

The True and False Spirits are defined by this understanding. The Spirit of Yahuah declares that Yahusha "came in the flesh" outside any Divine influence, not Yahuah. The Spirit of the False Messiah (*demi-god*) is that Jesus is "God in the flesh" or that "God" came to Earth as a man and we killed him.

345

Book 24
Heaven

It is in the stars and constellations that Yahuah made a spoken promise (LOGOS/DABAR) of a coming Kingdom ruled by a Righteous King. That "Kingdom" is a Divine Government made up of Yahuah's literal Spiritual Family... but does that mean there is no physical "Kingdom" in the sense we think of in the physical realm? These are questions I will answer in this book. This is a deeply spiritual concept, and we must train our minds to think outside this physical box we exist in...

Corinthians 2:14 "The natural man does not accept the things that come from the Spirit of God. For they are foolishness to him, and he cannot understand them, because they are spiritually discerned."

The parts I see people struggling with and what I will cover is:

- Is the Kingdom spiritual only, physical only, or both combined?
- What happens to this physical realm/Creation going forward?
- What happens to this physical realm/Creation going forward?
- Where does the Earth come into play?
- What about the 1,000-year reign on Earth?
- Is Yahusha a being with a body or a disembodied spirit?

- Will we have bodies that can interact with the physical realm?
- What is the Greater Exodus?
- What did the Messiah mean the Kingdom is not of this world?
- What did the Messiah mean the Kingdom is "inside us"?
- Will there be a physical second coming everyone on Earth will witness?
- Does Yahusha come back to Earth in a physical body riding on a cloud in the sky?
- Will there be another physical Altar?
- Will there be another physical Temple?
- Will there be another physical Sacrificial Offering on the Altar?
- What about the Ark of the Covenant?

And much more. Everything you need to know to fulfill the Great Commission "Repent! The Kingdom proclaimed in The Heavenly Scroll is at hand (inside you)"

Book 25
Enoch

This book is a study guide to the Book of Enoch sections 1 "The Watchers" and section 2 "Parables". In this book, I restore the context of these two sections, correct mistranslations, and properly interpreting the text in light of the complete revelation of Yahuah to mankind due to progressive revelation.

Progressive revelation is the way Yahuah has revealed Himself, his "hidden" plan to send Yahusha, and all aspects of the coming Spiritual Kingdom that will govern creation. Yahuah disclosed the full Plan of Salvatio and coming Kingdom over time through prophets and covenants over a 6,000 year period. Only at the end of the Age of Pisces can the full meaning of the Book of Enoch, the prophets, and His Word be fully understood in light of the full revelation.

The revelation of the coming King and Spiritual Kingdom began with Enoch the Scribe of Righteousness who was transfigured from the physical realm to the Spiritual Realm through the veil (cloud) that separates the two realms. Enoch's was a temporary transfiguration like that of Yahusha's. He was not transposed (resurrected) permanently to defeat death. The first born of the resurrection to defeat death was Yahusha. Enoch was transfigured and returned to the physical realm to live out his life and die as I will prove. He returned obviously to write the Book of Enoch, draw the diagram of The Heavenly Tablets (Scroll) he was shown called The Enoch Zodiac or Mazzaroth.

While many today believe you must approach the Book of Enoch from a Flat Earth perspective to understand it, I will prove the only way to properly interpret and understand the Book of Enoch is by putting into context of what he saw in his vision which was The Heavenly Scroll.

This knowledge is the key to unlocking the Book of Enoch in these last days, the end of the Age of Pisces. It was to those of us alive today that Enoch wrote his book and the keys to unlocking it (The Enoch Zodiac) has been passed down only to those initiated in the secret or hidden things which are not for the masses. Only the chosen few, the prophets, and the Zadok Priesthood had access to this knowledge.

Book 27 Passover Devotional

In this devotional book, I present a "study guide" to Passover in 12 lessons. Building the Scarlet Thread of Redemption from creation through when the Messiah gave his life as The Passover Lamb. I bring out the intent behind the Spring Holy Days or the Passover Season. I put Passover in the context of the Will of the Creator written in The Heavenly Scroll and the wedding it proclaims.

Each lesson builds on the one before it to a climax between the true sacrifice of a Lamb on Passover and the false sacrifice of a pig on Easter. This book contains the following lessons:

Lesson 1: The Spoken Promise, the Logos/Dabar.

Lesson 2: The Scarlet Thread of Redemption.

Lesson: 3 Contents of The Heavenly Scroll.

Lesson 4: Why Slaughter a Lamb on Passover?

Lesson 5: Crossing Over – The Greater Exodus.

Lesson 6: The Way of Mikveh, Circumcision, and Offering.

Lesson 7: The Narrow Gate.

Lesson 8: The Intent of the Passover Season.

Lesson 9: Passover Preparation Day.

Lesson 10: The Feast of Unleavened Bread, Wave Sheaf, Weeks, and Shav'uot.

Lesson 11: Baptized Paganism.

Lesson 12: The Abomination of Desolation.

NT Study Guides

Book 15
The Testimony of Yahuchanan
(Gospel of John)

Yahusha came at the fullness of time or rather the time of the fulfillment of The Plan of Salvation written in the stars. He came to fulfill what is promised and written (Logos/Dabar) in The Heavenly Scroll on Earth "in the flesh". Yahusha's Message was the same as John the Immerser's that we are to repent and follow The Way because The Kingdom proclaimed in The Heavenly Scroll is at hand as he came to fulfill it at just the right time. We have been blinded by tradition and religion to deny The Heavenly Scroll and commit what the Scriptures call the two evils by denying Yahusha was the fulfillment of ORION and AQUARIUS! The Bible is the story of The Battle of the Ages that plays out in the stars/constellations between ORION The Son of Man and The Dragon/Serpent. That battle then plays out on Earth and is documented from Genesis to Revelation.

This book restores back to the Messiah his mission and his message and for the first time delivers an accurate rendition of his teachings which astonished everyone who heard him speak. This book is the restoration of the Gospel of John bringing back to the text The Word of Yahuah's Testimony that Yahusha is the Messiah written in the stars and the Doctrine of Righteousness called The Way.

Book 16
ROMANS

This book is the study guide on Sha'ul's letter to the Roman Nazarenes will restore the intent and meaning of his writings by explaining the context in light of all Sha'ul's writings. I will define terms like "Faith of Abraham", I will restore references to The Heavenly Scroll, and I will overcome the false "Pauline Doctrine".

In this book, I will demonstrate the correct translation of Sha'ul's writings removing all pagan implications and false doctrines including any hint of "incarnation" which is the Spirit of the Antichrist.

In the end, this work on the Book of Romans will bring out the real Apostle Paul as a true "leader of the sect of Nazarenes".

This book on Sha'ul's letter to the Roman Nazarenes will restore the intent and meaning of his writings by explaining the context in light of all Sha'ul's writings. I will define terms like "Faith of Abraham", I will restore references to The Heavenly Scroll, and I will overcome the false "Pauline Doctrine".

In this book, I will demonstrate the correct translation of Sha'ul's writings removing all pagan implications and false doctrines including any hint of "incarnation" which is the Spirit of the Antichrist.

In the end, this work on the Book of Romans will bring out the real Apostle Paul as a true "leader of the sect of Nazarenes".

Book 17
HEBREWS

This book is the study guide on Sha'ul's letter to the Nazarenes in Jerusalem will restore the intent and meaning of his writings by explaining the context in light of all Sha'ul's writings. I will define terms like "Faith of Abraham", I will restore references to The Heavenly Scroll, and I will overcome the false "Pauline Doctrine".

This book goes into detail on Yahusha's role as the Ruling High Priest from the House of Zadok. This is what Melchi (ruler) Tsedek (Zadok) means. It is the highest title (name above every name) given to man. It means he hold the highest political office as King and the highest spiritual office as High Priest.

Book 18
1 Corinthians

This book is the study guide to Sha'ul's letter to the Nazarenes in Corinth.

The Apostle Paul's (Rav Sha'ul) writings have been twisted by pagan scribes and Hellinzed Jews into what we have today in our modern bibles. They have been altered to the degree they no longer reflect the beliefs, traditions, and teachings of the Nazarenes. This book correctly interprets the intent of 1 Corinthians by putting the text back into context of all of Sha'ul's writing and the historical beliefs of the first century Nazarenes who followed the Messiah.

The foundation of Sha'ul's teachings was "the Passover Lamb" which was a shadow cast by The Heavenly Scroll and a rehearsal of when the Messiah would come and die for the chosen few. I restore his writing in context of The Plan of Salvation written in the stars whereby the Creator's Will is recorded.

DANIEL 4:35
"ALL THE INHABITANTS OF THE EARTH ARE ACCOUNTED AS NOTHING, BUT HE DOES ACCORDING TO HIS WILL WRITTEN IN THE STARRY HOST (THE ZODIAC WHICH HOSTS CONSTELLATIONS. CONSTELLATIONS "HOST STARS").

EPHESIANS 1:9-10
9 HE MADE KNOWN TO US THE MYSTERY OF HIS WILL ACCORDING TO HIS GOOD PLEASURE, WRITTEN IN THE

HEAVENLY SCROLL WHICH HE PURPOSED TO FULFILL IN THE YAHUSHAIC COVENANT (DANIEL 4:35), 10 TO BE PUT INTO EFFECT WHEN THE AGES REACH THEIR FULFILLMENT (AGE OF AQUARIUS) —

PSALM 89:2
I WILL DECLARE THAT YOUR LOVE STANDS FIRM FOREVER, THAT YOU HAVE ESTABLISHED YOUR FAITHFUL PROMISE (LOGOS) OF SALVATION IN THE HEAVENLY SCROLL ITSELF.

PSALM 119:89
YOUR WORD (LOGOS / DEBAR), YAHUAH, IS ETERNAL; IT STANDS FIRM WRITTEN IN THE HEAVENLY SCROLL.

PSALM 89:2
FOR I HAVE SAID, "LOVINGKINDNESS WILL BE BUILT UP FOREVER; IN THE HEAVENLY SCROLL YOU WILL ESTABLISH YOUR FAITHFULNESS."

PSALM 119:105
105 YOUR WORD (LOGOS / DABAR ETERNALLY PRESERVED IN THE HEAVENLY SCROLL PSALM 119:89) IS A LAMP (THE DIVINE COUNSEL, WE AS HIS BRIDE ARE TO KEEP OUR LAMPS LIT BY KEEPING THE WORD OF HIS TESTIMONY ISAIAH 48) UNTO MY FEET, AND A LIGHT (REVELATION OF THE SUN/STARS/CONSTELLATIONS PSALM 19, ENOCH 35:3) UNTO MY PATH (THE HEAVENLY SCROLL IS 'THE PATH OF RIGHTEOUSNESS' CALLED THE WAY ... ISAIAH 42:5-7).

PSALM 19
1 THE SHAMAYIM/HEAVENS (THE PLACE IN THE SKY WHERE THE STARS ARE LOCATED I.E. ZODIAC) ARE TELLING OF THE GLORY OF YAHUAH (THE GLORY OF YAHUAH IS YAHUSHA! - HEBREWS 1:3); AND THEIR EXPANSE IS DECLARING THE WORK OF HIS HANDS (ENOCH 35:3). 2 DAY TO DAY POURS FORTH SPEECH, AND NIGHT TO NIGHT REVEALS KNOWLEDGE. 3 THERE IS NO SPEECH, NOR ARE THERE WORDS; THEIR (CONSTELLATIONS) VOICE IS NOT HEARD. 4 THEIR LINE (PATH OF THE SUN) HAS GONE OUT THROUGH (AND SEEN THROUGH) ALL THE EARTH, AND THEIR

(CONSTELLATIONS) UTTERANCES TO THE END OF THE WORLD. IN THEM HE HAS PLACED A TENT FOR THE SUN, 5 WHICH (AS IT TRAVELS THROUGH THE CONSTELLATIONS) IS AS A BRIDEGROOM (YAHUSHA) COMING OUT OF HIS CHAMBER; IT REJOICES AS A STRONG MAN TO RUN HIS COURSE (THROUGH THE ECLIPTIC).

This is what the Messiah came to fulfill.

HEBREWS 10:7
THEN I SAID, 'HERE I AM–IT IS WRITTEN ABOUT ME IN THE HEAVENLY SCROLL– I HAVE COME TO DO YOUR WILL, MY ELOHIM! (MATTHEW 6:10)

MATTHEW 6:10
YOUR KINGDOM (DECLARED IN HEAVEN MATTHEW 4:17) COME, YOUR WILL BE DONE, ON EARTH AS IT IS WRITTEN IN THE HEAVENLY SCROLL (PSALM 19, ENOCH 35:3).

EPHESIANS 1:9-10
9 HE MADE KNOWN TO US THE MYSTERY OF HIS WILL ACCORDING TO HIS GOOD PLEASURE, WRITTEN IN THE HEAVENLY SCROLL WHICH HE PURPOSED TO FULFILL IN THE YAHUSHAIC COVENANT (DANIEL 4:35), 10 TO BE PUT INTO EFFECT WHEN THE AGES REACH THEIR FULFILLMENT (AGE OF AQUARIUS) –

This is what Sha'ul calls "the Faith of Abraham".

ROMANS 10:17,18
17 CONSEQUENTLY, THE FAITH (OF ABRAHAM) COMES FROM HEARING THE MESSAGE (PROCLAIMED IN THE STARS GENESIS 15:5), AND THAT MESSAGE IS HEARD (PROCLAIMED BY THE STARS PSALM 19) THROUGH THE WORD OF HIS TESTIMONY ABOUT THE MESSIAH. 18 BUT I ASK (SHA'UL QUOTES PSALM 19 POINTING TO THE

MESSAGE/WORD ETERNALLY PRESERVED IN THE HEAVENLY SCROLL PSALM 119:89, PSALM 89:2): DID THEY NOT HEAR? OF COURSE THEY DID: THEIR (CONSTELLATIONS) VOICE HAS GONE OUT INTO ALL THE EARTH, THEIR WORDS (CONCERNING YAHUSHA) TO THE ENDS OF THE WORLD (PSALM 19:1-6)."

In additions to instructions for the assembly, In 1 Corinthians, Sha'ul teaches The Heavenly Scroll and how the Messiah came to fulfill it.

Book 19
2 Corinthians

This book is the study guide to Sha'ul's second letter to the Nazarenes in Corinth.

Most of us have been raised to believe the Bible is without error. "God-breathed" and in no need of untwisting or any further translation. It is complete and everything we need to know the truth. Unfortunately, this is not only a fallacy, but it contradicts the clear declarations in Scripture!

We read on the pages of the Bible that we would only "think" we have His Word (Jeremiah 8:7-9) but it would be twisted into a Babylonian Lie through translation at the hands of pagan astrologers (wise men) who twist The Word of His Testimony written into the stars into what we today think of as The Zodiac! Why twist the Zodiac into a pagan lie? Because the written scriptures are based on the Plan of Salvation written in the stars! Twist the meaning of the stars/constellations and then deny its message and the written Scriptures can be mistranslated and handled falsely by scribes:

JEREMIAH 8

7 BUT MY PEOPLE DO NOT KNOW THE ORDINANCE OF YAHUAH (ETERNALLY PRESERVED IN THE STARS PSALM 119:89). 8 "HOW CAN YOU SAY, 'WE ARE WISE MEN, AND THE WORD OF YAHUAH'S TESTIMONY IS WITH US'? BUT BEHOLD, THE LYING PEN OF THE SCRIBES HAS MADE MY WORD INTO A LIE. 9 "THE WISE MEN ARE DISMAYED AND

CAUGHT; BEHOLD, THEY HAVE REJECTED THE WORD OF MY TESTIMONY (THE HEAVENLY SCROLL), AND WHAT KIND OF WISDOM (SPIRITUAL UNDERSTANDING OF THE PLAN OF SALVATION WRITTEN IN THE STARS WHICH PROCLAIM THE GLORY OF YAHUAH PSALM 19:1, WHICH IS YAHUSHA HEBREWS 1:3, AND DECLARE HIS HANDIWORK PSALM 19 AND ENOCH 35:3 AND MANY MORE SCRIPTURES) DO THEY HAVE (BECAUSE THE SCRIPTURES ARE LITERALLY BASED ON THE HEAVENLY SCROLL/PLAN OF SALVATION/LOGOS WRITTEN IN THE STARS AT CREATION WHICH IS WHAT YAHUSHA CAME TO FULFILL HEBREWS 10:7 AND MATTHEW 6:10)?...

The Word of Yahuah's Testimony concerning His coming King who would rule Creation is found in The Heavenly Scroll. The Word of Yahuah's Testimony concerning His coming King who would rule Creation is found in The Heavenly Scroll. Sha'ul called this the "faith of Abraham" and is the foundation of his teachings and instructions. This book restores 2 Corinthians back to the beliefs and faith taught by the first century Nazarenes taught by the Messiah himself and then taken to the lost sheep of the House of Israel by the Apostle Paul (Rav Sha'ul).

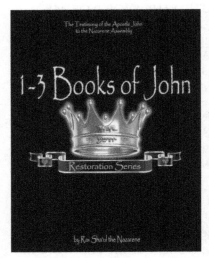

Book 20
1-3 Books of John

This book is the study guide In these three letters, John establishes the testimony that Yahuah gave of His first born-again son is that he was born fully human in every way "in the flesh". This means we must deny the doctrine of Incarnation and accept that Yahuah is the one and only "God" and Yahusha is the Human High Priest and Mediator (1 Timothy 2:5, John 17:3). It is in that declaration called the Shema that eternal life is found.

1 TIMOTHY 2:5
FOR THERE IS ONE GOD, YAHUAH, AND ONE MEDIATOR BETWEEN YAHUAH AND MANKIND, THE MAN YAHUSHA THE MESSIAH.

JOHN 17:3
NOW THIS IS ETERNAL LIFE: THAT THEY KNOW YOU FATHER, THE ONLY TRUE GOD, AND YAHUSHA THE MESSIAH, WHOM YOU HAVE SENT (TO FULFILL THE HEAVENLY SCROLL - DANIEL 4:35, HEBREWS 10:7, MATTHEW 6:10).

HE CAME INTO BEING THROUGH PHYSICAL ORIGIN THROUGH NATURAL GENERATION OR "TWO HUMAN PARENTS" APART FROM ANY DIVINE INFLUENCE (VIRGIN BIRTH IS A FALSE DOCTRINE), AND HE HAD HIS OWN WILL THAT WAS OPPOSED TO YAHUAH'S AND THEREFORE PRONE TO SIN:

G4561 'SARKI' FLESH - THAYER:
2A) THE BODY OF A MAN 2B) USED OF NATURAL OR PHYSICAL ORIGIN, GENERATION, OR RELATIONSHIP 2B1) BORN OF NATURAL GENERATION 4) THE FLESH, DENOTES MERE HUMAN NATURE, THE EARTHLY NATURE OF MAN APART FROM DIVINE INFLUENCE, AND THEREFORE PRONE TO SIN AND OPPOSED TO GOD.

Those who accept this have The Spirit of Truth. Those who deny this and claim "Yahuah came in the flesh as Yahusha" have the Spirit of the False Messiah and blaspheme the Creator who is Spirit and Immortal (cannot die – Romans 1). Yahuah cannot "come in the flesh" as by definition that means born to two human parents, opposed to Himself, and prone to sin against Himself. That is blasphemy. See my book Blasphemy of the Holy Spirit for proof.

Yahusha the Messiah must have been fully human (g4561 'sarki') for Yahusha to inherit (Hebrews 1:4) the right to serve as Eternal High Priest, be the mediator of the Covenant of Peace, and atone for humanity from the Zadok Priesthood (Numbers 25:13) given to The House of Zadok High Priesthood. He is the Ruling Zadokite High Priest or rather holds the title/name above every name Melchi Tsedek.

Book 21
Colossians

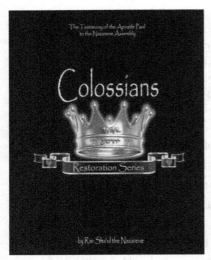

This book is the study guide on Sha'ul's letter to the Nazarenes in Colossi. In this book, Sha'ul proclaims the same message found in his letters to Nazarenes in Galatia and Corinth as he fulfills The Great Commission. Sha'ul teaches the Gospel proclaimed by the stars as the foundation of their faith (the Faith of Abraham). The Gospel was a hidden mystery concealed in the stars for ages going back to the beginning of Creation.

He goes on the compare and contrasts the main attributes of Yahuah as The Creator and Yahusha as the firstborn of eternal Creation and King of the Kingdom proclaimed in The Heavenly Scroll.

Sha'ul concludes by stating his commission by Yahuah is to proclaim the fulfillment of The Heavenly Scroll to the Lost Sheep of the House of Israel which is The Great Commission.

When Sha'ul refers to having faith and calls it the Faith of Abraham or just The Faith; what exactly was he referring to? He is referring to the original Gospel written in The Heavenly Scroll he calls "The Faith of Abraham".

PSALM 89:2
I WILL DECLARE THAT YOUR LOVE STANDS FIRM FOREVER,
THAT YOU HAVE ESTABLISHED YOUR FAITHFUL PROMISE

(LOGOS / DEBAR) OF SALVATION IN THE HEAVENLY SCROLL ITSELF.

PSALM 119:89
YOUR SPOKEN PROMISE (LOGOS / DEBAR), YAHUAH, IS ETERNAL; IT STANDS FIRM WRITTEN IN THE HEAVENLY SCROLL.

PSALM 119:105
105 YOUR WORD IS A LAMP (THE SUN IS A METAPHOR OF THE MESSIAH PSALM 19) UNTO MY FEET, AND A LIGHT UNTO MY PATH (THE HEAVENLY SCROLL IS 'THE PATH OF RIGHTEOUSNESS' CALLED THE WAY - ISAIAH 42:5-7 - ZODIAC MEANS "PATH OF THE SUN').

DANIEL 4:35
"ALL THE INHABITANTS OF THE EARTH ARE ACCOUNTED AS NOTHING, BUT HE DOES ACCORDING TO HIS WILL WRITTEN IN THE HOST OF HEAVEN (THE HEAVENLY SCROLL WHICH HOSTS CONSTELLATIONS. CONSTELLATIONS "HOST STARS")

EPHESIANS 1:9-10
9 HE MADE KNOWN TO US THE MYSTERY OF HIS WILL ACCORDING TO HIS GOOD PLEASURE, WRITTEN IN THE HEAVENLY SCROLL WHICH HE PURPOSED TO FULFILL IN THE YAHUSHAIC COVENANT (DANIEL 4:35), 10 TO BE PUT INTO EFFECT WHEN THE AGES REACH THEIR FULFILLMENT (AGE OF AQUARIUS) —

Book 22
Ephesians

This book is the study guide on Sha'ul's letter to the Nazarenes in Ephesus. In the Book of Ephesians, Sha'ul addresses the "Mystery of the Ages":

EPHESIANS 1:9-10
9 HE MADE KNOWN TO US THE MYSTERY OF HIS WILL ACCORDING TO HIS GOOD PLEASURE, WRITTEN IN THE HEAVENLY SCROLL WHICH HE PURPOSED TO FULFILL IN THE YAHUSHAIC COVENANT (DANIEL 4:35), 10 TO BE PUT INTO EFFECT WHEN THE AGES REACH THEIR FULFILLMENT (AGE OF AQUARIUS) –

The Mystery of Yahuah, hidden from the foundation of the Universe, is that Yahuah's predestined plan was to procreate a family of "godlike ones" called elohim. This family is likened unto a "body" which will be the Spiritual Temple of Yahuah in and through which Yahuah dwells. The head of this body is the first born son Yahusha and the body is the assembly of chosen sons of Yahuah known as Remnant Israel. It is through this family of "godlike ones" or elohim that the Universe will be governed in righteousness for eternity by The Kingdom of Yahuah.

Book 23
Philippians

This book is the study guide on Sha'ul's letter to the Nazarenes in Philippi.

In his letter, Sha'ul address the Spirit of Adoption and our hope, the need to deny the Spirit of the False Messiah and, like Yahusha, have the mindset that that he was not equal to Yahuah in any respect.

Sha'ul stresses how we should fulfill Yahuah's Purpose to adopt us as His children and accept whatever training this life provides without grumbling. Knowing that as we are lost among the pagan nations it will be difficult not to be assimilated and influenced by their behaviors. Sha'ul encourages the assembly of Nazarenes to follow the example of their elders, himself included, conducting themselves at all times in a manner worthy of their calling as sons of Yahuah.

Book 26
Ephesians

In the Book of Ephesians, Sha'ul addresses the "Mystery of the Ages":

Ephesians 1:9-10
9 He made known to us the mystery of His will according to his good pleasure, written in The Heavenly Scroll which He purposed to fulfill in The Yahushaic Covenant, 10 to be put into effect when the ages reach their fulfillment —

The Mystery of Yahuah, hidden from the foundation of the Universe, is that Yahuah's predestined plan was to procreate a family of "godlike ones" called elohim. This family is likened unto a "body" which will be the Spiritual Temple of Yahuah in and through which Yahuah dwells. The head of this body is the first born son Yahusha and the body is the assembly of chosen sons of Yahuah known as Remnant Israel. It is through this family of "godlike ones" or elohim that the Universe will be governed in righteousness for eternity by The Kingdom of Yahuah.

Book 26
Ephesians

In the Book of Ephesians, Sha'ul addresses the "Mystery of the Ages":

Ephesians 1:9-10
9 He made known to us the mystery of His will according to his good pleasure, written in The Heavenly Scroll which He purposed to fulfill in The Yahushaic Covenant, 10 to be put into effect when the ages reach their fulfillment —

The Mystery of Yahuah, hidden from the foundation of the Universe, is that Yahuah's predestined plan was to procreate a family of "godlike ones" called elohim. This family is likened unto a "body" which will be the Spiritual Temple of Yahuah in and through which Yahuah dwells. The head of this body is the first born son Yahusha and the body is the assembly of chosen sons of Yahuah known as Remnant Israel. It is through this family of "godlike ones" or elohim that the Universe will be governed in righteousness for eternity by The Kingdom of Yahuah.

More from Rav Sha'ul

Please visit my websites www.sabbathcovenant.com or www.ravshaul.com for in depth teachings, audio lessons, links to these books, and much more.

Be sure and check Amazon Books (search for author Rav Sha'ul) for new books released after this publication date.

If this book has been a blessing to you, please support this ministry. Email ravshaulfunds@gmail.com for more information or click on the donate link at the top of the page of www.ravshaul.com. Please visit my YouTube Channel for further video teachings and presentations.

https://www.youtube.com/channel/UCVLZgChmeSa78Mo7b228sjQ

All Glory belongs to Yahuah. He is our Creator, Author of the Heavenly Scroll, and Father of the called out ones (*Nazarenes*). And to Yahusha the Nazarene, the Messiah and Royal High Priest of Israel, I say...

"WORTHY IS THE LAMB! TO RECEIVE HONOR, AND GLORY, AND POWER, AND PRAISE" HALLELUYAHUAH!

LET IT BE SO DONE, ON EARTH AS IT IS WRITTEN IN THE HEAVENLY SCROLL."

Kingdom blessings, and much love... Rav Sha'ul